Studies in European Culture and History

edited by

Eric D. Weitz and Jack Zipes
University of Minnesota

Since the fall of the Berlin Wall and the collapse of communism, the very meaning of Europe has been opened up and is in the process of being redefined. European states and societies are wrestling with the expansion of NATO and the European Union and with new streams of immigration, while a renewed and reinvigorated cultural engagement has emerged between East and West. But the fast-paced transformations of the last fifteen years also have deeper historical roots. The reconfiguring of contemporary Europe is entwined with the cataclysmic events of the twentieth century, two world wars and the Holocaust, and with the processes of modernity that, since the eighteenth century, have shaped Europe and its engagement with the rest of the world.

Studies in European Culture and History is dedicated to publishing books that explore major issues in Europe's past and present from a wide variety of disciplinary perspectives. The works in the series are interdisciplinary; they focus on culture and society and deal with significant developments in Western and Eastern Europe from the eighteenth century to the present within a social historical context. With its broad span of topics, geography, and chronology, the series aims to publish the most interesting and innovative work on modern Europe.

Published by Palgrave Macmillan:

Fascism and Neofascism: Critical Writings on the Radical Right in Europe
by Eric Weitz

Fictive Theories: Towards a Deconstructive and Utopian Political Imagination
by Susan McManus

German-Jewish Literature in the Wake of the Holocaust: Grete Weil, Ruth Klüger, and the Politics of Address
by Pascale Bos

Turkish Turn in Contemporary German Literature: Toward a New Critical Grammar of Migration
by Leslie Adelson

Terror and the Sublime in Art and Critical Theory: From Auschwitz to Hiroshima to September 11
by Gene Ray

Transformations of the New Germany
edited by Ruth Starkman

Caught by Politics: Hitler Exiles and American Visual Culture
edited by Sabine Eckmann and Lutz Koepnick

Legacies of Modernism: Art and Politics in Northern Europe, 1890–1950
edited by Patrizia C. McBride, Richard W. McCormick, and Monika Zagar

Cinema After Fascism

The Shattered Screen

Siobhan S. Craig

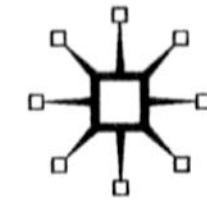

CINEMA AFTER FASCISM

Copyright © Siobhan S. Craig, 2010.

First published in 2010 by
PALGRAVE MACMILLAN®
in the United States—a division of St. Martin's Press LLC,
175 Fifth Avenue, New York, NY 10010.

Where this book is distributed in the UK, Europe and the rest of the world,
this is by Palgrave Macmillan, a division of Macmillan Publishers Limited,
registered in England, company number 785998, of Houndmills,
Basingstoke, Hampshire RG21 6XS.

Palgrave Macmillan is the global academic imprint of the above companies
and has companies and representatives throughout the world.

Palgrave® and Macmillan® are registered trademarks in the United States,
the United Kingdom, Europe and other countries.

ISBN: 978–0–230–10384–9

Library of Congress Cataloging-in-Publication Data

Craig, Siobhan S., 1958–
    Cinema after fascism : the shattered screen / Siobhan S. Craig.
       p. cm.—(Studies in European culture and history)
    Includes bibliographical references.
    ISBN 978–0–230–10384–9 (alk. paper)
    1. Motion pictures—Europe—History—20th century. 2. Fascism and
    motion pictures—Europe. I. Title.

PN1993.5.E8C73 2010
791.43094′09045—dc22   2009050869

A catalogue record of the book is available from the British Library.

Design by Newgen Imaging Systems (P) Ltd., Chennai, India.

First edition: July 2010

10 9 8 7 6 5 4 3 2 1

Printed in the United States of America.

For Leslie, with love

Contents

Illustrations

Acknowledgments

My fascination with the traces of fascism in postwar life dates back to my childhood in Rome in the 1960s and 1970s. Rome's many historical pasts persist, sometimes carefully excavated and curated, often messily and promiscuously mixed into the sights and textures of life in the present. Navigating Rome in the company of my art-historian mother, I learned to read these traces, and they conditioned my love for the city. Remnants of the fascist past, however, were not a readable element of the palimpsest. These signs are everywhere in Rome but, unlike the magnificent traces of the ancient or baroque city, seemed to me to be visible but not seen, hidden in plain sight. A memorable example of the half-suppressed persistence of the past could be found on a travertine plaque in my favorite neighborhood park, which thanked a noble Roman family for the donation of their villa and its grounds to the "people of Rome." Chiseled out of the inscription but still easily readable was the name of the first and primary recipient of their largesse: "Sua Eccellenza Benito Mussolini, Duce D'Italia." Fading paint on a few buildings in the newer parts of my neighborhood, Trastevere, revealed their age in terms of the chronology of the fascist *ventennio*; an inscription in the never-used communal laundry room of our apartment building, with its travertine sinks and constantly flowing streams of frigid water, dated its construction to "Anno XIV," or 1936. As I later began to think about film—having learned something about the constructions, coding, and illusionism of cinema in conversations with my father, a screenwriter—I returned to my fascination with the historiographic incoherence I first encountered so richly in Rome. I found that my vision was conditioned by the early awareness of these not quite concealed traces of a half-acknowledged past. My awareness of the ambivalent historiography that characterized the complex and deeply imprinted text that was, for me, the city of Rome led me to seek similar constructions in postwar film. In looking for the moments in which cinema "after fascism" glances ambivalently backward, I found myself returning to the history of my own intellectual formation.

This project was made possible by the help of many family members, friends, teachers, and colleagues over the years. I thank my brothers, Sean and Tommy, and Yolanda Ponzianelli. I owe special thanks to Don Eric Levine for invaluable help through the many stages of *Cinema After Fascism*. I am also deeply appreciative of the assistance, through early versions of this project, of Barton Byg, Sara Lennox, David Lenson, and Elisabeth Petroff at the University of Massachusetts. Many colleagues and students at the University of Minnesota have proven to be intelligent and insightful interlocutors and a crucial source of encouragement and support. I would particularly like to thank Richard McCormick and Maria Damon. I am also grateful for many helpful discussions at various points in the writing of *Cinema After Fascism* with Charlie Sugnet, Paula Rabinowitz, Lois Cucullu, Anna Clark, Andy Elfenbein, John Watkins, Michael Hancher, Jani Scandura, Carol Donelan, and Frank Adler. Omise'eke Tinsley, Christophe Wall-Romana, and Shaden Tageldin were perceptive readers of parts of the manuscript.

I also thank Sara Cohen and Will Kanyusik for many stimulating discussions that contributed directly to my work. Adam Schrag has provided invaluable help toward the completion of the manuscript, as has Anne Carter, whom I also thank for her friendship and support. Judith Katz and Riv-Ellen Prell have both been unfailing sources of warmth and encouragement. I am especially appreciative of Jack Zipes for his help, confidence, and friendship over the years. I would also like to thank Eric Weitz.

I have received crucial support for my research from the University of Minnesota over the years. A residential fellowship at the Institute for Advanced Study provided an especially congenial and stimulating environment for interdisciplinary discussion. I would like to thank the University of Minnesota for the McKnight and Faculty Fellowships, and the College of Liberal Arts at Minnesota for a research leave, which was instrumental to the completion of this manuscript. Parts of the fourth chapter of *Cinema After Fascism* and an early version of the second chapter have appeared in the *Quarterly Review of Film and Video*.

Without Barbara Meyer, this project would never have been completed; I thank her for her wisdom, support, and friendship over many years. Thanks to Catherine McNeel for presiding over the delivery of the manuscript, and to Sydney and Simon Rackenberg-Loisel, who offered me light, love, and more wisdom than they knew. Theo and Arthur Morris-Craig were loving companions. Finally, I would like to thank Leslie Morris who has, in every way imaginable, enriched my life and work.

Siobhan S. Craig

INTRODUCTION

Cinema After Fascism considers postwar European cinema, examining the ambivalent backward glances with which filmmakers acknowledge the saturation of the present by the fascist past. Fascism persists as the rubble-field of cinema after 1945, its constituent elements taken up as building blocks for new visions and new constructions, which never fully escape the mark of their origin. The ruins of war, a recurring image in postwar cinema, are emblematic of a broader condition: the failure of the familiar epistemologies of knowledge and of the self, in which all existing constructions, both literal and figurative, have been erased. There are no stable certainties left, only provisional configurations that are always threatening to collapse again into the debris. The rubble on the screen is matched by the ruin of cinematic representation as postwar directors engage with the fascist past of the medium. Attempts to reconfigure the idioms of cinema, ranging from the ambivalently postfascist neorealism of Roberto Rossellini to the "neomelodramas" of Rainer Werner Fassbinder, remain highly precarious. These new cinematic languages are never fully naturalized: the joists and scaffolding remain visible and indeed become a major preoccupation in themselves. In examining the embedded discourses about epistemology, representation, gendered subjectivity, and historiography in the work of several major postwar directors, *Cinema After Fascism* looks at the rubble of art and vision as filmmakers confront the fractured remains of fascist aesthetics, culture, and cinema. The geography of *Cinema After Fascism* is both trans-European and trans-Atlantic as it attempts to remap the territories of recent scholarship with regard to postwar cinema.

European filmmaking after the Second World War is haunted by a persistent "specter:" the fascist cinema of spectacle. Many of the films sanctioned by the fascist states in Italy and Germany invited the viewer to enter into narratives positing an unbroken arc between fascism and imperial Rome or heroic Teutonic myth, and retrospectively conferred upon the viewer an (illusory) mastery of history and a position within a unified, stable system of identity. Even though film under fascist regimes was not monolithic—plenty of genre or escapist fare was produced—grand historical films, such as Alessandro Blasetti's *1860* (1934) and Carmine Gallone's *Scipione l'Africano* (1937) in Italy, or the masterly documentaries by Leni Riefenstahl in Germany, represent particularly powerful examples of fascist uses of film. In *Cinema After Fascism*, I discuss films by several postwar European directors who all, I contend, must confront these "ghosts:" Much of the pleasure associated with cinema has become suspect, potentially contaminated by its association with fascism. In response, what develops is a highly self-conscious attempt to rebuild a cinema from the "rubble" of what preexisted it, an attempt that recognizes the impossibility of an entirely new cinematic language and takes as its building blocks the elements of previous cinema, at the same time acknowledging and interrogating the ideological taint that clings to them.

Cinema After Fascism reconsiders the relationship between fascist-era cinema and postwar film. The films considered here do not, in my reading, simply embody an artistic and philosophical break with fascist cinema; instead, they foreground the complex, ambivalent relationship between past and present that characterizes European film after 1945. All the directors discussed in *Cinema After Fascism* are indisputably "antifascist;" however, they are also engaged in an extended dialogue with fascist aesthetics and ideologies. Whether, like Rossellini, they served an artistic apprenticeship within the fascist film system or came of age later, they have all placed at the center of their work an interrogation of postwar film's dubious antecedents in the cinema of fascism. I argue that these particular films, in part through formal experimentation and a refusal to naturalize the diegetic worlds they offer, question the very possibility of representation. Using widely varying techniques and idioms, ranging from the ambivalent but compelling realism of Rossellini to the highly distanciated approaches of Fassbinder and Alain Resnais, these directors forbid us to enter into any sort of comfortable relationship with the screen. They force us, the film spectator, into a kind of epistemological abyss, a necessary paradox in which the only ethical imperative of cinematic representation is to fail *as* representation. What they present to us is not the possibility of knowledge or an opportunity, however illusory, to enact a unified self in the mirror of the movie screen; instead, they posit the bankruptcy of this wish. History, in consequence, is also radically denatured. Narratives of causality or continuity are disrupted and delegitimized.

All of the films considered in *Cinema After Fascism* engage with spectatorship as a crucial problematic; a complex and ambivalent discourse around spectatorship is integral to their examination of historiography and subjectivity, especially gendered subjectivity. The "ghosts" of past spectators imprint themselves on postwar celluloid; the traces and past accretions of different ways of looking are invoked as the films consider the history—aesthetic, ethical, and political—of the medium. Spectatorship is considered as a structure affording particular modes of subjectivity as well as in terms of a historically situated viewership. All of the directors I discuss consider the ways in which spectatorship is "trained," dependent on previous modes of viewing and preexistent cinematic texts—the spectator comes into being as constituted within the composition of light and shadow playing on the screen and flickers through various subject positions in dialogue with it. As we move from Riefenstahl to Billy Wilder, from Rossellini to Fassbinder, the spectator wavers in and out of view, encoded or in plain sight, but always determinative. This spectator, a creature of cinema, embodies a complex and shifting structure of subjectivity, of desire and identification, potentially occupying a succession of identities and positions. The scope of my discussion is necessarily transnational. In *Cinema After Fascism* I go beyond the classifications of period and national cinema that have conventionally delimited the boundaries of scholarly discussions of postwar film. Instead of thinking in terms of periods, movements, or nations (i.e., Italian neorealism or new German cinema) or avant-garde versus commercial film in defining my objects of study, I choose to cut across these categories. My definition of "postfascist," as outlined above, is conceptual rather than strictly chronological and encompasses films made in the latter half of the twentieth century, from the mid-1940s to the 1980s. I bring together a group of directors from different national cinemas who work in very diverse cinematic idioms and styles. For example, I draw films by an established Hollywood director, the German émigré Billy Wilder, into dialogue with nearly simultaneous work by a great "rebel" against the strictures of the commercial film industry, Roberto Rossellini, and place the self-conscious melodrama of Rainer Werner Fassbinder's postwar trilogy in juxtaposition to Bernardo Bertolucci's psychological dissections of fascism. However, a central preoccupation links the specific directors and films I discuss: all engage self-reflexively with the question of how to find a cinematic "language" in the aftermath of fascist film; all consciously grapple with their ambiguous inheritance as postwar directors. Much of the writing regarding film in relation to fascism has tended to limit its discussion to particular national contexts. For example, analyses of the cinema produced under European fascist regimes generally focus on Germany (e.g., Schulte-Sasse, Schoeps, Rentschler) or Italy (Landy, Hay, Garofalo, Reich), as do broader discussions about fascist constructions of subjectivity, gender, and aesthetics (de Grazia, Spackman, Ravetto, Pickering-Iazzi, Koonz, Theweleit, Hewitt, Kaes). Scholarly treatments of specific cinematic genres and movements in the postfascist period also generally respect these divisions, as exemplified by discussions of the German "rubble film" (Shandley) and Italian neorealism (Bondanella, Liehm, Brunelle). Discussions of the work of a single director (i.e., Brunette on Rossellini, Elsaesser on Fassbinder) necessarily limit themselves to a fairly restricted historical and national context. *Cinema After Fascism*, like recent work that takes a transnational approach to European film scholarship (e.g., Galt), works both within and between these intellectual traditions, examining complex theoretical and cinematic dialogues that cross national, cultural, and linguistic boundaries. *Cinema After Fascism* also engages with scholarly discussions of gender and film, especially masculinity studies, building on preexisting work in cinematic masculinities and queer film (e.g., Griffin, Benshoff, Aaron, Lehman, Kuzniar, Cestaro, Miller) and placing it in new contexts. Each chapter combines close analysis—often of a lesser-known film by a major director—with broader discussion, situating specific readings within the context of larger historical and theoretical debates. I argue that all the directors discussed, in their self-conscious preoccupation with the implications of cinema in a postfascist era, undermine presence, meaning, and authority.

I begin my discussion in the immediate postwar period, with a discussion of Italian neorealism. Roberto Rossellini's films *Paisà* (1946) and *Germania anno zero* (1947) posit subjectivity, historiography, and the cinematic medium itself as being in profound crisis. Discussions of Italian neorealism tend to conceptualize it primarily as a break with fascist film, a new start, and a radical reinvention of the medium; I argue, instead, that Rossellini makes an ambivalent interrogation of previous cinema into one of the central issues of his early work. Rossellini himself came of age as a director within the fascist film system and had made well-known nationalistic war films, even collaborating on a screenplay with Vittorio Mussolini, the son of the Duce. The connections between Rossellini's early films—*La nave bianca* (1942), *Un pilota ritorna* (1942), and *L'uomo della croce* (1943)—and his neorealist oeuvre are generally elided by scholars. It is my contention that Rossellini's great trilogy of the mid- to late 1940s glances ambivalently backward toward another trilogy from the early 1940s, which celebrated—albeit with reservations—fascist masculinity and militarism.

The "rubble" of fascist cinema is, I argue, a constant presence in Rossellini's neorealist films. As his camera moves through the postwar cityscapes, Rossellini builds into his new, perhaps precarious, neorealist structure a meditation on spectatorship and subjectivity, specifically foregrounding modes of spectatorship invoked by the cinema of militarism and hypermasculinity that flourished under the fascist regime. In these films about current and former soldiers, both fascist and antifascist preexisting constructions of masculinity are denaturalized. We watch men watching themselves and each other, consummate spectators and performers of a tainted, often absurd, always precarious male subjectivity. The director jettisons the conventional cinematic tools by which gendered selves are built and shows us instead the clumsy machinery of this process. In *Paisà*, heterosexual masculinity is perpetually in the process of breaking down and being arbitrarily reconfigured. The male protagonists in the six separate segments of this fragmented film spread across the geographic regions of Italy, are failures in potency and passion. They are ruled by scopophilia, the fascination with spectacle their only mode of desire.

Germania anno zero—a German language film by an Italian director shot in Berlin and Rome in 1946, and hence defined by its crossing of national and linguistic borders—uses the landscape of the shattered city to explore these transgressions and the slippages of identity. Rossellini's camera obsessively follows the child protagonist through the city in a series of endless tracking shots, the boy's affectless demeanor suggesting the inadequacy of any conventional system of representation to capture the crisis that he inhabits. As Rossellini reconfigures the elements of cinematic representation, the boy is caught in the destruction caused by the collapse of masculinity. The adult men we encounter—pedophiles, deserters, invalids, the broken wreckage of fascist masculinity—are photographed surrounded by voids, gazing out hungrily at ruined spaces. Heterosexual normativity, national and linguistic identities, and the limits of subjectivity itself are repeatedly undermined as the war-torn city emblematizes the collapse of masculinity as icon and ideal. In the ruins of Berlin, Rossellini also engages in a dialogue with fascist cinema, and with his own origins as a director, albeit at one remove. He glances back at the dubious past ethics and aesthetics of his medium—for him, the two are inextricably linked. He reanimates the cinema of the fascist past in Germany, inviting the "specters" of Nazism to walk the streets of Berlin—the maudlin ghosts of the children in the classic Nazi film *Hitlerjunge Quex* appear as trace and echo on his postwar celluloid.

A very different approach to the aesthetic and ideological implications of a world in rubble emerges at approximately the same time as the neorealists were establishing their unique cinematic idiom. Like Rossellini, Carol Reed and Billy Wilder confront the wreckage of past cinematic representations of gender, desire, and national identity, centering on new ways to consider masculine subjectivities after fascism. Once again, the medium of film itself is under scrutiny in Reed's *The Third Man* and Wilder's *A Foreign Affair*, two English-language films shot almost simultaneously with Rossellini's *Germania anno zero* on location in the rubble of Nazi capitals. Unlike Rossellini's neorealist work, these films do not reject the manipulations and stylizations of conventional cinema; instead, they embrace the pleasures of artifice, while continuously interrogating the terms of their own representation. Reed's *The Third Man*, set in the rubble-scapes and battered baroque theatricality of postwar Vienna, juxtaposes the ruins of Nazi subjectivity to American popular culture and its myths of masculinity, using each as an ironic comment on the other. The film presents us with a network of sly allusions to different icons and codes of masculine subjectivity that, like the giant Ferris wheel that appears, on film, to dominate the city through which Reed's bumbling protagonist obliviously wanders, cycle pointlessly and endlessly through possible positions. The iconic American figure of the cowboy—literally imported to Vienna by the film's protagonist, a naïve writer of pulp Western novels— and the shop-worn Aryan ideal represent equally bankrupt models of masculine subjectivity. I argue that the film's positing of a series of mirrors of selfhood—the multiplications, confusions, and slippages of identity—is ultimately a commentary on film spectatorship, the happy "misrecognitions" by which we attempt to instate a stable, unitary subjectivity as we gaze at the movie screen.

The Third Man is often read within the framework of American cinema, specifically in the context of film noir and the cold war. My reading of the film shifts that optic. Not only is *The Third Man* a film "about" the cold war, or an exploration of postwar alienation, but it must also be read in terms of its setting and historical moment in the ruins of fascism. The protagonist's simplistic moral code is encapsulated by the title of one of his books, *The Lone Rider of Santa Fe*; he brings his lonely "holy faith," his straightforward belief in unitary identity, to the epistemological simplicity of his search for "truth." He naively approaches the mystery of this world of "noir" in which the only illumination is the occasional beam of blinding light, not truth at all but a theatrical trick, the "limelight" to which the name of his friend Harry Lime refers. As we watch Holly—in the throes of his triangulated passion for his old American "buddy" Harry—attempt to navigate an intricate maze of masculinities that he is ill-equipped to understand, we are shown the complex links between fascism and American icons. One important shot clearly shows us the cover of Holly's novel *The Oklahoma Kid*—ironically offering for our ambivalent identification a self with unity and unproblematized masculinity. The face of the cowboy on the book cover is blocked by the head of a dark-haired passerby with a toothbrush moustache: Adolf Hitler by way of Charlie Chaplin in *The Great Dictator*. Reed "blows the cover" of American masculinity as constituted within popular culture and points out the similarities with other models of subjectivity—the dubious hypermasculinities of fascism. These diverse but ultimately equivalent masculine subjectivities are frankly presented as performative, offering an illusory coherence that is finally bankrupt.

Alongside *The Third Man*, I consider *A Foreign Affair* (1948), a Billy Wilder film set in the rubble of Berlin, during the postwar Allied occupation of the city. Wilder begins *A Foreign Affair* with a god-like panorama of the rubble-scape of Berlin as seen from an Allied aircraft, in a series of shots that directly quote from the opening sequence of the greatest fascist propaganda film of them all, Leni Riefenstahl's *Triumph of the Will*. This provocative opening sequence deliberately places Wilder's film in dialogue with Riefenstahl's: Wilder's image of the shadow of an American aircraft against the ruins of the German capital directly echoes a nearly identical shot of Hitler's plane approaching Nuremburg in *Triumph of the Will*; this sweeping panorama of the ruined city opens up a world in which the shattered vestiges of fascism are reconfigured into parodic caricatures of national identity, gender, and desire. *A Foreign Affair* posits a particularly suggestive series of questions about genre, gender, and national identity in both American and German cinema. I argue that, by simultaneously adopting and subverting the conventions of romantic comedy and film noir with a healthy dose of German expressionism and fascist propaganda thrown into the parodic mix, Wilder requires his audience to abandon any stable notions of identity, representation, or epistemology. *A Foreign Affair* keeps us off balance at all times, leaving us standing uneasily on the margin between genres and forcing us to consider how our ways of seeing and our positions of identification—whether through constructions of gender, nation, or desire—bring us inevitably to crisis. As the American and German characters negotiate the physical rubble of a defeated city—a mise-en-scène memorably employed by Wilder—they also traverse the chaotic territory of identity in ruins. Wilder, returning to his native country in the aftermath of Nazism, glances, like Rossellini, ambivalently backward at fascist cinema. While formations of GIs may have replaced the Nazi storm troopers on the airfields of Germany, fascist subjectivities and codes of representation still haunt the landscape of postwar cinema.

American masculinity—newly refurbished in military supremacy— collapses in *A Foreign Affair*, its vacuity as an epistemological category suggested by the silk stocking peeking out of the pocket of our splendidly uniformed leading man, a hero chronically unable to maintain gender stability as he crosses and recrosses its ruptured boundaries. The Nazi singer, played by Marlene Dietrich as an off-kilter comment on a femme fatale, is just as unmistakably a failure at femininity. Throughout *A Foreign Affair*, Wilder frames Dietrich in obtrusively theatrical and denaturalizing ways, emphasizing the frank performativity of the character's gender identity, a drag queen wreathed in smoke and silhouetted by spotlights. The corn-fed Iowa girl who is Dietrich's foil—memorably dismissed by her as having a face "like a scrubbed kitchen floor"—does not offer a naturalized female counterpart to the ambivalent femme fatale. Her clean-scrubbed American forthrightness is defaced as she too crosses the boundaries of nationality and gender, appearing—to her character's astonished dismay—as a German prostitute, a GI in uniform, and a film noir detective on a stakeout. It is my contention that masculinity in *A Foreign Affair* is a highly unstable commodity; we are left with a failure of conventional identities and a repeated foregrounding of that failure through denaturalization and parody. As we—and the cinematic audience—immerse ourselves in "the ruins of Berlin," any semblance of a credibly unified vision collapses.

The French new wave enters the rubble of the destroyed city as part of its radical destabilization of preexisting cinematic language, as did neorealism in the immediate postwar period; I turn in my third chapter to this continuing dialogue. Alain Resnais and Marguerite Duras turn to the east in the 1959 film *Hiroshima mon amour*; however, the European subject, shattered by its embrace of fascism, remains their focus. Here, too, the traces of fascism are inescapable, defining both the physical setting and the psychological and aesthetic geography of the film. *Hiroshima mon amour*'s exploration of the continuing trace of the past in the present brings back history and memory as echo and displacement. The dominant metaphor, once again, is the destruction of a city. The atomic bombing of Hiroshima produced trace images, ghostly relics of the past persisting into the present, literally burned into existence. This "photo-graphic" trace, formed by the unfathomable light of atomic detonation, underlines the discourse about cinematic representation that is central to this film. In the flash of the atom bomb, the physical world of Hiroshima was transubstantiated into something unknowable: so, too, was the possibility of representation according to any preexisting systems or codes. An exploration of the implications of spectatorship is central to my discussion: the film constantly foregrounds the act of looking and ultimately questions vision as a way of attaining epistemological mastery. It is my argument that Resnais' fracturing of the conventions of cinematic continuity—his rupture of the familiar codes of intelligibility—leaves us in the rubble of meaning, trying to reinstate some version of a "readable" artifact. The film's restless movement between its dual mise-en-scènes—a rebuilt Hiroshima, in which the present cannot obscure its unfathomable destruction, and Nazi-occupied France, seen in disorienting flashback—open up an epistemological abyss in which all possibility of "knowledge" is lost and the gendered subject is, by definition, shattered.

Past and present intermingle freely in *Hiroshima mon amour*. Resnais uses flashbacks in an innovative, and profoundly disconcerting, fashion: he catapults us between different times without providing cues or context.

His methods are associative and, perhaps, antinarrative—for example, a close-up of a man's hand and arm is suddenly replaced by another hand and arm in a brief and violent transition that is over long before we, the spectators, can even attempt to process it. We are left in an epistemological quandary, as temporal and narrative structures are destabilized, and all familiar contexts collapse. If "history"—the narrative of the past—is the central "story" of *Hiroshima mon amour*, it is represented in such a way as to disrupt the very possibility of knowledge, producing a continuing epistemological crisis. In a universe that contains post-nuclear Hiroshima—a town which, in Duras' memorable image, has risen into the sky and returned to the ground as ash—knowledge, history and subjectivity have all been fissured and fragmented, reduced to a tumbled heap of debris. Even the natural world participates in this disordering—the central section of the film is set overlooking a river, which, Duras specifically states, has no boundaries that are visible to the film spectator. The Frenchwoman's history is shown to us as a series of flashbacks; the differences between past and present break down as the characters on screen—and we, in the theater—begin to inhabit both simultaneously. The Japanese man stands in for, and becomes interchangeable with, a dead German soldier, the woman's wartime lover, as the "resurgence" of French town of Nevers—a collapse of temporal boundaries so complete that Duras refers to it as a "miracle"—begins to take over the film. In Nevers the Frenchwoman—mad with grief after her lover's death—was confined in a cellar by her family. In this cellar, with its imprisoning walls, we discover that all epistemological structures have been bankrupted: the "walls" between life and death, human and animal, male and female, have proved as unstable and fluid as the river. Even the cellar walls themselves have no existence as autonomous, stable constructions—the woman eats them, incorporating them into her body.

The exploration of spectatorship as a central focus of *Hiroshima mon amour* is evident from the first shot of the film; Resnais and Duras begin by questioning the viability of vision as a way of obtaining epistemological mastery. A confusing view of intertwined bodies is so dark and fragmented that we don't at first know what we are looking at. The initial dialogue—disembodied male and female voices—continues this theme. The first words we hear are a male voice asserting flatly: "you have seen nothing in Hiroshima." The man's words are addressed as much to the spectator as to the woman, his conversational partner within the film's diegesis. She places her claim to the viability of both vision and knowledge—"I have seen everything in Hiroshima"—only to have it undercut in multiple ways. We, the film's spectators, are put on notice. Our spectatorship will not yield knowledge or mastery, whether aesthetic or ideological; instead, we can expect only obscurity, fragmentation and a challenge to our own status as unified subjects. The subject-object dichotomy breaks down, as we see our own spectatorship represented on screen. We, too, are tenuous subjects: split, fragmented, and multiplied.

In chapter five I again move across the borders of national cinema to consider *Hiroshima mon amour* alongside Helma Sanders-Brahms' 1979 film, *Deutschland bleiche Mutter*. While these films may appear, at the outset, to have little in common—belonging, as they do, to different periods in the history of cinema and different national traditions—they share important preoccupations, and employ textual strategies that invite their placement in dialogue with one another. Like Duras and Resnais, Sanders-Brahms situates us at a symbolic "ground zero," the epicenter of destruction, both physical and epistemological; both films speak to us from a location without familiar constructions of knowledge or subjectivity. Sanders-Brahms, once again, foregrounds spectatorship as an act of both historiography and subject constitution, confronting us with the bankruptcy of these models, and destabilizing their structure. In both films, we see acts of spectatorship subjected to a very skeptical and challenging scrutiny—Sanders-Brahms presents us, repeatedly, with distillations of the gaze, tableaus that emphasize looking rather than what is seen, and defamiliarizes the process, presenting both seeing and what is seen as estranged. As do *Paisà* and *Hiroshima mon amour*, *Deutschland bleiche Mutter* employs its landscapes of unfathomable destruction to contextualize a meditation on spectatorship. All three films present us with landscapes, both literal and symbolic, of flow—whether rivers, lakes, or lava fields composed of congealed flowing rock—in which boundaries are flooded over. The film does not allow the possibility for any "natural" subjectivity to be enacted in the relationship between subject and object; indeed, these categories— again—dissolve, melting into water, ash and rubble. Subject and object, the self and the outside world, become untenable distinctions as separations disappear; the body of the female protagonist, in both films, becomes, as a signifying entity, the "theater" in which this denaturalization of unitary identity occurs. In our own (movie) theaters we (as, perhaps, increasingly uneasy perceiving subjects) watch the collapse of the subject/object split— its literal, physical dissolution, as the two elements are conflated—enacted in the bodies on screen that are the focus of our own spectatorship: it is a spectatorial loop, a mise en abîme. Historiography—any possibility of a stable construction of the relationship by which the present can "know" the past—is a casualty of the collapse of the subject. Sanders-Brahms, like Duras and Resnais, challenges the privileged epistemological status of "the document," foregrounding textual constructs that seem to carry this privileged claim to be "true," "real," or "objective fact" only to negate their existence as autonomous avenues for epistemological certainty and emphasizing their mediated artifactuality. "Subjective" and "objective" knowledge lie in the rubble with the constructs of subject and object on which they depend. Stable gender is yet another casualty: Sanders-Brahms foregrounds gender as a textual construct. She allows extradiegetic texts to intrude into the diegesis of the film, rupturing its continuity with eruptions of pure textuality. As unified, temporally limited subjectivity ("historical knowledge" depends on this premise) goes, so goes gendered subjectivity: the category of "woman"—along of course, with its binary partner, "man"—is denaturalized, appearing, literally, as a fairy tale suitable for children. Both Duras/Resnais and Sanders-Brahms break up the unity of the body, especially the female body, and the autonomy of the embodied subject: we are repeatedly confronted with bodies that are split, disunited, cut up like the celluloid of a film, broken into pieces never to recover any "natural" wholeness.

Italy in the 1970s, to which I turn in chapter four, was consumed by debates over the legacy of fascism. If the neorealism of the 1940s attempted, albeit ambivalently and incompletely, to turn away from what had come before and to develop a new cinematic vision and idiom, later filmmakers instead confront the past. Younger Italian directors like Bernardo Bertolucci appropriate and subvert what was left to them by their cinematic ancestors. His films *La strategia del ragno* (1970), *Il conformista* (1970), and *Novecento* (1976) are deeply concerned with the pitfalls and possibilities of the cinematic construction of subjectivity in the aftermath of fascism. Like Rossellini, Wilder, and Reed, Bertolucci focuses on masculinity as his crucial problematic: here also, I argue, we see an exploration of the continuities and correspondences between fascist and postwar masculinities. Postwar film, again, must look back at fascist subjectivities and fascist iconography; the saturation of the medium of cinema by the stain of fascism is Bertolucci's constant preoccupation in these three films. The rubble here is not so much literal—there is no ruined city dominating the screen; instead, we are presented with the ruins of fascist epistemology and iconography, and an ambivalent examination of the ways in which these ruins provide the only landscape in which postwar cinema can situate itself. *La strategia del ragno*, in particular, can be read as an intervention in the long and still ongoing debate within postwar Italian culture about the place of fascism in Italian history and national identity. Soon after the war's end, the philosopher Benedetto Croce, a towering figure in Italian intellectual life throughout the first six decades of the twentieth century—so influential, in fact, as to have been nicknamed "the lay pope"—famously "explained" fascism as a brief aberration in Italian history. Croce described the twenty-plus years of fascist rule as a "parenthesis," or even as the result of an alien "virus" infecting the otherwise healthy body politic; in the late 1960s, this and similar formulations were increasingly challenged.[1] In *La strategia del ragno*, the fascist and postfascist body politic as well as, literally, the fascist and postfascist body are represented seamlessly, in an apparent contradiction to the Crocean metaphor. If, for Croce and many liberal postwar intellectuals, there is a clear distinction between "health" and the pathologized (and temporally limited) eruption of fascism, in Bertolucci's film the reverse is true. The film zigzags dizzyingly between time periods—1938 and 1968—and between two identical protagonists, a father and son played by the same actor. Tara (a cinematically overdetermined name, indeed) is the town in which the film is set; it is, in both periods—to the extent that they can be separated at all, always a problematic issue in this film—a world from which all forms of difference, including sexual difference, are categorically banished. Femininity literally does not exist, along with national or racial difference, age distinctions, and "foreignness" of any kind. Neither does time pass: past and present do not exclude each other. The ghosts of the fascist cinema of spectacle haunt this film; an awareness of fascist iconography, codes of representation, and gendered subjectivity is inescapable.

It is my argument that Bertolucci both satirizes and mourns masculinity as construct—whether exemplified by a fascist icon or an antifascist hero, it never emerges as "natural" but as consisting of repetitions, stylizations, and performances of masculinity that verge on the parodic. The hypermasculinized figure of the Duce hovers over the film, remaining just off screen as Tara awaits his arrival in 1938. He never appears, but his iconic body literally becomes the film's template for masculinity, whether fascist or antifascist, as the protagonist substitutes his own body for Mussolini's in an elaborate assassination scheme that takes place as part of a gala performance of *Rigoletto*. (The use of the opera is a typically layered reference to Italian nationalist mythology; it is an allusion to Verdi's prominence as a symbol in the war of unification and consequently links both fascist and postfascist iconography to earlier uses of spectacle.) In addition to being substitutable for the Duce, the bodies of the protagonist are substitutable for each other—one male body is multiplied in the flesh and in heroic sculptures that again echo fascist iconography, albeit as a memorial for the antifascist resistance hero killed in 1938. The absent figure of Mussolini, therefore, dominates this screen on which it does not appear, repeatedly producing sameness, as difference is obliterated, reproduced in its symbolic equivalences as the template for masculinity. The ruined stone that we see in this film is not the rubble produced by bombs; instead, it is the defaced remains of a marble plaque and statue commemorating this overdetermined male body. Cities in rubble have been replaced by the rubble of fascist iconography, the spectacle of the hypermasculinized ideal body—indistinguishable from and interchangeable with that of the anti-fascist hero. The film invokes the fascist fascination with spectacle, playing with the conventions of theater, opera, and film, focusing our attention on our own scopophilic passion as we are forced to consider its dubious antecedents. Again, it is my contention that an epistemological crisis is produced in *La strategia del ragno* as "history" and identity collapse into rubble; the tottering edifice of spectacle rises in their place. This chapter also briefly considers *Il conformista* (1970) and *1900* (1976); I read this trio of films as Bertolucci's intervention in the contemporary debates about the echoes of fascism in Italian life and the political implications of cinematic pleasure.

The new German cinema returns repeatedly to the hollow myths of the Adenauer era, built as it was on the rapidly concealed ruins of Nazi society. Rainer Werner Fassbinder's *Die Ehe der Maria Braun* (1979) and *Die Sehnsucht der Veronika Voss* (1982) cast a cynical eye on the sanitized striving of the German economic miracle. Fassbinder's use of the ironically distanciating effect of the conventions of melodrama to destabilize feminine identity has been discussed extensively. My analysis in chapter five builds on this work and argues that Fassbinder's postwar trilogy is an extended contemplation of fascist spectacle as an ancestor of his filmmaking. The narcotic addiction of the character Veronika Voss, a former actress in Nazi cinema, as she desperately seeks relief for an unspecified pain, shows us our own addiction to the pleasure of cinema as it provides us with analgesia, the (mis)recognition of a unified self and the illusory "healing" of our broken subjectivity. Fassbinder, in presenting us with the characters of Veronika and Lili—both performers, stars in the fascist iconography of spectacle—parallels the pleasures of fascist cinema, the Hollywood "dream machine," and his own movies; visual pleasure itself is placed under his ironic scrutiny, both exploited and undermined in his films. My analysis of *Die Sehnsucht der Veronika Voss* links spectatorship and analgesia. Pain is both cause and effect of our desire for spectacle, and is both elicited and soothed by the pleasures of cinema. Film is simultaneously an irritant to the throbbing nerve and an analgesic. When frau Dr. Katz, the sinister "nerve-doctor," dispenses doses of morphine to her wealthy patients in her all-white clinic—itself a blinding composition of light, which erupts into our darkened spectatorial space—she, like the movie director, presides over their addiction, manages their indefinable, agonizing ache. Veronika has a double pain that needs soothing: her insatiable craving for morphine is parallel to her desire to inhabit once more the lost world of Nazi spectacle. She seeks her "fix" from the needle, and from both the movie camera and the projected image.

Die Sehnsucht der Veronika Voss, from its opening moments, invites us to contemplate our own "Sehnsucht," the compelling longing and desire—our own need, perhaps, to anesthetize the traumatic wounds of our passage into subjectivity—with which we approach the image on the screen. Our presence as spectators is "coded in" to the screen image, the distinction between spectator and spectacle virtually erased, from the first scene of the film. As, in a kind of mise en abîme, we watch the film's protagonist sitting in a darkened movie theater watching herself perform a snippet of melodrama in which a drug-addicted actress gazes at the morphine she desperately needs, and speaks a line that will be repeated later in this film, we enter into a kind of infinite loop of possible subject positions in which all the options—audience, actress, fictive character, "real" person, tormented addict, dedicated film consumer—are all interchangeable, all substitutable for each other. To complicate matters further, Fassbinder includes his own image in this scene, both as one of "us"—an audience surrogate—and as part of the spectacle as he leans forward with a sinister geniality in a seat behind Veronika. Fassbinder does not offer us a seamless diegesis to which we can surrender; rather, he repeatedly opens gaps in that diegesis, highlighting and denaturalizing the building blocks of his representations, and forcing us to contemplate the fissures in the images that we see. Veronika longs to return to her heyday during the Nazi regime when, it appears, she enjoyed the specular pleasures of unity in herself as both subject and object. The change that has occurred by 1955, when the film is set, is painfully evident in a scene in which Veronika is shooting a small part in a new film, a considerable comedown in status. The script calls for tears, which Veronika cannot produce. She bemoans the fact that in the old days she could always feel the appropriate emotion and cry when required. Eventually, rather than submit to the indignity of a glycerin tear applied by the makeup department, a vulgar simulacrum of the unity that was once so effortless, she collapses and is returned to the tender care of Dr. Katz for her analgesic treatment. The irony here is clear; the nature of her pain—the agony of the loss of a specular world—is signaled by her inability to embody, by crying for the camera, the image of pain. The "cure" she seeks is unity between self and image, subject and object. Like Veronika seeking to exchange a glance of recognition with her own image on screen, we long for completeness, for a narcissistic unity in which there is no distinction between subject and object. Ultimately, however, neither director nor doctor offers any lasting satisfaction of this desire; instead, they both bring us repeatedly to the scene of its failure and of our loss.

In each of the films discussed in *Cinema After Fascism*, our own acts of spectatorship are represented to us, almost obsessively foregrounded through an emphasis on the act of looking and the creation of a series of spectator-surrogates, denaturalizing the process. The relationship between subject and object is problematized, each reciprocally constituting the other until the opposition can no longer be sustained—for the directors discussed here, a denaturalizing of epistemology is essential to cinema after the fall of fascism. There is no longer a separate object that can be "known;" the subject is considered as itself an epistemological construct, and "knowledge" and the nature of "reality" are deeply compromised concepts. The gaze of the spectator is also invariably politicized: a historically situated subject emerges in specific contexts in the decades after fascism. This spectatorial subject, then, comes into being as a creature of ideology as well as aesthetics: indeed, for all the directors considered in *Cinema After Fascism*, the two cannot be separated. They are almost obsessively aware of the ideological history that marks their medium in the aftermath of fascism and rigorously cognizant of the embedded subtexts of their films; ideology as well as desire—to the extent that the two are discrete at all—is repeatedly foregrounded and subjected to skeptical scrutiny. The weight of this baggage, the taint carried by the medium itself in the world left behind after the fall of Hitler and Mussolini, burdens these films; the ideological and aesthetic traces of fascism are searchingly explored. On the shattered screen of cinema after fascism, the failure of representation is the only remaining imperative.

Chapter 1
In the Ruins of Fascism

Roberto Rossellini's neorealist trilogy demands to be read in the context of the past history of Italian cinema, especially fascist cinema, though it is not usually interpreted in that light. Two years before making *Roma, città aperta*, which opened in 1945 and is considered by many to be the first true neorealist film, Rossellini was operating within the fascist film industry, creating work that could be classified, perhaps somewhat reductively, as sophisticated military propaganda films.[1] He moved in this short time from producing work that glorified the fascist military machine—espousing, at least in large segments of these films, a jingoistic and hypermasculinized version of Italian national identity fully in keeping with fascist ideals—to a clear condemnation of fascist society.[2]

Rossellini's fascist-era films are intensely ambivalent artifacts, however—contradictions are rampant, and (at least) two opposing stylistic and political imperatives seem to coexist. It is in focusing on human weakness and suffering—the opposite of the hypermasculine, technologically enhanced ideal manhood of fascism—that Rossellini begins, in this first trilogy, to develop elements that will be identifiable aspects of the neorealist ethic and aesthetic emerging in the second trilogy. While technology is glorified, the human cost of the machines of war is also stressed. Extreme nationalism, and the consequent demonization of enemy soldiers, is evident in all three films, but so is the universality of human need. The fascist war trilogy, while glorifying war and Italian warriors, focuses its attention primarily on men who are noncombatants, or who become noncombatants through injury or capture. There is a turning point in each film in which the emphasis shifts from the glorious masculinity of the warrior to the damaged masculinity of warriors who fail, to their broken bodies and their suffering. As I will argue, Catholicism plays a large part in the vision of the fascist-era films—suffering, surrender, and willed sacrifice being models for masculinity in a religious context—but it is not the main determining factor in their marked ambivalence.

Rossellini's rapid transition from being an apologist (however ambivalent) for fascism, with its imperialist sense of entitlement and its militaristic and technology-glorifying iconography, to a staunch antifascist has received relatively little critical comment. Instead, scholars have tended to focus on neorealism as a decisive break from the past, politically and aesthetically the opposite of fascist film.[3] There is general agreement that the distinctive "look" of neorealism was dictated partly by the material conditions of postwar Italy: the necessity of moving away from the studios of Cinecittà (founded, of course, by the fascist regime and personally inaugurated by Mussolini) and relying on technical and narrative improvisation were constraints, fortunate perhaps in retrospect, that shaped the early films of the movement. There were, then, practical changes after the fall of fascism, which undoubtedly contributed to the neorealist aesthetic; however, this does not mean that postwar films were entirely divergent from fascist cinema. Fascist filmmaking was not monolithic, and it allowed different genres and styles to flourish. The industry was also not immune to commercial considerations, and it aspired to surpass Hollywood imports in providing popular entertainment in Italy.[4] However, there was a definite ideological "stamp" on some types of films, especially those depicting war or colonial struggles, particularly in wartime.[5] Mussolini himself was keenly aware of the ideological power of film and incorporated it as part of the national machinery, regarding it almost as an extension of the direct power of the state: he was photographed at the founding of Cinecittà near a slogan that read: *il cinema è l'arma più forte* ("film is the strongest weapon").

The heterogeneity of fascist-era film was a reflection of the contradictory attitude of the fascist regime, at least in its early days, toward intellectual and aesthetic influences that might have been considered subversive, especially if those influences reached only a limited cultural elite. Fascism tolerated a transnational and ideologically diverse flow of ideas: Vittorio Mussolini, the son of the Duce and a committed cinephile who often discussed his enthusiasm with his father, gave his powerful stamp of approval to publications in film journals that espoused Soviet film and sponsored screenings. Rossellini himself, for example, was clearly influenced by Sergei Eisenstein, the great Soviet filmmaker: His fascist-era war film *La nave bianca* contains montage sequences that bear a striking resemblance to Eisenstein's 1925 film, *The Battleship Potemkin*, which glorified precursors to the Bolshevik Revolution.[6] Under the Duce's regime, therefore, it was possible for Italian filmmakers to absorb influences that would seem to be subversive of fascism's ideals and to experiment with narrative and form. The innovative elements that would become the signature of neorealism after the war were developed by filmmakers working in fascist studios: the three so-called fathers of neorealism (a somewhat misleading formulation, specifically rejected by Rossellini[7]) including Vittorio De Sica—also a major star as an actor in the 1930s—Visconti and Rossellini were all actively making films during this period. Indeed, it was through their training at Cinecittà and, at least in Rossellini's case, on location with fascist armies in battle that neorealism was made possible.

Rossellini's vision in his neorealist trilogy of 1945–1948, therefore, cannot be considered in isolation from his work in the fascist war trilogy of 1941–1943. The later films, though very different from one another, all bear the distinctive stamp of neorealism as a movement. However, they must be read in the context of Rossellini's previous experience as a filmmaker within the fascist studio system where the antecedents of neorealism can be found. *Paisà*, like *Germania anno zero* and, perhaps to a lesser extent, *Roma, città aperta*, is an extended dialogue with the "ghosts" of fascist cinema. In these films, Rossellini engages in what seems to be a self-reflexive spiral, constantly foregrounding and questioning his own role as the constructer of a given "reality."[8] He seems to be acutely aware of the unique ideological function of film—and, perhaps, of his own complicity in furthering the ideological goals of fascism—and of its larger epistemological functions. In the neorealist films, Rossellini clearly positions himself as a national filmmaker, speaking for "Italy" in its new postfascist incarnation (as, indeed, he spoke in the fascist trilogy for the nation at war). The films often incorporate extradiegetic elements (e.g., voice-over, maps, and newsreels in *Paisà*, opening and closing titles that refer to the liberation of Italy in *Roma, città aperta*) to make this "speaking" function clear. The neorealist films are self-consciously historiographic; the nature of history, of our knowledge and representation of the past, and the relationship between past and present are an important part of the epistemological focus—even, perhaps, the epistemological crisis—that emerges in this oeuvre.

Rossellini also pays very close attention to spectatorship as an act with crucial ideological implications, and to the kinds of subjectivities that cinematic spectatorship invokes. In his later neorealist films, Rossellini foregrounds spectatorship as a dynamic, interactive process within which particular styles of subjectivity are enacted. He is acutely conscious both of the instability of these subjectivities—the mobility of identifications and desires, of mirrorings of all kinds—and of their implicit ideological content within the specific historical context in which he works. Standing in the rubble of fascist Italy, Rossellini highlights and reconfigures all these elements, helping to establish a new style and a new politics of the cinematic. He creates both a new ethics and a new aesthetics: the two are very closely bound together, inextricable from each other, in this work.

Paradoxically, this is built on a foundation of disavowal: the political and ethical dimension of his early work was not generally acknowledged by him, as is the case for many other Italian cultural figures who began their careers under fascism.[9]

The Fascist Trilogy

Roberto Rossellini is enshrined in the popular imagination and in film scholarship as one of the leading voices of antifascism in postwar European cinema. The relationship of his work to fascist aesthetics and ideology, however, is far more complex than is generally acknowledged. It has become a truism that Rossellini's neorealist trilogy of the late 1940s was a decisive break with fascism and the foundation of a new ethics and aesthetics of film. I argue, however, that the neorealist films look back to another trilogy from the early 1940s, shot in fascist film studios and on fascist battlefields. *La nave bianca* (released in 1942), *Un pilota ritorna* (from 1942), and *L'uomo della croce* (1943) are profoundly contradictory films. These early films venerate the fascist war machine—and glory unashamedly in the sounds and visual rhythms of war's machinery: tanks, artillery, aircraft. At the same time they present us with a distinctly paradoxical view of the fascist soldier. Masculine subjectivity in these films is a profoundly unstable commodity. Rossellini's heroes are at once military men and noncombatants. Priests, wounded hospital patients, and prisoners of war, they epitomize the fascist male virtues of patriotism and courage. They inhabit the battlefield, but they do not always fight; often, they suffer instead. Passivity becomes the quintessentially masculine posture. The heroic figure of the larger-than-life fascist hero flickers out of focus as the characters dissolve into illegible landscapes, human figure becoming increasingly indistinguishable from fractured ground. The male body is defined by paradox: it is presented both as a machine of war in itself, visually constructed as an extension of the tanks, aircraft, and artillery pieces that define the mise-en-scène of these combat films, and as permeable and organic, defined not by its aggressive capabilities but by its capacity for suffering and pain.

Rossellini, in the fascist-era films, employs a paradoxical visual vocabulary, oscillating between two immediately recognizable tropes of masculine representation. He simultaneously offers us the phallic, machine-linked male of fascist iconography—typically shot from a low angle, framed against the sky—and the body of the hero as utterly earthbound, bereft of its steel machines, a fragile organic object passively suffering indignity and pain. The film's fetishistic aggrandizement of military technology gives way to a primitive immediacy as the heroes tenderly carry other wounded men, anticipating—and regendering—the iconic pietà composition so prevalent in Rossellini's postwar films. Rossellini's implicit statement "behold the man" must, therefore, be accorded the full complexity of its ambivalence. It must be read both in its original context, as an invitation to view the all-too-overdetermined image of the body of the scourged and soon to be crucified Christ, and as an exposition of the hypermasculine body of fascism, epitomized by the ubiquitous image of the Duce as soldier and man of action, a countervailing icon to the crucified Christ in fascist propaganda. Rossellini draws extensively on images from Italian art, especially the early and late pietàs by Michelangelo, in his compositions on screen, as well as contemporary fascist aestheticizations of the human male. In either case, he gives us an invocation of spectatorship: the director stands in for Pontius Pilate—a most uncomfortable position—asking us to look at masculinity. As Rossellini, after 1945, turns away from heroic spectacle and embraces "realism"—"reality" being, of course, itself a highly problematic term—he still returns to an uneasy contemplation of spectacle and spectatorship. It is my contention that his postfascist films engage in an ambivalent dialogue with the films of 1941–1943. The *mani sporchi*, or "dirty hands," of neorealism—the grime of "reality"—are also the "dirty hands" of all postwar cinema in Europe after Hitler and Mussolini. Postwar film, even the stripped-down stylizations of neorealism, the ostensible opposite of fascism's militaristic spectacle or white telephone escapism, can never achieve any kind of purity; instead, it interrogates its own moral, political, and aesthetic ambiguity.

Rossellini's relationship to fascism has been the subject of considerable debate among scholars. His great neorealist films clearly and unambiguously reject fascism, and he later denied having been a member of the fascist party or having actively supported it. However, there is no question that he learned his craft in fascist film studios, and it was through his personal connections to dominant figures in the fascist culture industry, especially Vittorio Mussolini, the aviator son of the Duce who was an eager mentor to Italy's young directors, that he was able to become a filmmaker.[10] An interestingly double, ambivalent point of view pervades Rossellini's fascist-era films. Nationalism, hypermasculinity, militarism—the indispensable ingredients of war films made during the fascist regime—are certainly part of Rossellini's films of this period; in his later neorealist films, it is precisely these qualities, so identified with fascism, that are most ruthlessly criticized. In his war trilogy of the early 1940s, Rossellini presents these identifiably "fascist" elements in ways that underline, and even exploit, their seductiveness, while simultaneously undercutting their power. The films of the war trilogy focus on the exploits of the Italian fighting forces; they present audiences with the familiar seductions of patriotism, military heroism, and sacrifice. Most notable, perhaps, is their focus on the mystique of military technology. In the three films, we see aircraft, tanks, and ships in stunning montages, shot from low angles that exploit their gleaming phallic beauty. Long stretches of soundtrack are dominated by the roar of tank and aircraft engines; in these segments Rossellini is fulfilling the prescription of a fascist slogan we see painted on the superstructure of a ship in *La nave bianca*: "*uomini e macchine un sol palpito*" ("men and machines share a single heartbeat"). The men inhabit these machines and become part of them; pilots, sailors, artillery officers, and tank crews are visually linked to the modern technology that they control. They are efficient amalgams of flesh and steel, masters of battlefields in which, not incidentally, the enemy is often limited to antiquated technology, transported by horse or mule, or slogging on foot through the dirt.

Figure 1.1 *La nave bianca*: the ship in battle: "men and machines share a single heartbeat."

However, despite Rossellini's reverential treatment of these hypermasculine heroes and their technology and his enthusiastic surrender to the seduction of the machine, it is noncombatants who ultimately emerge as the paradoxical heroes of his war films. In the three films, our heroes are military men who do not fight: a priest who is a military chaplain with a tank unit, a pilot who is shot down and imprisoned, a crippled patient on a naval hospital ship. The chaplain and the pilot are both captured by the enemy that has been so ridiculed for its primitiveness. The technology ultimately fails, the soldier ultimately becomes a man of peace, and the fighter becomes a nurse, caretaker, even a pack mule. The splendid isolation of the machine, its effortless speed and elegance, give way to the dirt, cold, and drudgery of a prisoner on the ground, cowering under the bombs and bullets of his own comrades, delivered with unfailing efficiency. The machine is no longer a magnificent servant but becomes a vicious threat: in *Un pilota ritorna*, our point of view changes radically: no longer enjoying the god-like point of view of a pilot, we cower on the ground, looking up at a German Stuka as it roars out of the sky, strafing prisoners on a dirt road.

The contradictions at the heart of Rossellini's fascist oeuvre are evident from the opening sequences of *L'uomo della croce*, the last film of the war trilogy, released in 1943. The film is set during the Italian campaign in Russia in 1942. It was inspired by the story—much exploited for propaganda purposes—of an Italian army chaplain who ministered to Russian civilians and Italian troops alike, and who sacrificed his own life to do so.[11] *L'uomo della croce* is dedicated to military chaplains who died ministering to the "godless in barbaric lands." The film explicitly links the Catholicism represented by the chaplain to fascism: in one sequence, a handsome young Italian soldier who is being interrogated by repulsive Russian captors proudly claims ownership of a fascist party membership card: he is immediately taken out and shot, crying *padre* as the priest crosses himself. The first shots of the film, however, are, if anything, pastoral; they seem to be the opposite of what the audience expects from a patriotic film about the Italian fighting forces. Rossellini, as the opening minutes of the film continue, however, builds toward a completely different effect: we go from birdsong and a gentle depiction of men in communion with nature to being engulfed by the roar of engines, by the hard mystique of the machine. Rossellini opens the film with a shot of doves (obviously, a highly overdetermined image—a symbol both of peace and of Christianity; there are no fascist eagles to be seen) flitting around in the branches of a tree and slowly pans across an idyllic scene of shirtless young men wading in a stream and sunbathing in a field. There are no signs of war matériel and, at first, no indication that these are soldiers, except for a distant figure standing on a ridge who might be a sentry. Indeed, the men seem like schoolboys: young, skinny, and vulnerable. The rhythm of the opening is quiet, leisurely, and peaceful; it is focused on nature and on human beings nearly naked, unprotected within a natural setting.

The conversation of the men in this opening sequence gradually makes it clear that they are, in fact, soldiers—including a tank crew sidelined by mechanical failure. When they go to check on how their tank's repairs are progressing, we get our first sight, surprisingly ambivalent, of military technology. Their tank is a useless hunk of metal, unable to move, camouflaged prettily in its woodland setting. Like the shirtless young men, it seems harmless and slightly ineffectual, its contours softened and its menace blunted. In the opening sequence of *L'uomo della croce*, men and machine are indeed parallel. The fascist slogan, unifying man and machine, is fulfilled, but ironically, as men and their tank share a pastoral idyll, sidelined from their military role. All of this changes, however, as the long-awaited tank squadron returns from battle. The soldiers hear the engine noise and leap up to meet the tanks, immediately acquiring purpose, energy, and military bearing, hitherto noticeably absent. The tank crew lines up on a wooden bridge as the machines pass, churning up the streambed in which the men have been so peacefully wading. They salute their comrades in unison, shot from below, silhouetted against the sky (a shot that is almost identical to the one in which wounded sailors stand at the rail of the hospital ship in *La nave bianca*, saluting their battleship as she returns to port). As the tanks arrive in the camp, Rossellini places his camera low, almost at ground level, and films the machines charging straight at it, veering away at the last minute. The roar is deafening; we look up at the tanks and see their commanders standing in the hatches, visible from the waist up. They are modern centaurs, their upper bodies rising from the bodies of their machines, clad in steel and leather, as hard-shelled as the steel armor that surrounds them. The contrast with the skinny, naked torsos of the soldiers at the beginning of the film could not be more marked.

In all three films of his fascist war trilogy, Rossellini's heroes are defined by paradox. Their bodies are coded simultaneously as the hard-shelled, mechanized phallic figure of fascist iconography and as organic, vulnerable, permeable, and suffering. Long, almost wordless, sequences in all three films are essentially ballets between man and machine. They are stirring, often poetic. In the naval battle scenes in *La nave bianca*, for example, the connection between the Italian sailors and their vessel is profound—the men appear to move in rhythm with the mechanical systems of the ship without thought or hesitation. The huge naval guns fire, the shells are loaded by sweating crewmen, smoke and flame erupt from gun barrels, and the shells strike. The romance of fascist masculinity, the phallic fascination of the military hero, is expressed perfectly in the slogan painted above the targeting center for the guns that, in giving the pulse of the heartbeat to inorganic systems, links organic and mechanical. Man and machine indeed share a single heartbeat, gracefully united in their triumph. In all three films, however, this invulnerability, the hard-shelled grace of mechanical centaurs, is a highly perishable commodity. Military men are always eventually separated from their machines, cut off from their phallic romance, and become earthbound and broken. Masculinity, in Rossellini's fascist-era films, is defined both in the perfection of its link to technology and in the failure of that link, the betrayal of the romance. His presentation of the fascist iconography of the hypermasculine hero is, therefore, simultaneously hagiographic and highly critical. Rossellini glories in the dubious beauty of the phallic romance, but ultimately undercuts it. He seems most interested in his heroes when they cease to be supermen and become sacrificial victims.

In their sacrifice, always presented as voluntary, another symbolic system supervenes, with Catholic iconography substituting for the fascist sloganeering. In all three films, we see compositions strikingly reminiscent of the classic pietà pose, with one figure cradling another who is passive, either suffering or dead. It is important to note that Catholicism was, generally, not considered to be antithetical to fascism. Mussolini's "Accordi Laterani" with the church in 1929 created the Vatican as an independent state and allowed it a certain degree of control over some civic institutions and public education in return for the church's recognition of the Italian state. The movement from the hypermasculine stylizations of Rossellini's warrior bodies to the use of readily identifiable visual tropes associated with Catholicism also serves to link the fascist-era war trilogy to his later neorealist oeuvre: the pietà composition appears in many of Rossellini's films from both periods. The gentle cradling of a wounded or dead body becomes a defining posture of the hero in Rossellini's fascist war films. No longer are they visually linked to their machines, like modern centaurs; instead, they are inserted into another set of codes, another unmistakable visual iconography, employed with equal deliberation. Rossellini repeatedly frames the chaplain in *L'uomo della croce* in a classic pietà composition as he cradles his wounded soldier, for whom he sacrifices his freedom and, ultimately, his life. In *Un pilota ritorna*, the knight of the air becomes earthbound, cradling, carrying, and nursing another badly wounded comrade. The young wounded sailor in the white hospital ship of *La nave bianca* is cradled in his bed, his head held up so that he can look out and participate as his comrades salute the return of their battleship to port.

Gender is highly mobile in Rossellini's pietà compositions—a male soldier can stand in both for the Madonna, the sorrowing mother, and for the dead Christ, the sacrificed son. The mobile significance of this visual signature continues, of course, through Rossellini's later career, after the fall of fascism. One of the most famous shots in Rossellini's iconic neorealist film, *Roma, città aperta*, shows the body of a woman who has just been shot by the Nazi occupiers, cradled by a male priest in a traditional pietà pose. Rossellini, in *Roma, città aperta*, reverses the gender of the participants, a potentially subversive revisioning of this important image. In the fascist war trilogy, the fascist male body encompasses both the phallic, machine/man hybrid and the sorrowing maternal figure, undeniably feminized. The familiar Catholic iconography is not offered as an alternative system of codes to fascist hypermasculinity and the machine/human centaur. Instead, it is commensurate with it, another way of emphasizing the voluntary sacrifice of the military hero. However, the ambiguity and ambivalence implicit in reconciling such different codes, both of which are familiar and ubiquitous, is unmistakable. In his later neorealist films, Rossellini will return repeatedly to the pietà, relying once more on its familiar iconography. We see it in *Roma, città aperta*, *Paisà*, and *Germania anno zero*. However, the meaning of this composition has been radically altered: in the later films, the sacrificed figures are fascism's victims, not its martyrs. Rossellini's trademark pietà has been recontextualized: rather than an exaltation of the fascist ideal, it has been rewritten as a condemnation of it. Rossellini, like the pilot in *Un pilota ritorna*, returns to his origins, acknowledging, interrogating, and recoding the elements of his early films. Rossellini's neorealism, therefore, must be read in this context; it is a complex and coded ballet of revision and commentary, casting ambivalent glances back toward its fascist antecedents at the same time as it refutes them.

Paisà

With *Paisà*, his second film of the postwar period, Rossellini returns to the military themes and settings that characterized his work of the early 1940s, once more depicting war and focusing on soldiers as protagonists. *Paisà* is a film about recent history, specifically the events surrounding the American liberation of Italy in 1945.[12] The view of history presented here is, however, paradoxical. While on the surface the film advances a relatively unproblematic " factual" approach, I argue that unsettling questions about epistemology, about the ways in which we know truth and the reality of events, are at the center of *Paisà*. With this film, Rossellini is intervening in the running discussion among Italian neorealists about definitions of "reality," that elusive element that was, at least ostensibly, the goal of the movement.[13] This debate, carried on throughout the late 1940s and the 1950s, presented competing views about the nature of reality, and hence of the realism that this group was attempting to achieve. In attaining realism, the definitions of the real varied from quasiplatonic assertions about supersensory essences—the "ideal" or, more prosaically, the "typical" and "authentic" universal image—to a belief in scientific objectivity and observation. The basic assumption ostensibly shared by all sides in these debates was the idea that film is the most transparent of all media, providing the least impeded access to a reality that can be seen, and that has a prior existence separate from the medium through which we see it. In contrast, my reading of *Paisà* argues that the film works within a very different set of assumptions. For Rossellini, the luxury of an unproblematic assumption of transparency is never possible. He presents us here with a crisis of epistemology: knowledge and reality are, in the rubble of the war's end, extremely problematic concepts.[14]

These epistemological questions are developed partly by means of an explicit focus on spectatorship—visual pleasure in the act of looking at a constructed representation, assumed to be present for that purpose—throughout *Paisà*. The presence of the spectator—as an aesthete, a watcher of movies, both a consumer and a constructor of fictions, and a connoisseur of visual pleasures—is invoked in every section of the film. This, along with the use of a variety of distanciation techniques, helps to create a strong self-reflexivity. We are reminded at every stage of the film that what we are watching is a historical and technological artifact. Any illusion of transparency or unmediated access to a preexisting outside reality, whether by means of the familiar Hollywood codes, or the anti-Hollywood precepts of the neorealists, is undercut. In fact, the codes by which "realities" are mediated and constructed arguably become a major aspect of what the film is about.

Paisà is divided into six segments, each focusing on the effects of fascism and war in a different region of Italy, moving sequentially from south to north.[15] Each segment is introduced briefly by an interlude that looks very much like the sort of newsreel that accompanied the showing of contemporary films in movie theaters, a form that would have been very familiar to audiences and would presumably have had a certain amount of authority and credibility. The extradiegetic intercessions serve structurally to unify a film that otherwise seems like a series of "mini movies" that are remarkably heterogeneous in style. More importantly, the six narrative segments each seems self-reflexive in a different way; their varied styles create an assorted series of invocations of "cinema" as the system of codes and past representations from which neorealism as a movement ostensibly distanced itself, claiming that it was depicting "reality" and obscuring its own acts of mediation. These sections contain maps with arrows representing German and Allied troop movements with, at least in the version distributed in the United States, an authoritative voice-over in English—a vibrant and sonorous male American voice—narrating the public, "historical" events, creating a narrative movement that is progressive and teleological. The triumph of the Allies seems to be preordained.[16] Rossellini uses the familiarity of this form to achieve a subversion of its credibility, employing the codes and conventions that are traditionally used to claim the privileged position of objectivity and truth and to assert the primacy of the fact—and thereby generally glossing over any epistemological instability—to challenge these very constructions.[17] These "empirical" sections initially seem to assert unproblematic knowledge only to leave us ultimately with the paradox that all we can know is the impossibility of knowledge, the failure of epistemology.[18]

Sicily

The first segment of *Paisà*—following the initial pseudonewsreel section, which contains some actual archival footage—is set in Sicily, the starting point of the Allied campaign to retake Italy from the Germans. It opens on a landscape ravaged by war and nature: we see a nightscape, a scene of confused darkness and jumbled sound. Soldiers are fumbling over tumbled rocks and steeply eroded slopes, and move into populated spaces that are equally fragmented and unreadable. Rossellini deliberately refrains from clarifying the images that open the film's narrative, whether by lighting, continuity of movement, or the use of coherent establishing shots. (Since *Paisà* was made under the aegis of the American military, and with funding and equipment from MGM, Rossellini presumably had the means to achieve a conventionally "coherent" scene.[19]) The beginning of *Paisà* seems designed to provoke confusion, frustration, and disorientation in the spectator, which is intensified in the early dialogue between the GIs and a group of Sicilian villagers—the soldiers don't know where they are, the villagers don't know if they are encountering American or German troops, and no one can understand what anyone else is saying.[20] We learn soon that the landscape itself resists the imposition of structures of cartographic or spatial comprehensibility making linear navigation impossible. When asking later about roads they can take, the soldiers are told they must travel over lava fields: "just lava." The landscape here is based literally on a boundaryless flow.[21] Eventually the screen lightens, an Italian-speaking soldier (an Italian American from the proverbial and providential central casting department) appears, and the confusion—both within the diegesis of the film and as experienced by the spectator—eases. This multilayered lack of comprehensibility at the beginning of *Paisà* is in ironic contrast to the godlike overview and the reassuring certainty of the voice-over in the initial "newsreel." At the beginning of the film, the spectator is confronted with the limits of observation and direct knowledge. Mediation by film does not offer any clarification, but a distillation of the confusion. In *Paisà's* opening segment, we are also given an unmistakable reminder that "history," the unfolding of which we are struggling to make out on the screen, is a man-made construct, and that this film, like all films, is a palimpsest of previous mediations and representations.

A group of American GIs approaches the ruined tower around which much of the action of this segment is set. The following discussion ensues: "Hey, Joe, remember *Frankenstein*? This joint reminds me of the old mill in it." "It does, now that you mention it. What a place for a murder!"[22] The soldiers are referring to two well-established Hollywood genres: the horror movie (of which James Whale's *Frankenstein*, 1931, is a well-known example) and the murder mystery. The German soldiers in this segment have seen the same movies as the Americans. Bits of overheard dialogue among the Wehrmacht contingent convey that they, too, share the same culture of spectatorship, shaped by Hollywood romance and boys' adventure movies: "One could really get romantic here, if not for the Americans. ... This is a real pirates hole." Errol Flynn flickers momentarily to life on the lava fields of Mt. Etna as it becomes clear that the German soldiers see themselves as swashbucklers in a similar mode. As the Americans enter the tower, their dialogue continues in a similar vein, a constant chatter that makes clear the primary "reality" for these men is in fact Hollywood, rather than the life and death struggle they are actually engaged in: "I hope we find a treasure up here!" "What would you do with a million bucks?" "Ah, he'd go to a medic and get his face lifted." ... "This place has a trap door, a deep dark trap door—you're not scared, are you?" The references to a shared filmic culture (shared by the fictional GIs, the fictional Wehrmacht, and the spectator of *Paisà*) are obvious—two films that come immediately to mind are *Treasure Island* and *The Prisoner of Zenda*. The joke about a face-lift is especially interesting. This bizarre statement—"real" men, as we might suppose these GIs moving through hostile territory in the middle of a war to be, don't get face-lifts from army medics—ruptures the diegetic universe: we are reminded that these are not "really" GIs we are watching, but actors—actors who, in time-honored Hollywood tradition, may get face-lifts. "Joe from Joisy," a plainspoken soldier, engages in romantic banter—a moment heralded in almost parodic fashion by a shooting star in the sky—with Carmella, a spunky dark-haired local beauty (both, again, could have come straight from central casting). Joe from Joisy is concerned with cinematic lighting—during his conversation with Carmella, a moment is reached in which Joe obviously thinks it is time for his close-up. In order to demonstrate his resemblance to a family photograph he is attempting to show her (reality must follow the image rather than the reverse), he produces a flame from a cigarette lighter to show her his face. He obviously thinks of lighting in cinematic rather than military terms: he "forgets" that it is dangerous in a battle zone. Joe as a cinematic being, a creature of celluloid who requires a close-up, causes the demise of GI Joe: the Germans see the light and fire at it, resulting in his death and Carmella's. The movie-saturated dialogue and the Joe/Carmella incident, so early in the film, underline the fact that the soldiers on screen are preeminently spectators, creatures of film; throughout *Paisà*, we see soldiers doing a lot more spectating than fighting—it is the preferred masculine activity, despite all the accoutrements of war with which the men are surrounded.

Naples

In the second segment of the film, set in Naples after its liberation, spectatorship and representation are also a central concern. The "newsreel" segment that separates the first and the second sections appears to constitute an ironic commentary on both: after the schematized map, and a sonorous voice-over informing us that "the Allies sweep northwards," we are given a panoramic shot of the Greek temple at Paestum and a beautiful vista of the Bay of Naples and the city itself. The temple suggests, perhaps, both the "eternal truths" of classicism, with its decorous and seductive balance and certainty, and the edifices of "history" itself. The panoramic shot of a famous Italian landscape—one well known as having inspired writers and artists from antiquity on—gives us a god-like overview similar to that offered by the maps. Both, perhaps, offer a more comfortable and familiar model of constructing the past than the uncertainties and dislocations offered by *Paisà* as a whole. The opening of the narrative of the Neapolitan segment is in striking contrast to this placid certainty: Rossellini engages in radical and disorienting shifts in tone, using (false) epistemological reassurance to bridge two episodes in which chaos and epistemological dislocation have ruled.

Here, as in the opening of the Sicilian segment, there is no establishing shot or opportunity to orient ourselves spatially—we are plunged immediately into the middle of a confusing, chaotic street scene; this is very different from the deserted volcanic slopes that open the Sicilian segment, but the effect of disorientation is similar. Street performers emerge from the crowd: tumblers and acrobats career around, and hustlers call out their specialties: "Look, ladies and gentlemen, I defy death—man of steel!" declaims a fire-eater. This opening line of dialogue is, like the "newsreel" segment, also a bridge of sorts—it links the soldiers of Sicily to the teeming streets of Allied-occupied Naples. It is, of course, highly ironic: we have seen the "men of steel" in the previous segment: they get themselves killed because, like Gloria Swanson, they are "ready for their close-up." The fire-eater's statement only underlines the failure of the GIs at war as soldiers; instead, they insist on living within a world of movies. The reference to a "man of steel" is clearly a bridge in another sense as well, this time a historical and temporal one. Fascist constructions of the male subject through hypermasculinizing rhetoric sounded strikingly like this fire-eater's cry—here, the phrase links fascist rhetoric to American constructions of masculinity. The tank crews, airmen, and naval sailors of Rossellini's fascist war trilogy flicker briefly into view here: the glorification of the link between technology and the martial male body that was an integral part of fascist iconography suffuses these films, albeit in an ambivalent way—Rossellini's fascist military heroes were human–machine centaurs, truly men of steel, at least until the machines are destroyed or broken down. The phrase refers on the level of language, also: the "Patto d'Acciaio" or "Pact of Steel" was the name of the alliance between the Führer's Germany and the Duce's Italy, and Mussolini himself was sometimes referred to as *l'uomo d'acciaio*. The Pact of Steel lasted until another "man of steel" (Stalin's adopted name) helped to smash it. American popular culture is also, of course, inextricably inscribed into this statement: Superman, as an American icon of the (super)masculine, is glimpsed. (Italy, or course, also had its own hypermasculine comic book heroes, such as Sandokan). The fire-eater echoes and parodies a style of maleness, an iconic hypermasculinity that is operative in both the wartime fascist and the postwar American contexts. As the opening line of dialogue in this segment, this statement is, once again, an ironic reference to the expectations of the audience. We might be awaiting a familiar story of men at war, a tale of the military heroism, conquest, and liberation implied in the newsreel section bridging the segments, characterized by the sonorous certainty and retrospective teleology of statements like "the allies sweep northwards." However, instead of ideal masculinity and a heroic view of war, the Naples segment of *Paisà* gives us an extended meditation on spectatorship and the coconstruction of narrative.

It is significant that both the protagonists in this segment are characterized by their role as spectators: the Neapolitan street urchin who is the instigator of the segment's action is first introduced as part of a group of ragged children watching the street performers, and the black GI whom the boy "buys" from the others as his allotted theft victim is the ultimate spectator/participant in *Paisà's* most famous sequence: the puppet show. The boy takes the drunken GI by the hand and leads him into a traditional puppet theater. The audience of the puppet show is remarkable for its absorption and the avidity with which it consumes the spectacle before it. As the drunken, hulking GI shambles down the aisle of the theater, he elicits cries of outrage from the audience, who find their view briefly interrupted. Here, the consumption of spectacle is presented as having a distinctly ugly aspect: it is greedy and rapacious, almost violent if thwarted.

The scene depicting consumers of spectacle is, of course, self-reflexive: the puppet theater bears a resemblance to the scene inside the movie theater in which we are watching *Paisà*. We are seeing ourselves, the audience of this film, represented on screen. Here, again, we see the intensity of our own hunger for narrative, story, and "history" represented on screen: it is not a pretty sight.

After the GI and the boy find seats, the camera turns to the puppet show itself. Once again, the spectacle before the multiple diegetic and extradiegetic audiences represents "history:" we see a crude pastiche of the story of the Crusades, especially its most disturbing elements of racism and religious intolerance. The large marionettes represent "Christians" (white puppets) and "infidels" (black ones). The "voice" of one of the white puppets is clearly audible: "To arms, to arms! Christians, God has called us not for riches and gold, but for justice and liberty!" Another white puppet "says:" "You can't frighten me, you giant Moor, because I'm white and you're black!" The audience is fully engaged in the narrative shouting support and encouragement to the white puppets and abuse at the black ones. They are actively engaged in historiography—as are we, by analogy—coproducing "the past" and establishing a very specific relationship between past and present. These raucous representatives of working-class Naples, oppressed and dispossessed, more desperately poor than ever despite having been newly "liberated" by the Allies, are venting their hatred and intolerance toward a racially differentiated enemy. In this, there is apparently continuity between the Crusades (as retrospectively constructed by the historiographic performance of a puppet show), Italian colonialism, and American society. Fascist colonialism depended on racist constructions that ranged from pious pseudobenevolence to overt justification of mass murder; in this, of course, they are similar to American racist constructions. The black GI—also addressed, naturally, as "Joe"—echoes the figure of the "moor" and "infidel," which was itself echoed by fascism's version of the "native" inhabitants of the colonized Italian Quarta Sponda, the nation's "fourth shore" in North Africa.[23] This character also embodies a strong critique of American racial attitudes.

As a spectator, the black GI falls into the very trap that Rossellini warns us, the film spectators, about, throughout *Paisà*: he makes an epistemological mistake, confusing representation with reality. The drunken "Joe" rushes up onto the tiny stage to defend the black-faced puppet, the "infidel," who is being beaten by the white-faced "knights." In this segment, distinctions between spectator and participant disappear completely. We, the spectators of this black-and-white film, watch Joe watching another spectacle in black and white, and, of course, taking part in yet another, racially inflected black-and-white scenario himself—it is as if, in this sequence, spectatorship and its potential pitfalls are multiplied and repeated.[24] In his passionate confusion about what is real and what is fictive, Joe is trapped inside the very paradox that Rossellini foregrounds throughout *Paisà*. After Joe, still roaring and punching wildly in inebriated rage, is dragged from the stage by a furious audience, the boy again takes his hand and they flee the theater. After the puppet theater sequence, as the two protagonists wander through the ruins of the bombed city, we are given a performance from a very different theatrical tradition, albeit one that, like the puppet theater and this film itself, is also enacted in shades of black and white. Joe slumps drunkenly down onto a pile of rubble and begins to sing, in a rich bass: "nobody knows the troubles I seen/nobody knows my sorrow." *Paisà*, in citing a well-known American Negro spiritual, most memorably recorded by Louis Armstrong, is playing with stereotypes about blacks and American culture, once again placing "Joe" at the center of a scene that reinforces our perception of the artifactuality of what we are watching: we are being shown what we, within the prevailing filmic racial stereotypes, expect to see in movies or on stage. (It is, perhaps, worth noting that Paul Robeson's character in James Whale's 1936 film version of *Show Boat* is also named "Joe.") The constant emphasis on black and white in this segment subtly draws a parallel between the different spectacles and reminds us, once again, that the performances we see are essentially equivalent to the black-and-white film that is on screen in front of us.[25]

The next "show" begins when the drunken GI continues to perform, this time within yet another genre with which the audience would presumably be familiar: the adventure story. He narrates an elaborate fantasy of heroism, flying a plane to save America, culminating in a ticker tape parade in New York and a hero's reception at the Waldorf Astoria. This is somewhat transgressive: it goes without saying that, in the black-and-white economy of popular and cinematic culture in both Italy and America, it would have been inconceivable for the hero of such an adventure to be black. He physically acts out each stage of the story in vivid pantomime, spreading his arms to become an airplane and making chugging and huffing noises to represent a train. His youthful audience, the boy, is entranced; even though he doesn't understand a word of spoken English, he participates gleefully in the pantomime, identifying each element, with happy shouts, as it is acted out. The two of them, in a moment of complete harmony, put on their own cooperative theater performance. The sequence of Joe's spiritual singing and pantomime performance of a familiar adventure story breaks yet again into the diegesis of the film, rupturing any continuity of its illusion, revealing it, always, as a construction in black and white.

The rubble in which this sequence of the Neapolitan segment is set is not the rubble of nature, as is the volcanic Sicilian landscape, but of a great, historic city. Joe and the boy are surrounded by the random, tumbled, ruptured elements of civilization, a history dating back to classical Greece. The protagonists of this story inhabit a world similar to that created by Rossellini for the audience of *Paisà*, in which any landmarks, all certainty and familiarity, are destroyed and we are left to wander, disoriented, through their debris. Near the end of the Neapolitan segment, the boy is forced by an alert and sober Joe who is hoping to recover the boots the boy has stolen from him, to guide him to his "home." Joe is shocked and appalled when this "home" turns out to be a huge rocky cave inhabited by a ragged mob of bombed-out Neapolitans.[26] He asks the boy where his parents are and the boy replies with another "show," another pantomime of gestures: "boom, boom, boom, morti!" Rossellini insists, throughout *Paisà*, that his audience, like the Neapolitan street urchin, are epistemological orphans, living amidst rubble: we stand in the wreckage of our own certainties, the ruins of reassuring edifices of "history" and "knowledge." We have moved in this segment from the Greek temple of Paestum—though itself a picturesque ruin, its meaning is stable, even ossified. It testifies to the persistence of classical models of stability, of endurance over time, and of rational causality, in contrast to the far less picturesque world of a smashed city and a broken epistemology. The relationship between past and present is a palimpsest in black and white, the accumulation of layers of representation and spectatorship. "Reality" is profoundly problematized in this most famous segment of a very important neorealist film: clearly the concept of "realism" as traditionally defined is inadequate here. This segment of *Paisà* becomes a series of "shows" in which spectatorship and agency become entirely intertwined, and the distinction between subject and object disappears. Rossellini presents us with a model for subjectivity that is frankly performative and unstable. In Naples, we find no viable, secure epistemologies; instead, we are immersed in the far less impressive, provisional "truths" of narrative, spectacle, and spectatorship.[27]

Rome

The next segment of *Paisà*, set in Rome, begins with the expected voice-over: "every step of the path between Rome and Naples was fiercely contested by the Germans. The allies advanced through a wilderness of ruined cities." Accompanying these words is documentary footage of war-ravaged landscapes and towns, mostly anonymous although one well-known icon appears briefly, the destroyed monastery at Monte Cassino. Once again, therefore, Rossellini begins the segment by purporting to explain, clarify, and convey to us the "facts" about the war, only to undercut this by having what is—with brief exceptions—confusing, unidentifiable rubble precede the clarity and order of a map: cartography is useless when cities have become "wilderness." This is a landscape in which distinctions between the natural and man-made no longer hold sway, and all the clear lines of the map that follow have been obliterated; as happens continuously in *Paisà*, the audience's expectations of conventional categorization is challenged. The voice-over continues its sonorous summary, accompanied by the map: "the Allied landings at Anzio opened a new path to Rome and the German defenses crumbled. Through empty, silent streets the enemy withdrew from Rome." The German withdrawal is shown in documentary-style footage of tanks, lorries, and armored cars full of Germans driving past well-known Roman monuments, and units of soldiers on foot filing through cobble-stoned piazzas. One of the monuments shown is the Roman Colosseum, which will reappear as a backdrop for American GIs in the final scene of the segment.

The Colosseum functions in this segment as a multipurpose, even contradictory, reference. It was a symbol much beloved of Italian fascists, the centerpiece of Mussolini's attempt to confer legitimacy on his claims of empire through a grandiose redesign of the archaeological center of Rome. In this context, its presence invokes both "history" in the traditional sense, serving as a literally colossal reminder of the ways in which we, within our familiar historiographic models, purport to access the "truth" about the past—the Colosseum is the largest intact relic of imperial Rome in the city, and generations of archaeologists, art historians, and historians have examined and explicated it. Rossellini also employs a cynical comment on the readjustment, reconstitution, and manipulation of "history" in the service of politics, and the blurring of distinctions between "history" and "mythology," between fact and fiction. Most importantly, by bracketing the Roman segment with shots of the Colosseum, Rossellini is once again foregrounding spectatorship, as he does throughout *Paisà*. The Colosseum is the original venue for spectacle, the scene of bloody shows— perhaps a bit like war movies—that were used as a way to distract and control the population. The phrase, "bread and circuses," identified with ancient Rome, might just as accurately be used to describe the attitudes of the Italian fascist government: the fascists were masters of spectacle, both on screen and off. Mussolini's regime reconfigured the city of Rome to provide venues for nationalist spectacle that would visually link fascism with ancient Rome.[28] In creating a military parade route, designed for mass spectacle and for the camera, from the Capitoline to the Colosseum (Via dell'Impero, today's Via dei Fori Imperiali), the Duce's engineers bulldozed their way through invaluable archeological sites that had not yet been fully excavated. The epistemological paradox is clear here: rather than making possible excavations that would lead to actual information about ancient Rome, the Duce preferred to "discover" the links between past and fascist present by destroying the traces of the historic past and building new ones. It is a truism that the Duce's "recovery"/invention of the past caused much more damage to Italian cities than the Allies did. The presence of the Colosseum here also throws a highly ironic light on cartography, the vehicle for "knowledge" and certainty in the bridging voice-over sections—the Via del'Impero was well known for a series of large maps in bas-relief depicting the historic spread of imperial Rome and paralleling it to the Duce's modern "empire."[29]

The Rome segment in *Paisà* was generally disliked by contemporary critics who advocated neorealism's radical qualities; it was considered the most conventionally "Hollywood-style" part of the film.[30] Indeed, the narrative is about failed romance: a young, handsome, American soldier, Fred, meets a young beautiful Italian civilian, Francesca, during the liberation of Rome (depicted for us via documentary footage of cheering crowds and smiling Allied soldiers). After a flirtatious conversation, complete with comic sentences from an Italian English phrasebook, they separate. When they meet again months later, Francesca has become a prostitute and Fred her drunken client; he does not recognize her as the girl he met during the liberation and longed to see again. She leaves him her telephone number, hoping he will call her after he's sobered up, but he throws it away, dismissively saying to another soldier as they stand in front of the Colosseum waiting for transport to "chow" that the woman is "just a . . ." Much of the Rome segment is a deliberate echo of the many films we have seen in which handsome military heroes arrive, triumphant, to the adoring embrace of lovely and extremely grateful women. "Liberation" is synonymous with romance, and the screenplay of romance is given the full Hollywood treatment, with playful, enticing dialogue and a "cute" meeting. Large parts of the segment are shot in a fairly conventional way that is quite different from Rossellini's usual neorealist idiom: here, he uses three-point lighting for the interior scenes, dialogue handled in shot/reverse-shot fashion, and frequent handsome close-ups. Ultimately, however, Rossellini uses a conventional cinematic vocabulary to subvert the ideology, aesthetics, and epistemology of conventional cinema; in some ways, the Rome segment is the most disorienting part of *Paisà*, precisely because it appears, on the surface, to be the least challenging. It initially appears to be reassuring, reinterpellating us as spectators in a more familiar mode—as an antidote, perhaps, to the disturbing meditation on spectatorship that defined the Neapolitan segment. Ultimately, however, it casts a very dark light on its "romance." If the Naples segment is about deconstructing the "black and white" of cinema, creating a locus for epistemological slippage, Rossellini's Rome disrupts any stable kind of gendered subjectivity. This segment is a mini-movie of war and romance, Hollywood in microcosm, but lacking "real" men: what we are left with is the collapse of male desire—and what is left of Hollywood romance in the absence of desire?

Spectatorship and spectacle are again brought to the fore when Francesca and Fred meet for the second time in a crowded basement barroom; on the soundtrack we hear big-band classics. Unfortunately, Fred—our tall, dark, and handsome leading man—is, contrary to the musical injunction, never "in the mood" and is a failure when it comes to his most basic job requirement: desire. As in the Neapolitan sequence, the characters are first introduced to us as spectators: instead of watching a marketplace huckster swallow lit torches as the "man of steel," they watch a different kind of fire-eater: a GI performs tricks with lighted cigarettes, "swallowing" them for an appreciative audience. The conquerors—American soldiers—are directly paralleled here with the parodic representative of militaristic hypermasculinity whose words opened the previous segment. As the patrons of the bar, Allied soldiers and Roman women, gaze around the room at each other, the first axis of vision to which our attention is drawn is not the expected one of heterosexual desire. Instead, a shouting match explodes because one of the women objects to the stare of another: "all night long that ugly whore has been staring at me!" The challenged woman retorts, in a working-class Roman dialect: "Don't you know you're making a spectacle of yourself?" ("*Ma non sai che fai un spettacolo?*") Again, the production and consumption of spectacle is exposed for us as the primary machinery through which subjectivity is transacted; the "spettacolo" is named for us as such. This statement could be addressed to virtually every major character in *Paisà*—all are simultaneously obsessive spectators and constructors of spectacle, making it and watching it continually.

It is in this context of overtly named "spettacolo," then, that desire and its failure are enacted. Francesca, a woman trying tenuously to survive by prostitution—and presumably named, ironically, for the character in Dante's *Inferno* who is perpetually swept away by the winds of her illicit passion—could, perhaps, become viable as a character in a conventional romance. Her long lost Fred could come along and sweep her off her feet: unfortunately, Fred, the not-very-licentious soldier, no longer has any such aspirations. He lies sprawled passively, if perhaps rather voluptuously, on the bed to which Francesca takes him, immobile and without interest; he pushes her hand away, snarling "Don't bother!" Francesca (trying, perhaps, to salvage her "spettacolo" of romance) responds in an appropriate fashion for someone well trained in cinema, adjusting the lighting by throwing a shawl over the lamp. The rest of the scene is shot through filtered lenses, close-ups of both faces fully occupying the territory of the screen, in marked contrast to the style of cinematography normally favored by neorealists. In the flashbacks to the liberation of Rome, Fred spends most of the scene shirtless, showing a well-developed torso and the boyish, seemingly effortless all-American charm of a young Ronald Reagan, whom he resembles. Later, he hides from the gaze of the camera, and refuses the "spettacolo" required of him. In the flashback, his muscular, half-naked form fulfills the iconography of masculinity worshipped, and endlessly represented, in Mussolini's Rome—the implied homoerotic male-to-male gaze being as necessary as any heterosexual interaction, as it is, though perhaps in a slightly more coded way, in American constructions of maleness. In Francesca's bed, Fred remains fully dressed, retaining even his coat.

All the elements of conventional cinematic romance, the expected spectacle, are present between Fred and Francesca: the original "cute" meeting of two attractive, young, heterosexually matched protagonists, a touch of pathos requiring each to "save" the other, sprightly and flirtatious dialogue in the flashback scenes, a private setting with three-point lighting and a filtered lens. All that is missing is the desire of the leading man. When we see Fred again waiting, greedy only for food, for a truck to carry him off to his "chow," he throws his script for a romantic narrative, the scrap of paper Francesca has left for him, away onto the ground. In the shadow of the Colosseum, on the left-over stage set of Mussolini's Rome—the entire city reconfigured as a vast monument to hypermasculinity in travertine and marble—we find a scrapbook of Hollywood memories. Here, again, masculinity fails to live up to our expectations, to complete its required performance. The conventions of romance, so promising as Rome was "liberated" from the Nazis, are exposed as exactly that: conventions. They are not different in nature from the fictions of fascism, only in details of their coding: they are just as bankrupt. The expectant spectator—the well-trained watcher of movies to whom three-point lighting and lingering close-ups might denote a return to a certain, more familiar style of spectatorship, an opportunity to be "swept away," like Dante's Francesca—is left in an unsettling situation. Instead of "losing ourselves" in the story, we find ourselves, again, standing in the rubble—the ruins of conventional, especially conventionally gendered, spectacle. Projected before us, we can see only "ourselves." This projection is especially marked in the Roman segment: all the cinematic baggage, all the recognizable paraphernalia of medium and genre with which Rossellini loads this section are so obtrusive and in such contrast to the rest of *Paisà* that they create a sort of mise en abîme effect. We watch ourselves watching—and perhaps ask ourselves Francesca's revealing question: *"ma non sai che fai un spettacolo?"*

Florence

In the transition between the Roman segment and the next section, set in Florence, we are again given a brief return to the conventional certainty of the voice-over and animated map of the war's progress. Once again, Rossellini is laying out for us anew the terms of his epistemological questioning, giving us a little slice of ostensibly unproblematized "knowledge," the very concept of which will soon, once again, be radically undercut. The now-familiar map, with its moving arrow, reassures us of appropriate movement and causality—as we see the crisp cartographic evidence of the active triumphs of Allied soldiers, perhaps we may forget the languid and languishing leading man, the not-so-licentious soldier, of the Roman segment. On the screen, we see ambulances—converted military trucks with red crosses on the sides—moving through the undamaged streets of a city. This first scene of the Florentine segment again creates a visual link, a bridge to the end of the previous section, the last shot of which was a long view of Fred and his buddy climbing into the back of an army truck and being driven off, with the overdetermined signifier of the Colosseum looming behind them. In direct reverse of this, we see Harriet, the American woman who is the protagonist of the Florence segment, stepping down from the back of an army truck. In many ways, the entire segment can be read as a reconsideration of the main story line of the Roman section, one that takes many of the same elements and reconfigures them differently, picking up similar building blocks and creating a new, though perhaps equally unstable, epistemological and historiographic edifice.

After the Roman and the Sicilian segments, we are left with the scattered remnants of the Hollywood love story. All the stock elements were there—from the Sicilian moonlight to the scarf-softened lamplight Francesca provided in her bedroom, to, in both cases, the "cute" flirtatious multilingual dialogue between a lonely soldier far from home and a pretty girl—but both scenarios were abject failures as romance: the whole structure came crashing to the ground. In Sicily, "Joe from Joisy" was done in by his inability to separate spectacle from reality, in this most "classically" neorealist of the segments—in arranging the lighting for his close-up, he "forgets" that he is a soldier and not a movie star on set, and gets shot. The Naples segment gives us a different kind of romance, a cross-cultural mutual seduction between a GI and a Neapolitan street urchin, that also focuses on the relationship between spectacle and reality. (Even Rossellini, overtly critical here of American race relations, would, perhaps, not go "too far" beyond existing cinematic codes to depict the unrepresentable, an interracial heterosexual romantic relationship between a black American and a white Italian woman.) Rome gave us the languid Fred in the shadow of the Colosseum. In the Florentine segment, Rossellini regenders the story of intercultural romance. Harriet, the main protagonist of this section, appears to be a "revision" of Fred. She once lived in Florence and has returned as an American Army nurse; the main action of the section consists of Harriet and an Italian friend, Massimo, making their way through the fighting in the city so that Harriet can find her former lover, Guido, who has since become the legendary partisan commander, "Lupo."

In a sense, therefore, Harriet is fulfilling the role that Fred had previously refused. Harriet is active, courageous, and resourceful: she is motivated to risk her life—coming closer to sustained combat than any "soldier" we have yet seen—by an intense and idealistic romantic love. Rather than waiting for her soldier to find her, as Francesca so disastrously does with the haplessly passive Fred, Harriet goes out into combat to find him. She is not culturally incompetent and incapable of learning, like the other Americans we have seen, but speaks good Italian. Rossellini here seems to be presenting us with an experiment in cinematic coding: if the men in *Paisà* have, so far, failed to embody a viably masculine subjectivity, then perhaps divorcing the masculine role from the male body provides an alternative construction. The Florentine segment is a miniature war movie; however, as Rossellini subversively appropriates this most stereotypically "male" genre, he gives it a significant twist. Harriet is unquestionably the most successful incarnation of masculinity, at least as it is usually coded into genre cinema, in the film. She is a brave soldier navigating a battle, steadfastly remaining true to her goal, and an ardent lover, driven by desire. Harriet explains her quest with a statement about her absent lover, "*vorrei* tanto *verderlo*" ("I want *so much* to see him"). This places, perhaps, her motivating desire into the visual economy that Rossellini analyzes in the film as a whole—Harriet is still a spectator, driven by desire that is expressed visually. However, scopophilia and visual craving/obsession are not what primarily define her; consumption of visual pleasure and the construction of cinematic viewing conditions, the confusion between spectacle and reality, is, as in the previous segments, associated with failure. Harriet's quest does, ultimately, fail—but for not for these reasons.

Harriet's search is for a ghost, for an ideal type of masculinity that has so far not emerged in *Paisà*, from which "real men," in terms of preexisting cinematic coding, have been notably absent—except for Harriet herself who has obvious disqualifications for the role. Guido is never actually seen—we later discover that he was already dead when the action of the segment began, making Harriet's journey through battle even more quixotically courageous. His absence looms over the segment, as the absence of successful masculinity is eternally present in the film as a whole. His double name contains complex historical references that appear to place his character—present only, appropriately, as a name, semantic trace and echo of both fascist and antifascist iconography—squarely within the context of the recent history of constructions of masculinity in Italy. Guido, though a fairly common name, has a suggestive literal meaning: "I lead," "I guide," or—more prosaically—"I drive." This is, once again, an overdetermined echo, similar in meaning to the Latin word *ducere* from which *dux* and, ultimately, "Il Duce" or "the leader," are derived. Guido, then—the famous partisan leader, destined for martyrdom—ironically carries in his name the trace of the Duce, the *uomo del destino*.

As a model of masculinity, whether as soldier, statesman, or erotic icon, Mussolini fulfilled expectations that appeared to be contradictory. (For example, he managed to be perceived simultaneously as loyal husband, incarnating the patriarchal virtues in his role of *paterfamilias*, and as the Latin lover par excellence, active pursuer of women and possessor of several more or less "official" mistresses.) Guido, as a figure on the border between fantasy and actuality, a legend to whose name a mystical quality is attached, seems to share something of the Duce's protean quality. He, like Mussolini, is a vehicle for projection, spoken of with reverence and longing as a mythic hero, a new masculine ideal. His very elusiveness underlines his status as an object of desire for both women and men, hero-worshipped by young male partisans who longingly whisper his name, and deeply longed for by the remarkable Harriet. Guido's alias, "Lupo" ("Wolf") is equally suggestive. Mussolini enshrined and formally codified preexisting symbolism for the city of Rome, adopting the wolf as its official symbol, and reproducing the image of the famous Etruscan bronze sculpture of a wolf. (Interestingly, this image, which was ubiquitous throughout Italy, depicts a female: according to Roman mythology, the founders of Rome were suckled by a she-wolf. Infants suckling at the wolf's teats were added to the sculpture during the Renaissance.) It had a strong nationalist connotation, part of the discourse of continuity between ancient Rome and the fascist "empire." "Lupo," therefore, is a name that, like "Guido," seems to carry a particular weight of associations with fascism. Once again, new models of masculinity cannot escape the echoes of the past—they are haunted by the ghosts of fascism, perceptible at every level, including semantically. Guido, a legendary and perhaps even a "true" hero, may appear to be a more viable icon than the passive, narcissistic, and almost pathologically dense GIs, "Joe from Joisy" and Fred, or the compassionate but confused black MP, Joe—however, it is crucial that he doesn't actually "appear" at all. He is, from the moment we first hear his name, always already missing and, as we eventually learn, already dead: existing only as the trace of a vanished presence, he represents absence and loss. Ultimately, then, this model also fails, leaving us Harriet as the only successful representative of those two masculine archetypes, the brave, resourceful soldier and the ardent, desiring lover. Obviously, Harriet can't ever be naturalized as an example of "seamless" masculinity: the roughness of the construction, the separation of male body, and "successful" performance of a masculine role, is all too evident.

Spectatorship is an absolutely crucial concept in the Florentine episode, as it has been throughout the film. Florence, like Rome, is a city built on spectatorship, a world capitol of scopophilia. If Rossellini, through his use of the Colosseum as a bracketing image, focused in the previous segment on spectacle in the context of fascist reconstructions of ancient Rome, here the Italian Renaissance comes to the fore. The originality of the cinematography in the Florence segment has been widely commented on and is in clear contrast to the deliberately familiar, almost parodically genre-linked, "look" of much of the Rome section. As Millicent Marcus has pointed out in her discussion of this film, Florence is a "museum city," converted here to a battlefield.[31] People have, for centuries, traveled to Florence to look at beauty; it was a required stop on the "grand tour" agenda of any cultured or sophisticated English or American tourist from the nineteenth century on and is a presence in many examples of art and literature by foreigners—notably German, English, and American, the three nationalities represented in the narrative of the segment—from romanticism to modernism. This section oscillates between a forced and discomfiting contemplation of spectatorship as such—we witness a kind of static über-aestheticism in which people obsessively focus on beauty, divorcing it from all other considerations—and a frantic enactment on screen of a limited vision and ceaseless movement, through a Florence without, as Marcus points out, the familiar touristic reference points. We see two different types of scopophiles, visual connoisseurs who are consumed, again with parodic overtones, by their desire for visual satisfaction. Harriet and her travel companion, Massimo, first encounter two British officers and frantically try to gain information from them about conditions in the city. The Englishmen are sitting on a hillside overlooking Florence, gazing hungrily through binoculars—technological mediations of looking are foregrounded in this segment, as the technology of Rossellini's filmmaking is foregrounded by his breaking of continuity rules and expected visual conventions. As the officers, speaking in braying upper-class voices, comment with dubious erudition on the historic architecture before them, one touches the other suggestively on the shoulder. They are clearly coded as effete and probably homosexual; again, they are military men, shown at the fringes of a desperate battle that they seem to be quite successful in ignoring, and complete failures as exemplars of naturalized masculinity. All the Englishmen want to do is look, to consume the magnificent visual spectacle before them; their expertise as art connoisseurs intensifies their delectation.

Figure 1.2 *Paisà*: Harriet and the British officers look down on Florence.

We meet another enthusiast—this time a connoisseur of battles rather than art—as Harriet's journey into the city continues. This man, a fairly high-ranking officer (he is addressed as "Signor Maggiore," or "Major") is also a soldier, now retired, who has no interest in fighting. He may have been valiant in the past but now, far from going away to war, he is on the rooftop of his own apartment building, with his wife downstairs and all the comforts of home. (A servant is sent up to see to his needs and to convey his wife's peremptory and slightly peevish messages: "the signora says you are to come down now!") He is gathering information about military movements, but, primarily, he seems to be enjoying himself. Busily watching through binoculars, his own private spectacle of war, the major is a happy armchair warrior (literally), avidly consuming the scene before him, evaluating and commenting on the ordnance used, delighting in the delectable demands on his expertise. Thoroughly enjoying the aesthetics of war, he is a connoisseur of weaponry, a gourmand of battles. Oddly charming in his single-minded absorption (unlike the Englishmen, who are repellent), he greets Harriet and Massimo genially, but offers no real help—like us in the audience, he is a voyeur, not a participant, essentially passive, a consumer.[32] He states the credo of passive masculinity as he resists the blandishments of female voices calling him downstairs: "*Ma no...è impossibile...non mi posso muovere adesso.*" ("But no, it's impossible...I can't move [myself] now.") His intense visual focus has created a kind of impotence, stasis, and passivity, an inability to move.

In the Rome sequence, we saw a man who could not desire, who could not be moved, even by the lovely Francesca whose name distills representations of female romantic love reaching back to Dante. In Florence—which is, of course, the city of Dante—we see men who cannot move themselves to do or desire anything other than visual pleasure. These military men, unlike Harriet, are all lookers, not fighters. Harriet, too, is looking—looking for Guido, an active endeavor in which she "moves herself" constantly and, motivated by desire, enters into a battle zone. Rossellini's highly mobile camera "moves itself" and consequently constructs our vision as disconcertingly and sometimes almost vertiginously mobile. There is no privileged, stable point of view offered to us, even as we watch others—the scopophiles who remain still, high up and on the margins, avoiding immersion in the battle zone—trying to attain such privileged vision. There is no shot analogous to the views of the Colosseum in the Rome segment—we see the monuments and "sights" of Florence fleetingly. These locations are important for their role in the action, not lingered on to underline their iconic status. (The Piazza della Signoria is seen functionally as an open space in which Harriet can see German soldiers; the Uffizi—stripped of its treasures—is an essential, and dangerous, passageway, for a scene of constant movement, not static looking.[33]) These two scenes involving noncombatant military men underline Rossellini's insistence on showing us "ourselves" looking, offering audience surrogates who, in their obsessive scopophilia, represent an exaggerated version of our own search for visual pleasure through film. Technologies of vision are foregrounded, emphasizing the artifactuality of the film, showing us the seams in the illusion, the constructed nature of the "reality" it offers. This has the effect of denaturalizing the total experience, forcing a conscious and critical distance from the film's embedded aesthetic and ethical presumptions. As part of this aesthetic and ethical challenge to past representations and past historiographies, Rossellini requires us to be equally skeptical of how his own work enacts these fundamental, inescapable constructions. His creation of a doubly directed, constantly flipping, reversible axis of view does not provide us with a pretty picture of our own spectatorship.

At the end of the Florentine segment, Rossellini gives us, yet again, a bridge into the next one. The fifth segment, set among monks in an isolated Apennine monastery, proposes for our examination yet another style of masculine subjectivity, this time based in imagery and narratives of religion. In Florence, we see Harriet's bitter grief when she learns that Guido is dead—and has been throughout her brave odyssey. The final shot is of Harriet—back, perhaps in her "proper" gender, though those categories have by now become more or less unsustainable—standing in for the Madonna in classic pietà pose. The segment ends with a close-up of her sorrowful face as she cradles a dying partisan. Here again, as in the fascist trilogy, Rossellini evokes Christian imagery as an alternative interpretive matrix, perhaps offering us a model for a gaze, reverent and sorrowful, that seems, at least initially, less problematized than it has up to now in *Paisà*. Harriet, as a character, has been treated with less irony than any of the other "soldiers," emerging as a truly heroic figure: smart, resourceful, determined, and fearless—and perhaps symbolically regendered as the very model of military masculinity. Here, she is given the "last word," as we look at her posed in an unmistakable echo of what may well be the most familiar visual image in Italy: the Madonna cradling her dead son. This image raises an important question about how it should be read: does the religious framework we encounter so often in Rossellini's work have a privileged status in his films as more "true" than other systems for understanding the world, or is it essentially equivalent to them? The events surrounding the final shot of Harriet's pietà are disturbing, to say the least: at the fringes of the action we see the summary mass execution of local fascists—whom we hear weeping and pleading for their lives—by the partisans. This scene is set apart from the central action around Harriet and the dying partisan and could easily be missed: Rossellini doesn't call our attention to it. However, it clearly complicates the moment of apparent moral transcendence—Harriet's return to "femininity" and her transformation into a Madonna figure. Lupo may initially seem to be a candidate for the status of a hero, even possibly a guide or a leader, but ultimately he is defined by his absence and is a mere ghost, a trace that never translates into a presence; his comrades here, all those who are the allies of Harriet—our one "real man," a paradoxical position made untenable by her female body—are also murderers, able to kill helpless, pleading human beings, albeit fascists. The end of the Florence segment creates a religious discourse, presents us with (characteristically overdetermined) religious imagery, making Harriet the Madonna, and a partisan into the sacrificed Christ figure; however, mass murder is the context. The temptation to see religiously inflected images as providing a qualitatively different or ethically privileged way of looking, as constituting a different kind of spectator—less morally compromised than that instated by cinema in the light (and under the shadow) of its fascist and Hollywood history—is called into question, in Rossellini's habitually ambivalent fashion.

The Apennine Monastery

The Apennine monastery segment of *Paisà* suggests an alternative style of both epistemology and subjectivity, one less tainted by the obsession with spectatorship than the others we have seen.[34] In the monastery there are no GIs quoting Hollywood film, languishing their way through a mini-melodrama, or rewriting the historiography of a racist puppet show. This segment is set in a world into which neither desire nor war is supposed to enter, inhabited solely by reverently Christian men.[35] This setting suggests, perhaps, a sort of anti-Hollywood idyll: the Franciscan brothers of the monastery—with their vows of poverty, chastity, and obedience, and their rejection of "the world"—may, at least initially, be assumed to be innocent of the obsessive scopophilia that has cast a dubious light on the erection of a secular male subjectivity throughout *Paisà*. We can assume, perhaps, that they, unlike ourselves and most of the characters we have "met" during the film, are not highly trained and dedicated critics or spectators. The opening shots of the segment are much less confusing, more reassuringly legible, than in previous sections; they appear to emphasize the distance of the monks' world from the hurly-burly of ordinary life. We are given a panoramic view of an ancient monastery, perched high on a hill, on which we very slowly zoom in; muffled, distant gunfire can be heard. The sound continues as the screen fades to a shot of a monk in a dark habit outlined in a full-length window as he gazes out; his stillness is striking after ceaseless movement and the frenetic battle scenes of the Florence segment. We are then shown a series of activities: a monk is sweeping the steps to an altar with a handmade twig broom; another reads peacefully; yet another is shown vigorously ringing a huge metal bell; another shooes clucking chickens out into a courtyard; gradually, a group of cowled monks gathers around the chickens, ignoring their avian indignation. A young monk bows his head and intones a monotone chant, a prayer of thanks for being spared from danger. The monks kneel among the clucking chickens; a single very long take lingers on the praying group. These short sequences deemphasize the individuality of the particular brothers: they seem almost interchangeable, anonymous figures in identical long habits.

These scenes, showing the monks performing their various daily tasks, seem calculated to emphasize both the orderly structure and the simple virtue and piety of the life of the monastery. We could not be further away from the chaotic, bombed out Neapolitan slums, the shared "immorality" of the nightlife of Roman prostitutes and GIs, or the tense, frenetic atmosphere of street warfare in Florence. We are told near the beginning of the segment—the Father Superior of the monastery is writing in his diary, and we are shown the page—that the war has not affected the monastery.[36]

What defines these monks, therefore, is precisely the fact that they are not soldiers; in fact, Rossellini goes to considerable trouble to inform us that not only are they innocent of war, but they have had no contact whatsoever with it, even as civilians. The sound of gunfire may be heard, but it remains outside the monastery walls. Throughout the segment, Rossellini lingers on the monks' movement within the monastery walls, frequently showing them walking in "real time," surprising us, perhaps by the amount of screen time he spends on this activity which does nothing to advance the narrative. He gives the monks a slow, stately, almost hypnotic style of movement, in which they glide serenely along long corridors and up long flights of stone stairs. This establishes a contrast to the previous segment—it could not be more different from Harriet's frantic, kinetic race through Florence. The cinematography is much quieter, consisting of long takes and a relatively stationary camera.

The visitors to the monastery from the outside world—three U.S. Army chaplains of different faiths seeking shelter for the night as they travel toward the frontlines—are, once more, defined by their focus on visual consumption. They sound, in fact remarkably similar to the British officers we saw in the previous segment, looking over Florence from the Boboli Gardens. The age of the monastery makes it aesthetically desirable, a rare and precious commodity, to the American connoisseur. The clergymen are, once again, connoisseurs and aesthetic gourmands, consumers and sensualists, glorying in the picturesque antiquity of the scene: "Just think, by the time this monastery was built, America wasn't even discovered yet. It was an immense wilderness. These walls, those olive trees, that church bell, were already here. This time of the evening, five hundred years ago, everything had the same soft color." "Wilderness" is an environment without structure, resistant to epistemological "mapping," like the landscape of flow that is the lava fields of Etna, or the "wilderness of ruined cities" evoked in the voice-over at the beginning of the Rome segment. The monastery is initially posited as the opposite of epistemological "wilderness," a respite from bewilderment. It is defined spatially by its walls—Rossellini places a strong visual emphasis on them, and spends a lot of time showing us the complicated process of traversing the wall to enter the convent. We see the priest who is the porter, the custodian of this defined boundary, making a long journey through different visual zones to perform his duty of opening an entrance in the wall—he moves from light to shade and though spaces that appear immense, emphasized by the great depth of focus afforded here by Rossellini's camera, and underscored by one of the few point-of-view shots in this segment.

However, the walls of the monastery provide only an illusory barrier against epistemological slippage. At first, Rossellini seems to suggest that contagion is brought in from outside, when "the world" encroaches on this sacred precinct. The character of Bill Martin, the Catholic chaplain, is initially presented as a contrast to the monks. He is the same man, essentially, that we have seen throughout *Paisà*. His dual appellations of "Captain" and "Father"—two archetypal images of a conventionally successful masculinity—fail to conceal the fact that he bears a strong resemblance to the two "GI Joes" of the Sicilian and Neapolitan segments and the officers we meet in the Florentine segment. Martin and his companions, the Protestant and Jewish chaplains, are obviously close friends and colleagues, able to joke about their differences, and seem to be the embodiment of American religious pluralism. The monks, by contrast, are horrified to discover that they have a Protestant and a Jew in their midst—much of the content of the episode concerns this clash of paradigms, which is approached as mild comedy. However, the subtext of the segment is consistent with the focus on spectatorship that defines the film as a whole. At arrival, the chaplains are characterized by the avidity of their visual consumption, in contrast to the simple satisfaction of the monks.

Throughout the interaction between the American chaplains and the monks—between foreigners who, despite being clerics themselves, embody scopophilia and visual desire, and the apparently innocent and undesiring brothers—there are suggestions that this distinction does not really hold up. Soon after their arrival, the Americans present the monks with various scarce food items: chocolate, condensed milk, powdered eggs, and canned meat. The monks receive this bounty with enthusiasm and obvious comic greed; they may not, apparently, be consumers of spectacle, but they are willing to consume other commodities, with great relish. In another brief but very suggestive scene, the chaplains are led away to their rooms, leaving their helmets behind on a table. A young monk, left alone in the room, picks up one of the helmets and, smiling playfully, holds it up over his head (in the position a halo might occupy in Christian iconography, obviously a deliberate irony) before hurrying out. In this sequence, we see that "the world," with its culture of spectatorship, has, in fact, intruded into this cloistered life: the young monk is imagining himself as a man of action, a helmeted warrior, though Christian iconography slips into the scene—he can't seem to "decide" what genre of movie he is starring in. He fantasizes himself as a figure in a war movie—not unlike the war movie we are watching—placing himself simultaneously as spectator (he gets the idea, presumably, from having watched movies, and is also watching his own "act") and spectacle, embodiment of the imagined action. He is, therefore, another audience surrogate, occupying, like us, the positions of both subject and object—we are watching the film, and our gaze constantly finds ourselves reflected and represented on screen.

This piece of byplay, seemingly minor, serves to further collapse the distinction between the worldly American spectators and the innocent monks, supposedly free of scopophilic temptation. This separation is revealed as false. As models for the construction of masculinity, these monks do not provide an alternative to the culture of spectatorship, offering any possibility of a distinct, viable version of stable, unitary male subjectivity—however illusory such a structure might inevitably be. Instead, they prove themselves to be imbued with the desires that have defined the other men we have seen. Indeed, it might be argued that not only are the monks, as represented by Rossellini, infected by the scopophilia of the outside world, but that their life of Christian contemplation comprises, in itself, its own particular culture of spectatorship. The monks' lives are ruled by carefully choreographed rituals, their verbal exchanges—they intone predetermined ritual phrases at every encounter with each other—scripted according to preexisting protocols that are much more rigid than the improvised dialogue neorealists claimed to favor (but seldom actually produced). The ubiquitous crucifixes are present in every room, there to be looked at; they draw the gaze of the believer, inviting the contemplation—the mental reenacting of a visual tableau—of the great spectacle of the passion and crucifixion, both of which are experienced in churches primarily through the eyes, omnipresent as visually iconic. The Catholic Mass, the defining ritual of the monks' faith, is itself of course a superb piece of theater, the ultimate spectacle. Rossellini highlights the debt of the monastic world to visual precedent, the extent to which its inhabitants are trained spectators and reflexive consumers of scripted aesthetic experiences, by choreographing the culminating scene of this segment—a dinner in which Martin praises the monks' way of life—so that it bears a striking resemblance to countless artistic representations of the last supper, especially Leonardo da Vinci's most well-known fresco. The mainspring of life for the monks, therefore, is revealed to be the same as that of the other men we have watched throughout *Paisà*: scopophilia is the order of the day here also. The walls of the monastery cannot exclude desire; they are a false boundary, enclosing a "wilderness" just as bereft of epistemological maps as the world outside. Again, instead of knowledge or any kind of "truth," we must settle for spectacle.

The Po Valley

The last section of *Paisà*, set in the marshes of the Po Valley in northern Italy is, like the Sicilian segment that opens the film, notable for its preoccupation with the constraints and limitations of vision.[37] Rossellini repeatedly presents us with physically limited or confusing spaces, deliberately obscures our vision with screens and barriers, and carries out the main action of the segment in darkness. Therefore, the geographic setting of the Po Valley segment, with its contrast between claustrophobic marshland forests of tall reeds and its wide riparian vistas, becomes a major factor in extending and deepening the epistemological crisis that has characterized *Paisà* up to this point.[38] Once again, Rossellini foregrounds the slippage and instability inherent in the conceptual categories of subject and object, blurring the distinctions, undercutting and complicating the relationship between these positions: he creates a multiple and mobile subjectivity, repeatedly offering us surrogates and stand-ins in our role as audience and spectators, and continually introducing new surveillances and spectacles. *Paisà*'s final segment begins in the way to which we have now become accustomed, with the machinery that creates supposedly unambiguous certainties and invokes an unproblematic and stable relation between the epistemological subject, which "knows," and its separate object of knowledge. The familiar map shows the Allies' continued advance—now encompassing most of Italy—and the voice-over confidently proclaims: "Deep in the desolate marshes of the Po Valley, far behind enemy lines, special service troops of the OSS and British Intelligence were fighting an isolated action beside Italian Partisans." Again, however, cartographic certainty is immediately disrupted: this landscape, again, like the Sicilian lava flows and the dislocated linearity of Neapolitan and Florentine urban streetscapes in rubble, turns out to be another epistemological "wilderness," a place that resists boundaries and problematizes vision.

The first shot of the segment seems, initially, to offer some sort of coherent perspective, at least visually. As he has done in several other segments (the Bay of Naples, the monastery on its mountain, the Roman streets and monuments), Rossellini begins with a panorama—this time integrated into the narrative. From the map, the camera cuts to a panoramic shot of a wide calm river, with an unidentifiable object floating in the distance. The camera remains steady as the river's current carries the object closer, also rotating it so that we can see it is the body of a man, propped upright by a flotation ring. This shot is not a zoom or dolly shot: the agency here belongs to nature—the moving river current—rather than the camera, and the point of view is passive. On a placard held above the body by a stick is the word *Partigiano* (partisan). Clearly, this opening is linked structurally to the end of the Florentine segment rather than the monastery, showing the death and mourning for an antifascist fighter—we have moved away from the (spurious) isolation of a space with (permeable) boundary walls back to the war.[39] However, this shot doesn't read as chaotic, as the opening of the action in Sicily, Naples, Rome, and Florence did; there is more continuity with the tone of the monastery segment. The contrast between the chaos of careening crowds encroaching on the camera in the earlier opening of the Naples narrative, for example, and the static, stable panorama shot in this sequence is striking. The effect of the contrast is, again, to foreground the artifactuality of this constructed vision, and the processes of mediation by which our knowledge here is constructed. The wildly divergent opening sequences of the segments appear to denaturalize vision at the same time as, in the Po Valley, we are offered what seems to be a privileged, stable, overarching viewpoint. The camera pulls back to another wide panoramic shot, showing us the posed corpse slowly floating with the current as buildings gradually appear on the distant riverbank. We then cut to a large group of figures, mostly black-clad women and young children, standing on a bluff high above the river, staring out at the water. The camera angle is low, giving these figures a larger than life status and a heroic, almost mythical presence as they are outlined against the sky. The camera cuts to show more people arriving, hurrying in order not to miss the "show" on the river; we see that the group also includes a few Wehrmacht soldiers, with rifles and bayonets. One of the soldiers shouts: "Partigiani, banditi!" in a tone that is more instructive than vituperative. The group of civilians moves along the bluff, gazing at the river, solemn and silent, following the partisan's corpse as it floats downstream.

In the Po Valley scene, the movement of the spectators seems to be determined by that of the spectacle—they are drawn along almost involuntarily, transfixed by the act of looking. The moral context of this act of spectatorship initially appears different. The crowd represents a brutalized population looking at a warning against resistance, an admonitory tableau arranged for them by the Nazi occupiers; this has been a murder that deliberately manipulates spectacle. The silent movement of the crowd can be seen as a kind of reverence for a heroic victim, the dead freedom fighter, even as it fulfills the Nazi's wishes for an audience to their instructive tableau. However, it is not a contradiction to also read the watchers on the riverbank as yet another instance of the scopophilic obsession with which we are all too familiar in *Paisà*. The spectators are physically removed from the object of their gaze, occupying a different spatial plane. In this they resemble many other watchers we have seen in the film: the various military men we meet in Sicily who live their lives as if they were in a movie theater, constantly imagining cinematic scenarios, their actions—the shooting of Joe—determined by distant flickers of light; "GI Joe" in the puppet theater; the Roman spectators—both the ancient ones whose trace is implied by the presence of the Colosseum and the contemporary ones watching a performance of barroom stunts; the various military officers looking down over Florence. They share a similar unobstructed view of the object of their gaze.

Rossellini, once again, provides us in this scene with an interpreter and a "critic," a connoisseur, whose role is similar, perhaps, to that of the British officers of the Florentine segment, or the antiquity-conscious American chaplain visiting the Apennine monastery. The German soldier, another outsider, gives a gloss on the scene, explaining to the Italian civilians the meaning of the carefully arranged "show" in the river. His reaction appears to be, at least in part, an aesthetic one: the scene before him, with its handsome composition, its verbal caption, and its implied narrative of guilt and retribution clearly gives him satisfaction. This reminds his audience of the ways we, in our scopophilic hunger, may enable and participate in similar attempts, perhaps even including this very film. However, the function of the dead partisan—a piece of fascist "art" and a carefully choreographed spectacle in its own right, with the power to draw an intent audience—is, perhaps, to deliver a similar reminder and warning. Along with its foregrounding of the processes of spectatorship and its political or repressive manipulation, this sequence, coming toward the end of the film, also underlines historiography as a construction intimately linked to spectacle and the aesthetic: how will the events of "the past" remain to haunt the future and what kind of explanatory "captions" will be supplied?

This message is emphasized in the next scene by a radical change in the conditions structuring our vision. From the dead partisan in the river, and the crowd following along the bluff, the camera cuts to a confusing shot of reeds, tangled and interwoven; suddenly, we see movement behind the reeds, the barely perceptible figure of a man rising to a standing position, and pointing. An Italian partisan and an American Special Forces soldier are hiding in the reeds, in a space defined by its lack of boundaries—there is no distinction between land and water. We see the two men positioning themselves both as spectators and as creators of spectacle. They are watching the German produced propaganda "show" with the same intensity as the crowd on the bluff. They are also choreographing their own action as a spectacle for German eyes: in order for the Italian to retrieve the dead partisan safely, the German soldiers' gaze must be seduced in another direction, toward the "show" of a diversionary explosion—a rock on the beach is blown up. The purpose of the explosion is to be looked at: it has no other function. The next event in the action, the diversionary explosion and the retrieval of the floating corpse, is not arrived at for quite some time: Rossellini spends the next several minutes following the slow movement of the men through the reeds. There is a long take in which we see, from behind, the American stepping into a small wooden boat, which he almost swamps, and poling along among the reeds; our vision is drastically limited by the vegetation, and we, like the soldier, can see only a few feet in any direction. The next shot is deliberately disorienting. It is an overhead view of a small, partly overgrown clearing in the reeds. An unidentifiable object appears from the right frame; only belatedly do we realize it is the prow of the boat. Throughout this sequence, it is impossible to discern the border between land and water. We see the American soldier punting the boat, floating it through what look like several fairly solid stands of reeds. Moments later, he approaches another identical looking patch of vegetation, but this time he steps out of the boat and, with the other man's aid, picks it up and walks on dry land, dropping it back into the water after a few steps. In this entire sequence, therefore, the river landscape becomes a world in which visual perception cannot be trusted. Vision is severely limited among the reeds. Sight is also problematic in the wide-open riparian vistas like the one that opens the segment; there is no clear horizon, and sky and water cannot easily be distinguished. Figures appear to merge into the landscape, presenting us with a repeated figure-ground problem. Land as distinct from water is, in most places, an opposition that can be taken for granted; here the delineation vanishes. In the Po Valley segment, the landscape, yet again, emerges as an epistemological "wilderness," resisting the imposition of any reasonable cognitive grid or structure.

The narrative of this section continues to focus on actions performed mainly to be looked at, as spectacle. The diversionary explosion set off by the American soldier is seen by two German sentries, stationed in a wooden observation tower above the reeds. One exhorts the other: "Schau!" and then, immediately afterward, on seeing the American soldier's cigarette lighter flicked on to light a fuse, "Feuer!" ("Look!" "Fire!"). In a visual joke, the other sentry then hands him a cigarette—"Feuer" in German, can also be a request for a light. The sentry says "Schau!" again, and this time the camera shows us, from the Germans' point of view, the Italian partisan, fully visible in the center of the river, rowing frantically out to the body of his dead comrade. There is a rapid cut to a shot—not, however, from the sentries' point of view, as Rossellini again refuses to privilege any position at which vision originates—to what the sentry has seen, the American lighting the fuse from his cigarette. This is rapidly followed by a panoramic shot of the landscape, showing billows of smoke from the staged explosion. The German sentries here are, once again, the now-familiar audience surrogates. As in the preceding segments, they are dubious stand-ins: the misunderstanding of the word "Feuer" makes them into comic figures, classic stupid soldiers. The limitations on vision in this segment are not merely physical—a matter of one's field of view being limited by weeds—but also due to misinterpretation and misperception. This problematization directly connects the final story to the episode with which the film began: "Joe from Joisy" and Carmela in the Sicilian segment are linked to the stupid German sentry—again, the flickering flame of a cigarette lighter is seen and misunderstood. We are being shown "ourselves" yet again, as we watch distant flickers of light on the screen: it is an unflattering view, as the acuity of the observers we observe does not inspire confidence. The "history" that Rossellini represents for us in the Po Valley segment, as in the film as a whole, is history as spectacle: the soldiers on both sides "fight" by choreographing shows, purely visual events, to be consumed by their enemies.

Figure 1.3 *Paisà*: the Po Delta. German soldiers as spectators.

Later in the segment, there is more military activity focused primarily around vision. The group of partisans, with their Allied helpers, are attempting to set up a drop zone for supplies from an Allied plane. The partisans must have signal fires ready to be lit as soon as they hear the supply plane approaching in the dark—again, the orchestration of light by characters functioning as their own cinematic directors, determining the conditions under which they will be viewed, is crucial here, and again produces disaster. We hear the sound of engines, then a cry of "light the fires," immediately followed by "put out the fires—they've spotted us!" The operation goes badly, and there is massive confusion in pitch darkness: the Germans are destroying the partisans' hideout and massacring their civilian supporters. It is notable that this sequence, lasting several minutes, is barely lit: we know what is happening mainly through sound, and a confused impression of movement. The audience, like the characters on screen, is literally in the dark; the limitations on vision have become more extreme even than those created by the river landscape in daylight. Once again, like the diversionary explosion that enabled the retrieval of the dead partisan from the river, the military activity on the part of the partisans is designed only to be looked at, and has no other function: their role is limited to lighting the signal fires for the Allied pilots to see. (In this instance, however, they lose control of how their "show" is perceived—instead of guiding the Allied planes, the bonfires bring the Germans.)

At the end of the Po Valley segment yet another visual "show" is staged, this time by the Germans. The partisans and their Allied companions have been captured; the American and British soldiers are treated well, offered drinks and pleasant conversation. The Italians are not considered by the Germans to be covered by the Geneva Convention and are treated, like their dead comrade at the beginning of the segment, as "bandits." The Germans stage the mass execution of the Italian partisans as a spectacle, for which the Allied soldiers are the intended audience. We are shown the deck of a small ship, with a row of men standing facing the water, their hands tied behind their backs. The camera then cuts to the group of American and British soldiers, standing on land under guard, staring intently out at the ship. There is another cut: we see the ship in the middle distance, with the figures of the men silhouetted against the broad river and skyscape, at twilight. The partisans lined up at the edge of the deck are pushed, one by one, into the river: there is the sound of a loud splash as each man falls. The camera cuts back to land, where one of the Americans screams a protest, and starts to run to the water's edge, where he is shot down, his body falling partly into the water. The camera returns to the ship: another man is pushed into the river. The camera pans to the water, and remains there, in a fairly tight shot that shows perhaps ten or fifteen square feet of water. There are several more splashes as bodies fall in, and then a lengthy moment in which the screen is filled with rippling water: this is the last shot of *Paisà*. We hear the familiar narrator's voice saying: "This happened in the winter of 1944. A few weeks later spring came to Italy and the war in Europe was declared over." The word "FINE" appears against the water. This final shot, a screen full of water, is expressive of the preoccupations of the film as a whole; as a lingering last image, water represents a meditation, perhaps, on the epistemological crisis that haunts the film. Instead of "reality," "knowledge," or "history," we are left with ambiguity and ambivalence, an epistemology "writ in water." We have arrived, with the end of *Paisà*, at the most cartographically impossible landscape yet, a world of water, occupying our whole field of vision. It is an intensified version of the other "wildernesses" we have seen that resist boundaries and structure: we have moved from the landscape of flow of the Sicilian lava fields, through the shattered linearity of city streetscapes in rubble, to a landscape in which water and land flow together to become, finally, simply water.

The first scene of the Po Valley segment, therefore, seems at the beginning to offer clear, unobstructed vision: it shows a wide, calm river, with a clear view to the horizon miles away. However, the admonitory "show" of the partisan's corpse, which so magnetically draws the eyes of the watchers on the bluff, carries with it an admonition for us also. It is a warning against any assumption of transparency: it tells us that we should not attempt to regard this or any film as giving us unmediated access to true "reality." Rossellini makes his medium opaque, forcing us continually to confront it *as* medium, and emphasizing the innate limitations of vision, with its potential for blind spots, distortions, and limitations. Any "history" this mediated vision gives us will be at best partial and probably, like the dead soldier who is the main actor in this riparian spectacle, "partisan"—a word that, as noun and adjective, has the same double meaning in Italian and English. The process of creating "history," therefore, is provided with a helpful caption for us, a literal signpost: all historiographic constructions, partisan and stage-managed as they inevitably are, should evoke skepticism. Those who assemble the scene may have motive just as questionable as the Nazi propagandists—and the uses and implications of spectacle are, by definition, always multiple and always exceed their "authors'" intention. We have seen this polysemic potential realized in almost every segment: the stories hang on varying perception of visual "shows," whether the distant flicker of a cigarette lighter or a performance in a puppet theater.

The adversaries in the final Po Valley segment, like the Hollywood-focused American GIs and Wehrmacht troops in the film's opening Sicilian segment, are united by their scopophilic passion, which they reciprocally whet and feed for each other, at the same time that they, as characters in a film, are satisfying the audience's identical desire. In all the segments of the film, when we see ourselves represented on the screen as desiring spectators, it is in the context of a comedy of errors—a series of mistakes, misinterpretations, and misrecognitions arising out of the scopophilia itself. Spectatorship as a foundational act, the cornerstone of the subject, is inherently absurd; it leads not to trustworthy perception or to reliable knowledge of an object by the subject, but to a ridiculous series of epistemological pratfalls. In the opening Sicilian segment, for example, the entire sequence of events turns on several crucial misperceptions by our Hollywood-trained Wehrmacht and U.S. Army surrogates. "Joe from Joisy" is the chief incompetent: he begins his clumsy courtship of Carmela by getting her name wrong, referring to her as Maria because, due to his training as a film spectator, he can only see her as a generic, dark-haired Italian beauty straight out of central casting. His mortal mistake in striking a light for his close-up, inviting Carmela to compare his face to his photographs, sets in motion the main plot line of the segment. The German soldier who shoots at the flame of his lighter is himself making a "mistake" in vision: he isn't sure he has seen anything at all and does not know that his bullet has found an enemy target. Finally, the American soldiers who find Joe's body misread the spectacle before them, producing a melodramatic narrative of female betrayal that is not the same as the story we have watched on screen. In the Neapolitan segment, Joe, the black MP, stumbles in a drunken haze through most of the section, with his perception distorted throughout. In rushing the stage of the marionette theater, the second "GI Joe" reveals that he embodies the epitome of spectatorship—he makes no distinction between spectacle and reality, treating them as identical. He multiplies his role as a black soldier, entering into the puppets' "war." In the Roman segment, the plot revolves around Fred's misrecognition of Francesca, his inability to see in the weary prostitute the former object of his own Hollywood-style romantic longing. He cannot move from one hackneyed "plot" to another: he, tragically for Francesca, remains trapped in the wrong movie.[40] In the hills above Florence, we meet the two British officers, incompetent and obsessed aesthetes, who, in their busy misidentifying of historic structures, "forget" that they are in the middle of a war and that people are dying while they stand transfixed. The vision of the retired Italian major, intoxicated as he is with aesthetic pleasure, is absurdly limited: all he can see is the beauty of military ordinance as an art form, and he acts as though he were watching a sort of pyrotechnic ballet, rather than the destruction of a city. Harriet, the heroine of this segment, is the closest thing *Paisà* offers us to a "good" soldier, and presents a biting, ironic contrast to the professional military officers she meets, since she is more honorable, courageous, and determined—in every sense a better "man." But even the heroic Harriet, throwing herself headlong into the boys' adventure-movie world of romantically ferocious aliases like "Lupo," makes a crucial mistake in searching so intently for a "phantom" who is already dead, and appearing to gloss over any moral ambiguity, such as that represented by the apparently almost incidental act of mass murder taking place behind her as she performs her pietà. Captain Martin, in the Apennine segment, also makes crucial mistakes: in addition to the incoherent babbling and confusion of languages caused by his scopophilic ecstasy on viewing the monastery, he makes the much more important error of misrecognizing as saintly the group of monks who are, in fact, alarmingly bigoted; in addition, he romanticizes their isolation, assuming their wall is impermeable when in fact training in spectatorship has penetrated this monastic world. In the Po Valley segment, the plot turns on a series of visual mistakes: the partisans depend on confusing the vision of the Germans by ducking in and out of the concealing reeds, and staging various diversions. The partisans themselves make a deadly mistake, misdirecting their "show" of light and darkness, in botching the lighting of fires to signal the landing zone for a night air drop, and drawing German fire instead. In our very scopophilia, therefore, is revealed the basic epistemological crisis at the heart of *Paisà*: all vision, all spectatorship, all history and knowledge are inherently limited, distorted in potentially dangerous ways, subject to constant misreading and misinterpretation. In the attempt to satisfy our insistent gaze, our aesthetic longing, our desire for spectacle, we misrecognize as "reality" that which we ourselves perpetually constitute and reconstitute. In this wilderness of untrustworthy mirrors, we also perpetually constitute and reconstitute "ourselves" as unstable, perpetually collapsing subjects.

Germania anno zero

Roberto Rossellini's "Trümmerfilm," *Germania anno zero*—filmed on location in Berlin with dialogue in German—uses the landscape of postwar Berlin to explore transgression and slippage of gender identity and heterosexual normativity, national and linguistic confines, and the limits of "truth," narrative, and subjectivity itself. All of these boundaries are repeatedly ruptured and crossed as Rossellini insistently problematizes the category of German national identity. Any possibility of "true" national identity is rejected; perhaps, the film suggests, the main moral imperative in post-Nazi Germany is for "Germanness" to fail as a naturalized category. Rossellini's skepticism is embedded in the cinematic language he employs, to very powerful effect. As Rossellini's camera obsessively tracks an Aryan child in the ruins of Berlin, its focus becomes synonymous with the gaze of the failed men the film most closely identifies with national identity: unrepentantly Nazi pedophiles, military deserters, crippled fathers. In Rossellini's deceptively simple neorealist idiom, "Germanness" has dissolved into the fields of rubble into which his protagonist is lost: nationalistic icons of masculinity have become spectral echoes, like the recorded voice of Adolf Hitler we hear reverberating through the ruined Reichstag.

Rossellini's ambivalent exploration of "Germanness" in the rubble of the postwar city is part of his interrogation of the cinematic medium itself in the aftermath of fascism. *Germania anno zero*, whose mise-en-scène places us literally in the ruins of fascism, concerns itself with the ideological implications of spectacle. The fascist regimes in both Italy and the Third Reich raised the political art of spectacle to new heights. Leni Riefenstahl and Albert Speer are inescapable phantoms in the streets of Berlin; the trace of their unique and monstrous vision of the Nazi body politic and the Nazi city necessarily permeates any later cinematic representations of the former capital of the Third Reich, especially in the rubble (inevitably ironic, in this context) of the immediate postwar. Just as postwar Rome contains the echo of Mussolini's grandiose reconfiguration and resignification of the physical remnants of ancient Rome—explored by Rossellini in the Roman segment of *Paisà*—postwar Berlin contains the trace of Speer's city-that-never-was, the planned capital of the new "Germania," as the ultimate Nazi empire was to be called. When we see Rossellini's boy protagonist standing in the ruined Reichstag, Speer's never-built redesign of Unter den Linden—a grand boulevard leading to a dome that would be many times larger than St. Peter's Basilica in Rome, which features prominently in the background in a crucial scene at the end of *Roma, città aperta*—hovers at the edge of our vision.

Germania anno zero—a German language film by an Italian director, its exteriors shot in Berlin and the interiors in Rome—is defined, therefore, by its crossing of national and linguistic borders. Rossellini, the outsider in Berlin, engages this German context to return at one remove to his past. In an ambivalent consideration of his own fascist antecedents and origins, he employs the landscape of this most famously shattered city to approach the ruin of his own cinematic history. In *Germania anno zero*, Rossellini engages in dialogue with fascist film at one remove, looking away from Italy and by extension his own work in fascist film studios. Here, he reanimates an icon of Nazi cinema; the handsome Aryan children of *Hitlerjunge Quex* can be glimpsed behind his child protagonist moving like an automaton through the rubble of postwar Berlin. Rossellini's vision is structured around a fascination with destruction, a particular aesthetic of the void—his representation is oddly alluring. Like Wilder's version of Berlin in *A Foreign Affair*, Rossellini's shattered city seems, at moments in the film, to become fully aestheticized, beautiful as an abstract composition might be, far removed from the suffering humanity of the film's narrative. This experience of aestheticization is thoroughly unsettling, if only because its appeal as a formal composition seduces the viewer into "forgetting" the human element.

Rossellini brings us the maudlin shadow of Nazi childhood, referring repeatedly to the idyllic vision of Nazi youth embodied in the character of Heini in the film *Hitlerjunge Quex*, directed by Hans Steinhoff and released in 1933. The beautiful and doomed blond boy of the Nazi film appears again as Rossellini's traumatized child protagonist, Edmund. Nazi film injects itself forcefully onto postwar celluloid, in a series of startlingly direct visual parallels.[41] The war-torn city, with its scattered, tumbled ruins, its empty shells of broken buildings, embodies the collapse of masculinity as icon and ideal. Rubble becomes a metonymic term for this failure of male subjectivity. Familiar constructions of gender and sexuality are exposed as no longer tenable as Rossellini shows us the dissolution of German identity as, in part, a collapse of the masculine subject. In the rubble, we look for ghosts of streets and men. Even the cinematic past reappears in spectral form. The adult men we encounter—pedophiles, deserters, invalids, the broken wreckage of fascist masculinity—are photographed surrounded by voids, gazing out hungrily at ruined spaces, spaces in which the ruins of the present afford fleeting glimpses of past glories mediated by celluloid, spectrally visible, a flickering of presence and absence. The soundtrack also creates spectral presences: we see a man and a small child standing hand in hand in the ruins of the Reichstag as Hitler's recorded voice exults over German triumphs. The ghosts of the actual city that was ruined, and the potential city that existed only in the models of Albert Speer, are what we see looming around Rossellini's sad Aryan child as he makes his epic journeys through the rubble.

Figure 1.4 *Germania anno zero*: Edmund in the rubble of Berlin.

In this film, Rossellini presents the patriarchal German family in ruins. Edmund lives with his family in a half-destroyed apartment building. His father, the family patriarch, is a physical wreck of a man, crippled and bedridden; the youthful virility of Edmund's handsome older brother is a tattered facade—he is a deserter, hiding at home, and encouraging his sister to prostitute herself to support him. The only adult male to whom Edmund can turn is a former teacher, a still-devout Nazi, and a seductive pedophile. As we follow Edmund through the city, in a series of extremely long tracking shots in which Rossellini's camera never leaves him, our own gaze as spectator becomes implicated in the erotic matrix of the film: our own desire follows the loving eye of the camera as we obsessively watch this blond young exemplar of Teutonic beauty. Edmund is the embodiment of the Nazi Aryan ideal, truly a fitting stand-in for Heini in *Hitlerjunge Quex*, with his blond hair and Nordic features; our desiring gaze and the gaze of the fascist pedophile become one when faced with this seductive spectacle. Any presumptive link between antifascism and heterosexual normativity collapses. Rossellini is often criticized for making this connection in his films, especially *Roma, città aperta*, in which the fascist protagonists are clearly and unpleasantly coded as homosexual and depraved, in contrast to the "normality" of the heterosexual resistance heroes and the presumably chaste priest. *Germania anno zero* clearly demonstrates the untenable nature of this reading of Rossellini's oeuvre, however. The spectator is seduced by the eroticized, fetishized body of a male child moving through the rubble, a child whose appearance fulfills the Nazi racial ideal. In several lengthy point of view shots, our gaze is directly paralleled with that of the unrepentant fascist and overt pedophile, Edmund's former teacher, who becomes a trusted father figure. (It is interesting that many readings of *Germania anno zero* mention that Rossellini made the film immediately after the death of his young son, and that Rossellini himself placed the film in that context. It is as if a "safe" familial explanation—a father's grief—must be found for the film's noticeably intense and unwavering gaze, of which Edmund is the continual focus.[42])

The opening moments of *Germania anno zero* set the stage for the crisis of male subjectivity that will be the main concern of the film. Rossellini begins with a lengthy sequence in which he shows us—in long, sweeping takes and a series of aerial shots—the devastated landscape of Berlin in 1946: the scope of the destruction is stunning.[43] The extraordinary mise-en-scène, this vast universe of rubble, is the essential matrix within which all the issues of the film are embedded. It suggests not only the collapse of familiar definitions of masculinity, but also of our own subjectivity as spectators. Watching *Germania anno zero,* we find our own unity and stability as subjects ruptured and fragmented; our subjectivity is multiplied, as spectatorship again becomes a central focus. As in *Paisà*, we see our own acts of looking represented again and again on screen: as we watch characters watching, we are invited, through a series of point of view shots, to share in their gaze. Our own scopophilic desire for spectacle, therefore, is conflated with the politically and erotically charged gaze of the unrepentant Nazis who appear in *Germania anno zero*. The undead past of Nazi Germany persists in men who are ghostly revenants, walking the shattered streets of Allied-occupied Berlin: we recognize it by its erotics, the fixations of a desiring gaze.

Pedophilic desire becomes the sign of this spectral presence: our gaze parallels it as we watch a beautiful Aryan boy navigating a city in ruins. We are introduced to Edmund, the film's thirteen-year-old protagonist, as he misrepresents his age in an attempt to find work as a gravedigger. The family lives in a small, shared apartment in a half-ruined building. Edmund's father is ill and bedridden. In our first view of the father, we see on his body a graphic echo of the Nazi past, the trace of which is omnipresent in this film about the newly "democratic" present. His pajamas, the only garments we ever see him wearing, are striped in gray and white, immediately reminiscent of a concentration camp uniform. The father—sick and powerless—is the only adult male who was never a Nazi. (In fact, we later discover that he tried to prevent his sons from joining the Hitler Youth.) In his illness, he is symbolically still a "prisoner" of fascism. The family is starving because they are trying to feed four on ration cards for three. Edmund's older brother, Karl-Heinz, is in hiding, bureaucratically invisible. In an early familial conversation, in which the father is berating Karl-Heinz for allowing his young brother and adult sister, Eva, to carry the entire burden of supporting the family, we learn that Karl-Heinz had been a committed soldier of the Third Reich, a true "war hero"—we later find out that he been at Stalingrad and Tobruk, and fought with his unit in the streets of Berlin until the last moments of the war. He is afraid that if he comes forward to be assigned a ration card, the Allied government will discover that he belonged to a regiment that "fought to the very end," and will imprison him. Karl-Heinz, therefore, is as housebound as his father. (One is reminded, in an ironic reversal, of the Nazi code for women: hearth and home. The two adult males are fulfilling this dictum; it is the woman and child who interact in the public sphere.) Afraid to go out, Karl-Heinz is sulkily dependent on his younger brother and adult sister for sustenance, and seething with resentment at his father's reproaches. In this rubble of the traditional family, therefore, the patriarch is weak, the Oedipal "prisoner," through his illness, of his Nazi son who is symbolically killing him—as Edmund later does literally, poisoning his father at

Henning's bequest. The adult son has—as a paradoxical consequence of his very role as a "brave soldier" for his country—completely abdicated any recognizable masculine identity.

Rossellini shoots Karl-Heinz in ways that show him as embodying the bankruptcy of masculinity that is at the center of *Germania anno zero*. He is surrounded by symbolic voids—in a key scene, he is framed against a background of empty kitchen cubbyholes; shortly afterwards he stands against blank window frames. In addition to underlining Karl-Heinz' passivity, and the vacuity of his existence as a man, Rossellini, in his approach to filming Karl-Heinz' body, creates an unmistakable gender ambiguity. Karl-Heinz appears stereotypically feminized as a long, soft lock of dark hair falls down across his cheek and he shouts to his father that he will go and register if the father takes responsibility for the consequences; he then throws himself sulkily—and perhaps a little voluptuously—on his mattress in the corner. During the course of the conversation between his father and older brother, Edmund moves between them: he keeps stepping into the long takes—typical of Rossellini—centered on one or the other speaker, and settling down just in front of the camera. His sleek, contained blond beauty is in marked contrast to his father's decrepitude and his brother's dark, peaked, thunderous face. By emphasizing this contrast, Rossellini is both serving the narrative—Edmund's youth and delicate vulnerability underline the seriousness of Karl-Heinz' abdication of responsibility—and serving the eroticized scopophilia of the spectator. We want to see beauty, and Rossellini feeds that desire by keeping the camera on Edmund.

Eva, like Edmund, is active in the public sphere, effectively supporting the family by going to bars to meet Allied soldiers, and selling the cigarettes she is given. Eva's and Edmund's involvement in the barter economy is telling. *Germania anno zero*, like Billy Wilder's *A Foreign Affair* is, in general, obsessed with exchange. Eva and Edmund are involved in a constant series of complicated transactions involving exchange and substitution—a bathroom scale for a can of meat, cigarettes for food, soap for potatoes, and the like. Similarly, there is a broader system of displacement and substitution at work throughout the film. Characters stand in for each other; we, the film's audience see our displaced "selves" represented on screen, as figures in the film substitute for "us" in our scopophilia and spectatorship. It is this economy of exchange that, ultimately, places us, the spectators, as equivalent to the Nazis, pedophiles, and exploiters of children that we see in the film. Rossellini creates visual parallels between Eva and Edmund in several sequences: they become interchangeable figures in some respects. They tend to mirror each other's body position—at one point they stand with their heads together, identical in their blondness. Later, Eva accuses

Karl Heinz of forcing her to prostitute herself for him. Edmund also effectively "sells" himself as an erotic object to Herr Henning, in an attempt to get food for Karl-Heinz and his father. We, too, are brought into this system of erotic exchange, since our gaze at points is identical to Henning's. Rossellini makes us all watchers, all sharing in eroticized desire for Aryan perfection.

Herr Henning, Edmund's former teacher, is the most important, and most disturbing, spectator surrogate in *Germania anno zero*. Like Karl-Heinz, Henning mourns his lost fascist "manhood." In the first moments of our meeting with him, he and Edmund run into a friend of Henning's who, as Henning sarcastically states, is doing the "women's" work, the heavy labor of clearing rubble. To Henning's sarcastic comment "nice work," the man, framed ironically against the tumbled remnants of his former life and self, replies "back then we were men: National Socialists." Among Henning's first words to Edmund are "How is your father?" and "Didn't you have an older brother?" With these questions, Henning inserts himself into the chain of shattered maleness that encircles Edmund, insisting on the privileges and authority of traditional masculinity, unaware of its demise. The father, Karl-Heinz, and Henning are all substitutable for each other as bankrupt men. Edmund has gone to Henning for the physical and emotional sustenance that neither his father nor Karl-Heinz can provide, offering himself, as does his sister Eva in the bars, as an erotic object in exchange, allowing himself to be kissed and caressed. When Henning gives Edmund a record of Hitler's speeches to sell, cementing his quasipaternal role in the child's life by helping to support him, the former teacher sutures himself even more firmly into the economy of exchange developed in the film. Hitler's recorded voice echoing through the ruins remind us that we have entered a system in which fascism and masculinity are interchangeable commodities, and in which we find ourselves transposed onto the screen in a series of very uncomfortable resemblances.

Spectatorship is again brought to the fore as we see a group of British soldiers, Edmund's eventual customers, acting as tourists in the ruins of the chancellery of the Third Reich. Rossellini begins this sequence with a long pan of the rubble-scape that was the epicenter of the Nazi state, the symbolic heart of the lost masculinity mourned by Karl-Heinz and Henning and his friends. Into the shot walk British soldiers, the new conquerors. A guide is pointing into the ruins and saying, "Here is where they burned the bodies of Hitler and Eva Braun;" he then offers to take the soldiers' photograph. We cut to a medium close-up of the head and shoulders of two British soldiers, shot from a slightly low angle that emphasizes their confidence and mastery as they stroll through the rubble. One points out to the other the site of the burning, as they smoke and look around.

Slowly, they saunter away from the camera and out of the shot. Later, they encounter Edmund, who plays the record of Hitler's speeches for them, and they buy it from him for the vast sum of two hundred marks. As Hitler's voice rings through the rubble, Rossellini's camera pans through the empty ruined halls of the chancellery, pausing on the figures of a father and young son as they stop, transfixed, to listen—it is a heavily ironic moment, as we see the nostalgia passed on to another generation of males in the rubble that is all their "fathers" and "older brothers"—the military heroes of Nazism—have left them. The foregrounding of spectatorship in *Germania anno zero* is strikingly similar to Rossellini's thematization of it in *Paisà*, especially the Florentine segment, in which we also see British soldiers acting as "tourists," gourmands of visual pleasure; in Berlin, they are uncritical consumers of a sensationalized "history," raising again the question of historiography. In the prevailing structure of substitution and exchange, echoing the equivalences of the black market on which the literal economy of occupied Berlin is based, we watch the Englishmen as they, seekers of sensationalism like us, are also the "audience" for a narrative about the end of the Third Reich. Theirs is mediated by the visual technology of the photograph, as ours is by the movie camera. The spectatorship of the British soldiers is, like ours, suspect and contaminated. Though not, presumably, pedophiles or disappointed fascists, they are men entangled in the nostalgic allure of Nazism, part of the chain of displacement that defines a shattered masculinity in the postfascist rubble; they are substitutable for Edmund's father, Karl-Heinz and Henning, and also, in their spectatorship, for us. They, too, are the fascinated consumers of the trace of Nazism.

It is Henning, however, who is the most consistent embodiment of the principle of spectatorship in *Germania anno zero*. The moment in which his unrepentant Nazism is most evident, and his pedophilia relatively undisguised, is also a moment in which he is clearly, again, a stand-in for the cinematic spectator. Edmund, alarmed about his father's illness, seeks out Henning for advice just as Henning is bringing another handsome young boy home to his apartment. Henning responds to Edmund's concern with an impassioned speech, which Edmund takes as an instruction to kill his father: the weak must die to give way to the strong, and the strong must have the courage to bring this about without false sentimentality—a familiar fascist ideology. The boy who is with Henning is in the background, perfectly framed by the bodies of the two conversationalists, neatly served up for our delectation, as he is for Henning's. This is an ironic and self-reflexive shot, which is so clearly artificially posed that it acts as a distanciation device, forcing us to remember our own spectatorship, to notice ourselves looking. As Henning is lecturing Edmund, another man comes, looks at the other boy and leads him into the apartment building. Henning is obviously upset and jealous—as he continues speaking, he walks frantically along the side of the building, staring up at the windows. Again, the emphasis on looking as an act is marked—the Nazi is looking for the object of his desire, the same object we too have so recently been invited to gaze upon, while spouting his poisonous fascist creed. Later, when Edmund returns to tell Henning that he has poisoned his father, and then runs away, our view and Henning's are explicitly paralleled. Henning watches from a balcony as Edmund flees; we share in his gaze through a lengthy point of view shot. Once again, our spectatorship is directly evoked, and Henning is "us," as we are invited once more to consume the spectacle of fascist aesthetics, our desire equated with that of the fascist pedophile.

Edmund's flight from Henning is followed by the most famous sequence in *Germania anno zero*: the solitary "death march" that culminates in Edmund's suicidal leap from a ruined building. We follow him, through a virtuoso series of tracking shots, as he walks through the rubble of Berlin, pausing to play hopscotch on a sidewalk, carefully removing his jacket before using a fallen steel girder as a slide. He spies from across the street as his father's body is removed from the house, carried on a stretcher to join a truckload of shrouded corpses, perhaps all also "fathers" who, in their brokenness, have left their children only the shattered remnants of subjectivity. Throughout this long, virtually wordless sequence, the camera never leaves Edmund; its loving gaze, and ours, are fixed obsessively on him. We watch this beautiful Aryan child moving through the rubble, the smashed and tumbled structures that are metonymic for a fragmented and ruptured masculinity, a male subjectivity that carries the fractured trace and echo of fascism. At the end of the film, Edmund has himself literally become part of the rubble, both symbolic and literal, that has been his universe: his body lies, shattered, at the base of a ruined building.

Rossellini's Berlin is haunted by the "revenants" of fascism. Edmund kills himself by jumping into the ghost of a building that isn't there, falling "through" floors that exist only spectrally, as trace and echo of both the physical "brick and mortar" Berlin that is now gone, and Speer's grandiose wood and plaster models.[44] Similarly, the Nazi idylls of *Hitlerjunge Quex* flicker in and out of focus, the visual trace perpetually both present and absent, as we look at Edmund moving through the ruined Berlin of Rossellini's film.[45] The handsome Heini's maudlin death—his body held up in the arms of his comrades, his dying words a muttered invocation of his cherished Nazi flag—is both echoed and refuted by Rossellini's framing of Edmund's solitary leap into the void that was once a building, his death marked by the arrival of a woman who places herself by his body to form one of the director's signature pietà compositions.[46]

Edmund's fallen body echoes precisely the posture of Heini's—the two blond boys lie on the ground in exactly the same position, arm twisted outward and head to the side, nearly identical shorts, suspenders, and bare legs denoting the same childlike vulnerability, emphasizing the fragility of their immature bodies.[47] As Edmund's celluloid body substitutes for that of Heini, it is clear that Rossellini is engaging in dialogue with Germany's Nazi past and indirectly with his own fascist history, allowing it to flicker in and out of visibility, echoing it, reconstituting it, and ultimately rejecting it. For Rossellini, postwar Berlin is full of celluloid ghosts—perhaps it is easier to confront them in Germany than the more intimately familiar Italian version, which he himself helped to create. In *Germania anno zero*, we see again Hitler's capital and the never-realized city of Speer's grandiose imagination; Aryan Heini's maudlin death imprints itself on the celluloid on which we see the tragic leap of Rossellini's Edmund. Fascism is the specter that haunts these films, always present in its very absence. In the ruins of Berlin, postfascist identity is constructed in uneasy dialogue with past representations of national identity and masculine subjectivity.

Chapter 2
The Ghost in the Rubble

At approximately the same time that Roberto Rossellini was shooting *Germania anno zero* on location in the rubble of Berlin, Billy Wilder and Carol Reed were also making films in the former capitals of the Third Reich. Wilder's *A Foreign Affair* and Reed's *The Third Man* employ a dramatically different cinematic idiom from Rossellini's neorealist work. Despite their profound differences, however, these three almost simultaneous films share some important preoccupations. A central concern of the Wilder and Reed films, one that echoes Rossellini's ambivalent dialogue with the ghosts of Italian fascist cinema, is how to navigate the landscape of past cinematic representation. The literal rubble of Berlin and Vienna corresponds to the epistemological ruin of a post-Nazi world in the cities most identified with that regime. Both Wilder and Reed, like Rossellini, bring us characters who circulate obsessively through the rubble, traversing the traces of the past. All three directors repeatedly confront us with a visual summary of what has been lost and of the ad hoc quality of new constructions in these landscapes of destruction. Like Rossellini, Wilder and Reed focus their films on a confrontation between the fascist culture that now lies in physical and symbolic ruin and the postfascist world as offered by Allied "liberators." In all three films, Americans and American popular culture are placed in ambivalent opposition to the preexisting structures of subjectivity and representation. As the American characters in these three films—naive "innocents abroad" who now hold all the power—stumble through a complex world that they are ill equipped to understand, the inescapable traces of fascism become a central focus. So, too, does the question of whether there are any valid alternative systems of representation, or viable new ways of constructing the subject in relation to representation. Fascism is bankrupt and broken, but it is not clear whether what will succeed it has any more moral credibility. In *A Foreign Affair* and *The Third Man*, American popular culture, nominated for hegemony by the new Allied rulers, is scrutinized along with fascist culture. Structures of gender, racial, and national identity are undermined through an interrogation of cinematic representation. Unlike Rossellini's neorealist masterpiece, these films by Wilder and Reed do not attempt to distance themselves from the pleasures and perversities of conventional cinematic representation. Instead, they glory in it, offering us a kind of festival of artificiality, in which—through sly allusion, coded citation, and direct quotation—they immerse the spectator in a dizzying cascade of references and constantly foreground the terms by which they construct their own illusion. The ghosts of Nazism haunt the streets of Vienna and Berlin, but so too do the stock figures of American culture. The Nazi soldier, the Hitler Youth, and the dirndl-wearing "Mädchen"—disquieting revenants whose presence is inescapable in these films—share their landscape of rubble with American cowboys, detectives, GIs, and "gals." All are subjected to the same skeptical scrutiny.

Wilder's *A Foreign Affair* and Reed's *The Third Man,* both released, like *Germania anno zero,* in 1948, are haunted by similar "specters." Both films bring contemporary American popular culture—in the form of pulp fiction, cinema, and the visual arts—into dialogue with the aesthetic and political remnants of the Nazi past, situating themselves both literally and figuratively in the rubble of the former regime. Fascist aesthetics, ideologies, and modes of subject constitution are posited as irrecoverably broken; however, the American paradigm that appears poised to replace Nazi culture is no less bankrupt. American cultural models and institutions are shown, in both films, as backed up by the full force of the occupying armies: we see specifically Anglo-American cultural activity—ranging from literary lectures to baseball games—organized by men in Allied military uniforms. However, the superiority or inevitability of these cultural forms is not in any way naturalized for the spectator. Even as we watch these two films made by American studios with American financing and Hollywood stars—films which represent for us postwar Vienna and Berlin, the now literally fractured cultural and governmental capitals of the defeated Nazi regime—we are offered no comfortable assumption that there has been a morally, politically, or aesthetically unproblematic replacement of discredited fascist models by more familiar American ones. The artifacts of Hollywood are treated just as ambivalently as those of Nazism, and both are equally dependent on the politically and morally dubious processes of spectatorship.

In both films, spectatorship is foregrounded as inescapably problematic; both Wilder and Reed refuse to allow any sort of stable or comfortable relationship between the audience and the images on screen to develop. In both *A Foreign Affair* and *The Third Man,* we are repeatedly forced to confront the question of how we see and how we construct meaning; both films repeatedly and consistently denaturalize both the machinery of spectatorship and any implicit epistemologies that may emerge. Wilder and Reed both offer to the viewer a series of surrogates, outsiders in the German or Austrian culture who, like the films' spectators, attempt with mixed success to create a viable set of meanings with which to approach this post-Nazi universe. Both films make vision itself highly visible, emphasizing the complex processes by which we see or are blinded. Vision is obsessively foregrounded by both directors, as we look at people looking and are forced to consider the ways sight is enabled, limited, and constrained, both for the characters on screen and the spectators in the movie theater. The consciousness of vision as mediated construction rather than any sort of naturalized access to "reality" is intensified by the way both directors also posit vision as constituted by a complex series of codes established by our prior experience as spectators. The way we see, then, is doubly denaturalized: vision is emphatically shown not only as dependent on constrained, limited, and manipulated perception, but also as requiring us to read every image through a preexisting interpretive matrix. Mise-en-scène is crucially important in both films: the settings against which the main action takes place, the complex assemblage of elements on the screen, posit a sort of visual metacommentary on the aesthetic and political dilemmas that are central to the vision of both directors. Both films use mise-en-scène to establish a complex web of allusions—references to past cinematic movements, to iconic images from art and literature—to create a dialogue between past and present. Both directors engage in a dialogue with different past genres and styles, in a dizzying, sometimes gleeful and sometimes grief-stricken spiral guaranteed to keep audiences off balance.

The haunting of *A Foreign Affair* by the ghosts of fascist cinema is evident from the first shot as we see an elegant silver aircraft gliding in through a dramatic cloud and flying low over a city.[1] Wilder's unmistakable quote from the famous opening sequence of Leni Riefenstahl's *Triumph of the Will*, in which Hitler arrives like a god from the skies over Nuremburg, foregrounds the intense ambivalence that suffuses this film about the aftermath of Nazism. As the opening sequence continues, we see the plane flying over an unfathomably vast landscape of rubble. In a startlingly direct quote from Riefenstahl, Wilder tracks the shadow of the aircraft as it passes over the destroyed city; in *Triumph of the Will*, Hitler's plane casts a triumphant shadow over the sunlit, picturesque, populated streets of Nuremburg, as we see people on the ground moving in orderly militarized formations, preparing for the Führer's visit.[2] In referring so explicitly to this iconic moment in film, Wilder, perhaps with some glee, underscores the contrast between the Nazi's (literally) elevated view of their own civic accomplishments and the wreckage that was the ultimate result. This opening sequence also, however, highlights the meta-discourse about cinema and aesthetics that is central to Wilder's entire project. By simultaneously adopting and subverting the conventions of romantic comedy and film noir, and alluding parodically to German Expressionism and fascist propaganda, Wilder requires his audience to abandon any stable notions of identity, representation or epistemology. *A Foreign Affair* leaves us standing uneasily on the margin between genres, an unsettling position for any spectator, and forces us to consider how our ways of seeing and our positions of identification—whether through constructions of gender, nation, or desire—bring us inevitably to crisis. As the American and German characters negotiate the physical rubble of a defeated city—a mise-en-scène memorably employed by Wilder—they also traverse the chaotic territory of identity in ruins.

Riefenstahl's storm troopers seem to walk the streets of Wilder's postwar city, slightly out-of-focus denizens of Hitler's Nuremberg that keep cropping up in unlikely ways in this tale of the American occupation of Berlin. They lurch into view at unsettling moments, the repressed swastika appearing with comic persistence—it is a running joke—in this city where the stars and stripes hold sway. The never-built fascist city so chillingly envisioned by Albert Speer appears as a ghost on the celluloid of *A Foreign Affair*; we are guided (literally—there is a guided tour for the visiting congressmen, allowing Wilder to make full use of an unprecedented urban environment for his location shooting) through the ruins of the Nazi city. As we pass under the Brandenburg gate, and by the ruined Reichstag, which were intended to anchor planned parade routes in Speer's magnificent new Nazi capital, the axes of his fantasy landscape emerge. There are two sets of ruins, therefore, as the American victors gaze on Berlin: the actual rubble of the capital—vast fields of destruction—and the bones of Speer's "world capital," to be renamed Germania. The traces of the Nazi city invade the postwar scene, as a world that is often more "real" than the present. There is also, however, another specter, apparently paradoxical: a future from the past, one which never happened but still permeates the urban environment.

American masculinity—newly refurbished in military supremacy—collapses, its vacuity as an epistemological category underlined by the chronic inability of the American soldier to maintain gender stability as he crosses and recrosses its ruptured boundaries. The American soldier in Berlin ostensibly represents triumphant masculinity; however, the gender identity of Captain Pringle, the romantic hero, is as much in ruin as the Reichstag or Unter den Linden. We first encounter Pringle as part of the military formation that awaits Congresswoman Phoebe Frost's plane—in a position analogous to that of the imposing storm troopers holding back the Nazi crowds as Hitler lands in Nuremberg in *Triumph of the Will*. The masculinity of this American body that has unaccountably substituted itself for Riefenstahl's fascist figures is, however, highly ambivalent. If suppressed homoeroticism "haunts" and, perhaps, undercuts the iconic masculinities of *Triumph of the Will*, the male impersonators of the conquering allied forces are compromised from the beginning. Pringle—though he appears, in his perfect uniform, to incarnate the military ideal of the latest army to occupy the airfields of Germany—has one important element distinguishing him from the Nazi Brown Shirts: throughout the reception ceremony we see a sheer nylon stocking hanging from the front pocket of his pressed uniform trousers. His impeccable military exterior is, therefore, marred by an accidental sign of gender instability. A series of "slips" begins to show, as Pringle tells his superior about the laundry mishaps of a fellow officer who "sent out his shorts and got back a girdle." We are shown the apparently seamless facade of American military masculinity while we are invited to speculate about what might be hidden under the faultless uniforms. Pringle tucks the offending nylon out of sight when informed by his colonel that he "is losing something," but the proverbial cat is already out of the bag, and the sign of the failure of gender classifications cannot be erased. In this introduction to American masculinity "in the ruins of Berlin," it is clear that much—undoubtedly for the better—has been lost, including stable gender identity. The apparently effortless masculinity of Riefenstahl's storm troopers, however illusory it may itself have been, is a fading echo on the tarmac at Tempelhof Airport. Wilder's aircraft, unlike Riefenstahl's, delivers its "very important passengers indeed" (as they are called by the senior military officer, a phrase that would also describe Hitler in the Riefenstahl film) into a German cityscape in which subjectivity is unmistakably in crisis and the parameters of unitary identity, always problematic, can no longer be successfully maintained.

Our first sight of the city of Berlin is calculated to produce astonishment and awe; we have already been told, immediately after the opening credits, that "a large part of this picture was photographed in Berlin." Wilder, therefore, introduces an apparent contradiction from the film's earliest moments: we are told both that this is "real"—the authentic, actual rubble of the destroyed city—and, through intertextual allusion, that what we are watching is a film about film, steeped in cinematic quotes, citations, and tongue-in-cheek references. This tension between an appeal to the seductive authority of "reality" and a sophisticated metacommentary on how realities are constructed and reinforced pervades *A Foreign Affair*. Its depiction of the rubble cityscape bows in the direction of newsreel footage, a genre with which both American and European audiences would have been intimately familiar.[3] The newsreel genre, from which Wilder liberally borrows, presents an ostensibly unproblematized claim of authenticity, providing the spectator with a view of what is "really" before the camera and tending to bypass any consideration of itself as a mediated construction. In their appeal to the idea of "reality," and the voyeuristic attractions of some sort of direct access to the "truth" of the aftermath of the war in Berlin, the exterior shots of rubble-scapes seem to offer a way out of the moral dilemma alluded to by Wilder's Riefenstahl-inspired first shot. If alluding to Riefenstahl raises the specter of film as propaganda, reminding us of how our pleasure in images can be manipulated and how thoroughly politically compromised our enjoyment may be, presenting footage that assumes the mantle of unmediated "reality" might seem to be a more palatable alternative. However, no such escape is possible: the moral simplicity of a clear epistemology is not on offer. Like Helma Sanders-Brahms in *Deutschland bleiche Mutter*, Wilder alludes to the familiar idiom of the newsreel only to subvert its authority. Instead of placing emphasis primarily on the content of the footage itself, thereby privileging it epistemologically as some sort of relatively unmediated access to "reality," Wilder focuses our attention on it as image and, more importantly, on why and how we look at it. Any assumption about film as a transparent medium is definitively undercut.

If Wilder, alluding to Riefenstahl, begins *A Foreign Affair* by situating us squarely within the context of the fascist propaganda film and then evokes propaganda's seeming opposite, the documentary, with its claim to unvarnished, relatively unmediated "truth," he ultimately subverts any such epistemological distinction. (Of course, the newsreel's claims to any sort of unproblematic relationship to a prior external "reality" are always highly problematic.) A metadiscourse about spectatorship comes more clearly into focus as the first sequence continues: by emphasizing the constraints and conditions under which we "see," the film problematizes all epistemologies and raises important questions about our models of how subjectivity itself is constructed. Wilder presents us immediately with a set of surrogates for "ourselves:" a group of "spectators," an American congressional delegation flying into Berlin to investigate the progress of the military occupation. We are invited to inspect these inspectors, to watch them watching; as the film cuts between panoramic "God's eye" shots of the city, the plane's interior, and shots of the rubble from the point of view of individual passengers on the plane, we are forced to think about our own status as spectators. The fascination exerted by the rubble outside the plane is echoed by the fascination—and perhaps dismay—with which we view our own spectatorship. The political and aesthetic implications of vision, knowledge, and spectatorship are very much in play from this first sequence onward. The film, at the outset, emphasizes its own production as artifact: the presence of the camera becomes literalized for us, as one of the congressmen points a hand-cranked movie camera out the aircraft's window and films the approach over the city. The gaze of the plane's passengers, therefore, is directly equated with the eye of both the spectator and the film's director and the equivocal "reality" outside frankly presented as construction, with the process of its production an unavoidable focus. Wilder does not allow us to approach "Berlin"—which, as we have already been told, we are "really" seeing—without considering the ideological and aesthetic implications of that vision.[4]

A refusal of vision, myopia as a deliberate choice, is what succeeds our first sweeping views of Berlin in rubble. Inside the plane's cabin, Miss Frost—a gelidly blond congresswoman from Iowa and one of the film's romantic leads—is seated in a window, refusing to look out; she is concentrating on the paperwork in her lap and seems to have no curiosity about the city she has come to see. Even after her rumpled and faintly distasteful male compatriots have woken up, overcome their airsickness, and begun to look out the window, Miss Frost steadfastly refuses to move her eye away from the documents she is holding. When asked to look outside by a companion, who seems to be made slightly anxious by her lack of interest, she, packing her writing materials neatly away in a number of bags of increasing size, replies: "one thing at a time." Miss Frost's character type is clearly identifiable within conventional Hollywood iconography: she is the repressed and repressive female whose femininity and sexuality will, in the course of the film, be duly awakened by the right man. "One thing at a time" refers in part, perhaps, to this familiar plot sequence—in a sense, this statement is a synopsis of *A Foreign Affair* read as conventional romantic comedy; as well-seasoned film spectators, experienced in the economy of images to which Wilder refers, we know that in due course Miss Frost will be defrosted, her hair will come down, and her spine will unbend. The romantic lead will get her man, and the all-American virtues will be upheld; the clean certainties of Iowa will triumph over the unsavory ambiguities of Berlin.[5]

Identity slippage is characteristic of Wilder's protagonists in a number of areas. Miss Frost may be a sublimely unconscious spokeswoman for genre conventions, giving us a synopsis of the orderly progression of the type of movie her character initially seems designed to inhabit, but she herself seems to be increasingly "unsure" which genre she belongs to and moves between them with startling fluidity. Nationality and gender both fail to confine Miss Frost, despite her initial appearance as the apotheosis of American womanhood. She ostensibly represents all American women, claiming at one point to speak for all "the wives, mothers and sisters" who are waiting at home, presumably happily ensconced in environments in which they don't risk the destabilization of identity that Miss Frost encounters in "the ruins of Berlin." Her identity fluctuates wildly as she morphs into a series of stock movie figures. The corn-fed Iowa girl who is the foil to Marlene Dietrich's worldly femme fatale—and is memorably dismissed by Dietrich as having a face "like a scrubbed kitchen floor"—does not offer a naturalized female counterpart to the highly theatrical nightclub singer. Miss Frost's clean-scrubbed American forthrightness is defaced as she crosses the boundaries of nationality and gender identities, appearing—to her character's astonished dismay—as a German prostitute, a "country cousin" from Stuttgart, a GI in uniform, a film noir detective on a stake-out, even Scarlett O'Hara, dressed in a swatch of brocade pilfered from the domestic décor. Ultimately, the conventional limits of gender disappear entirely as she becomes an aggressive sexual predator, forcing the object of her desire, the now fully emasculated Captain Pringle, to adopt the classic posture of a lion tamer, protecting his virtue with a brandished chair and a frantic recitation of Longfellow.

Longfellow's poem, "The Midnight Ride of Paul Revere," its instantly recognizable bombast standing in for the entire constellation of American national mythology, is recited twice in the film, invoked on both occasions as a shield against the chaotic encroachment of sexual desire. The American soldier, the military conqueror who looms over the ruined landscape of Berlin, unsuccessfully deploys the ultimate weapon against emasculation, his heroic nationalist myth. The Longfellow poem, far from succeeding as a bulwark against identity slippage, only serves to underline the spirit in which Wilder handles both nationality and gender throughout the film. By linking the poem's recitation with two scenes of aggressive seduction that border on violence, and in which conventional gender positions are first upheld and then reversed, Wilder unmasks nationality, gender, and sexuality as inherently ridiculous categories, whose binary configurations cannot be sustained, and to which parody is the most fitting response. If the familiar cadences of Longfellow invite caricature, so too does the familiar rhetoric of cinema. *A Foreign Affair* invokes Hollywood romance only to satirize it. War films, film noir detective stories, and spy thriller are given the same treatment; the only sustainable form, ultimately, is parody.[6]

If *A Foreign Affair* is haunted by the ghosts of fascism, as evidenced by Wilder's quotations from Riefenstahl, it is also inhabited by more genial American phantoms. Various classics of American popular culture appear frequently as quotation and parody in *A Foreign Affair*. It is as if Wilder is taking the audience through a range of preexisting cultural models for this film: its content is contextualized for us in a series of sly references. We are led through a dizzying cascade of allusions, from the hyperbolic sonority of Longfellow to the high romance of *Casablanca*, stopping along the way to revisit such cinematic icons as *The Great Dictator* and *Gone with the Wind*. John Lund and Jean Arthur are parodic stand-ins for Bogart and Bergmann in *Casablanca*, as we find ourselves looking once more at a fogged-in airfield at night, with light refracted elegantly from a gleaming aircraft. At one point, Pringle's superior officer—a certain Col. Plummer who acts as deus-ex-machina by preempting the military weather report and keeping Miss Frost's plane from taking off—draws a target on the foggy window pane. As we look through the target at the tarmac on which this romance in the ruins of Berlin began, we see how this film takes deliberate aim at both the conventions of cinematic romance and at previous Hollywood treatments of Nazism and its effects. The visual elements that come together to create one of the most memorable moments in *Casablanca* are reconfigured here as absurd pastiche. Our all-American couple, of course, eventually reunites, leaving Erika, the German nightclub singer contaminated by Nazism, out in the cold and erasing the "foreign" element in the love triangle of *A Foreign Affair*. Instead of the noble self-sacrifice expressed in Bogart's famous statement in *Casablanca* that "the problems of three little people don't amount to a hill of beans in this crazy world," this film offers us a tongue-in-cheek look at solipsistic self-satisfaction and American triumphalism. Rather than asserting a moral vision, the film brackets all moral issues, even remaining neutral on Erika's relationship to Nazism. The heroism and moral seriousness of the standard rendition of the Allied anti-Nazi effort—which were, by 1948, so familiar in Hollywood films—return in *A Foreign Affair* as parody and pastiche.

Another film that flickers briefly into view in Wilder's off-kilter revisitation of Hollywood classics has a status as iconic as *Casablanca*: for a moment, Phoebe becomes another celluloid revenant, Scarlett O'Hara in *Gone with the Wind*. Racial politics—so notably absent as an explicit concern in this ostensibly lighthearted and apolitical film improbably set in the immediate aftermath of racial genocide—appears indirectly, caught in the corner of the viewers eye, as a passing reference. As Miss Frost—having metamorphosed temporarily from an asexual Midwestern prude to a beautiful woman in love with her handsome soldier—prepares to go out for a night on the rubble with Captain Pringle, she makes a grand entrance down a staircase, dressed in an evening gown. After Pringle adjusts the neckline of the black-market dress, he decides to add to the effect by appropriating an article from the household furnishings: he pulls off an elegant brocade tablecloth and drapes it around Miss Frost as a shawl.[7] This is, perhaps, a reference to the famous use of Tara's curtains to make Scarlett's dress in *Gone with the Wind*. In using a brocaded fabric from the domestic decor as feminine apparel, Pringle turns Phoebe into Scarlett, and the moral "superiority" of the Americans is suddenly cast into a different light. By recontextualizing "Americaness"—replacing its garb of post–Second World War virtue with the messier trappings of slavery and the history of race in America—Wilder allows, however indirectly, a subtext to emerge that highlights the buried discourse about racism in *A Foreign Affair. Gone with the Wind* may be one of the watershed films in the history of American cinema, but it shares a darker past with other iconic American movies, such as D. W. Griffith's *Birth of a Nation.* Racism is one of the "specters" haunting American film, one that is always present even, and perhaps especially, when it is unacknowledged. The highly ambivalent discourse about American nationalism and national identity that is coded into *A Foreign Affair* is placed into dialogue with another embedded discussion about the genocidal racism of Nazi Germany—also present in the film mostly as reference and allusion.

Miss Frost's character seems to unite these discourses. An aggressive whiteness is inscribed in her name and on her body in ways that are readable in both the German and American contexts. Miss Frost is as white, cold, and pure as the driven snow. Her mission at the beginning of the film is to extend her "frostiness" across the overheated moral morass that is postwar Berlin, making sure that the boundaries that limit appropriate identities and behaviors are not allowed to melt.[8] Aggressive whiteness is also emphasized, perhaps, within an American context in Miss Frost's constant stress on her Iowa origins and her insistence on singing "The Iowa Corn Song" in situations that might more properly call for jazz. Miss Frost's body itself is coded in ways that are highly suggestive of a broader racial discourse. Her hairstyle—a tight blond braid encircling her head—seems strikingly restrictive and old fashioned.[9] More importantly, it would not be out of place at a Nazi rally. It is precisely the style associated with dirndls and fetishistic "Germanness" and often appears in photographs of the Bund Deutscher Mädel, the girls' organization associated with the Hitler Youth. Miss Frost, therefore, appears in Berlin as a "ghost" representing two different, but overlapping, racially inflected discourses. By having her flicker into view, however briefly, as Scarlett O'Hara, *A Foreign Affair* places itself in the context of American cinematic discourses about race and engages in an ambivalent dialogue with that very checkered black and white history. Phoebe Frost also walks the streets of Berlin as the "ghost" of Riefenstahl's Nazi women, who themselves appear only briefly as peripheral figures in *Triumph of the Will.* The German "Mädchen," the Aryan feminine ideal with her halo of braided blond hair, represents racism carried to its logical extreme: genocide. The body of Miss Frost as "revenant," the ghost of cinema past, is readable as a sign that parallels, perhaps, America's history of racism and slavery with Nazi genocide and brings the Holocaust into this film from which it is, on the surface, so unaccountably absent.

The Nazi singer Erika von Schluetow, played by Marlene Dietrich, is also a "revenant" of sorts, strikingly familiar but oddly off-kilter, a walking comment on past cinematic "femmes fatales." Wilder shoots her in ways that make her unmistakably a parody of naturalized femininity.[10] Throughout *A Foreign Affair,* Wilder frames Dietrich in obtrusively theatrical and denaturalizing ways, emphasizing the frank performativity of the character's gender identity, a drag queen wreathed in smoke and silhouetted by spotlights. Wilder frames our first sight of Dietrich's in a hole in a shattered bathroom door. From that moment, we see her as the ultimate creature of the rubble, a shattered self for whom the world-weary disillusionment suggested in songs about the "black market" in both merchandise and love refer just as surely to the loss of any illusion of a "natural" gendered subjectivity. The cabaret songs written by Freidrich Hollander for his fellow German émigrés express cynical detachment. If the American Miss Frost seems genuinely, and comically, astonished to find the parameters of her selfhood utterly fluid, as she cycles through a dizzying range of stock cinematic identities, Dietrich's Fraulein von Schluetow does not seem to expect it to be anything other than a convenient fiction, a painted-on simulation created in the glare of the spotlights. When she ridicules her competitor from the cornfields of Iowa for a lack of makeup, it is Miss Frost's naïve assumption of authenticity that she is targeting. Dietrich's character appears on stage at a nightclub to which Wilder has given a tongue-in-cheek name that is deeply infused with the past—the oh-so-overdetermined "Lorelei." She, like the American soldiers who are her patsies and lovers, injects a variety of spectral cinematic presences onto Wilder's postwar celluloid. Dietrich is, of course, always unmistakably Dietrich—the great Hollywood star (perhaps a little past her prime) who also became an international icon as a German who rejected Nazism. (The Nazis tried repeatedly to find a substitute for her, attempting to elevate stars of their own, but none even approached her stature.[11]) On the spotlight stage, Erika's Germanness is a highly unnatural condition: the specters of previous cinematic representations flicker into view in the glare and smoke. Dietrich's character here is seen through the prism of all the other world weary, glamorously cynical performers she has played, from *The Blue Angel* to *Morocco* to *Blond Venus.* From the stage of the Lorelei, as the Rhine-maiden of the rubble, she sings into being her past cinematic roles.

Miss Frost's first utterance, "one thing at a time," can be read as invocation of Hollywood convention, an exhortation toward narrative neatness and clear genre boundaries; it could also, conversely, be interpreted as a futile if stubborn credo, a gesture toward the kind of rigid conventionalism—cinematic, moral, and political—whose bankruptcy is made all too clear by the scene of ruin she is refusing to contemplate. As Miss Frost turns her gaze away from the vast landscape of rubble outside the window in the opening sequence of *A Foreign Affair*, she literalizes the conflict at the center of the film. Her rigidly averted eye implies a desire to control the circulation of images and to hold excess and disruption at bay. Miss Frost, epitomizing the prudish refusal of experience of all kinds, holds knowledge in abeyance with her willful myopia. The rubble at which she will not look suggests an aesthetic and an epistemology that cannot be contained by the Hollywood genre of the romantic comedy; it is in every way the antithesis of the orderly universe of "one thing at a time." The rubble exemplifies a reality in which all boundaries are erased and all structures collapsed; no orderly temporal or spatial succession is possible.

Along with our heroine's frosty refusal to contemplate the scene outside her window—her unflappable insistence on maintaining an optic which is, in some ways, as blinkered as the triumphalist optimism of Riefenstahl's propaganda film—Wilder offers us a somatic response as another possible model for how to cope with the situation: nausea and (off-screen) vomiting. When Miss Frost's interlocutor is trying to persuade her to look out, he exclaims, with relish: "Don't you want to see it? Look at it—like pack rats been gnawing a hunk of old, moldy Roquefort cheese!" At this, another member of the delegation covers his mouth and is hurriedly helped toward the rear of the plane. This is the first of several food metaphors used to verbally describe the vast destruction; here the image suggests both rapacious consumption and disgust. The gregarious congressman, with his jolly bonhomie, consumes the sight before him with relish; his appetite for looking, and his desire to convert vision into consumption, to eat it all up with his eyes, continues as he later says: "You've got quite a sight coming. It looks like chicken innards at frying time." The jolly congressman is inviting Miss Frost to be a consumer, albeit of a somewhat tainted commodity, appealing to her appetite. She later transposes his cheerful greed into a somewhat different idiom when she anticipates what the effects of the bombing will look like: "after all the taxpayers' money that was poured on it I don't expect it to look like a lace valentine." Miss Frost is also a purveyor of metaphors describing cinematic representation. If the congressman's scopophilic desire is frankly one of consumption— appetite and the nausea potentially provoked by its excess are both played out for us, to comic effect—Miss Frost's view also offers a commentary on film viewing, telling us that we should interpret what we see within the conventional framework of romance. This invocation of the "lace valentine" of romance films as a genre offers us, again, a way of glossing this film and especially this character; at the same time, the statement is negative—this strategy, ultimately, will not work for this film. Genre conventions are commented on, evoked as a familiar framework, repeatedly in *A Foreign Affair*. However, genre is one of the things that does not survive intact in the rubble of cinema.

The beginning sequence of *A Foreign Affair*, therefore, demands that we consider our own spectatorship by undercutting the preexisting habits and assumptions by which that spectatorship has been structured. The "lace valentine" of genre, which might have been "sent" to us as viewers— with its familiar and predictable evocations and calibrations of desire— has been replaced by a world "delivered" by American bombing rather than Hollywood film. (It is financed by taxpayer's money rather than the investments of movie moguls, as Miss Frost points out—in either case, "made in America" is the inevitable label.) Rather than the graceful patterns and stylized voids of lace, we see the irregular, gaping holes and craters of a city in rubble. In fact, this scene, as framed by Wilder, does look rather like lace at times. The remaining walls of apartment buildings, with their rows of empty spaces where windows once were, march off into the distance in a kind of graceful symmetry, an aesthetically pleasing composition of voids; the impossible-to-comprehend, already radically denaturalized mise-en-scène of the rubble-scape is further defamiliarized by this aestheticization.[12]

The "lace valentine" of Miss Frost's imagination, therefore, is "sent" to us, but not as genre comedy; instead of frothy familiarity, the lace represents a frightening new aesthetic of the void, of collapsed structures, the beauty of an epistemology in rubble. The lace, a highly overdetermined image, takes on other meanings also: the congresswoman's reference to a valentine as one possible structure that might make this new world legible, might impose some sort of aesthetic and epistemological structure—even though she, in the same breath, disavows its potential as an explanatory framework, saying it is not to be "expected"—suggests a metadiscourse on the limitations of vision. Miss Frost is the kind of woman who would never be seen in public without gloves, hat, and a veil, and, in fact, she wears a lace half-veil through much of the film. The elegant band of black lace hanging over her eyes both restricts and shapes what she can see—and, by extension, tells us to pay attention to the way our own vision is constructed and constrained. Lace represents pure pattern; it has no "content," no "substance," but rather is the composite of elegantly structured contours that do not outline anything except empty space. It is a stylization of voids, representing nothing but itself as structure. If Wilder, in *A Foreign Affair*, takes as his "subject" the processes by which this film, and film in general, mediate reality, then lace—as "valentine" or as veil—becomes a symbol that suggests to us the necessity of focusing on what we see *as* representation, as structure, rather than on the "content" of the image. The voids that characterize the rubble-scape—the gaps where the structures of everyday life once stood, the empty sockets that had framed windows through which our gaze upon the world was once directed—echo the void at the center of identity. In the ruins of Berlin, therefore, the "lace valentine" of romance fails to cover up the void at the heart of identity, and gendered subjectivity cannot maintain itself as a credible structure. The American officer waiting on the Berlin tarmac, echoing by implication Riefenstahl's confident Brown Shirts, has shed any claim to naturalized masculinity and has indeed become "GI Joke," asserting identity only through a series of parodic impersonations.

The Third Man, like *A Foreign Affair*, situates itself at the interconnection of several different historical and filmic discourses, challenging the taxonomies of national cinema and genre. The vision of Reed and Graham Greene, the director and writer of *The Third Man*, respectively, resembles that of Wilder, in that subjectivity has lost any claim to unity or "authenticity" and has become purely performative. The subject in *The Third Man*, as it is in *A Foreign Affair*, is constituted both as a spectacle and as an obsessive spectator, with voyeurism and scopophilia the primary forms of desire. Both films are highly self-reflexive in their allusiveness and insist on placing themselves in an intertextual context that complicates any possible strategies of reading.[13] *The Third Man* is, again like *A Foreign Affair*, intimately concerned with the "machinery" of selfhood, specifically the specular constitution of the subject in film. However, this preoccupation can be looked at in a variety of historical contexts. *The Third Man* is usually read within the framework of American cinema, specifically in the context of film noir, and the cold war.[14] However, *The Third Man* is not only a film "about" the cold war, or an exploration of modern alienation, but it can also be read as a specific response to another facet of its historical moment, the collapse of the fascist state. Film noir, in general, is intimately engaged in questioning the basis of subjectivity; in this, *The Third Man* is no exception. However, the film adds a unique dimension to this engagement, inserting itself into a varied cinematic discourse that problematizes postwar subjectivity, the broken and denaturalized self that is provisionally erected in the rubble of Fascism, retaining elements from the preexisting structures but never their apparently "natural" wholeness. As a film whose mise-en-scène places us literally in the rubble of fascism, *The Third Man* must concern itself with the ideological implications of spectacle.

Riefenstahl and Speer are inescapable phantoms; the trace of their unique and monstrous vision of the Nazi city necessarily permeates any later representations of Berlin and Vienna, the former capitals of Nazism. *The Third Man*, therefore, is intensely self-aware about the ideological context of its own production of spectacle. Like *A Foreign Affair*, *The Third Man* is a haunted film. The specter of fascist cinema repeatedly returns, and the fascist man walks as a revenant through the ruined streets of postwar Vienna.

In the Vienna of *The Third Man*, Reed and Greene open to us a broken world in which instability, slippage, and displacement are the only structuring principles. The film presents its historical moment, after the war and the defeat of fascism, as one in which even the physical realm has no solidity or stability. In the brief montage that opens the film, we see—interspersed with images of the black market and the occupying allied armies—shots of rubble-scapes, as the voice-over casually informs us that Vienna "doesn't look any worse than many other European cities—bombed a little, of course." Legibility and coherence are lost in the rubble, as Reed disorients us with the rapid cuts of the opening montage (twenty-eight different shots in sixty-six seconds).[15] Viennese history is always symbolically present, but the past is irretrievably lost. The first words of the film are an almost elegiac description of a mythic—if clichéd—past: "I never knew the old Vienna before the war, with its Strauss music, its glamour and easy charm." We are standing in the ruins of fascism, in which visual references to Vienna's illustrious history only make more obvious the city's appearance here as disunified and incoherent, divided into occupied zones between which even the most basic communication is problematic. The occupation armies and the divided zones may initially appear to represent stability, an enforcement of an orderly taxonomy of space. However, in this film, all taxonomies break down; we learn in the opening voice-over that the visually impressive soldiers are impotent and that the four occupation zones are in fact highly permeable, as Harry Lime later demonstrates as he passes effortlessly between them by means of the sewers, appropriating the unrecognized space beneath the streets. Language itself has ceased to signify as we are presented with Babel.[16] Beneath the opening voice-over, we see a shot of a joint patrol of the Allied occupation force, as the narrator says: "Wonderful! You can imagine what a chance they had...no two of them speaking the same language." There has been a total breakdown of understanding and transparency, both in the mutual incomprehension of the Allied officials and our own incomprehension of the long sequences of unsubtitled German speech that rupture this English language film.[17]

Figure 2.1 *The Third Man*: Harry Lime in the sewer tunnel.

The Third Man casts many a sideways glance at Vienna's history as a capital of fascism. Nazism represented the ultimate specular society, in which the Führer, that former resident of Vienna, provided the "mirror" in an invitation to create, in jubilant "misrecognition," a unified, masterful self, and an accompanying annihilation of difference, the alterity that might disrupt specular bliss.[18] The film nominates a variety of other "mirrors" drawn from different contexts, including American popular culture. Near the beginning of *The Third Man*, the film's protagonist, Holly Martins, arranges a meeting with one of the shady characters who inhabit the venal world of postwar Vienna. When Holly asks for an identifying sign, his interlocutor replies that he will be holding a copy of Holly's book, "The Oklahoma Kid," a pulp Western bestseller. This initiates a drama of recognition that goes far beyond a simple arrangement to allow two strangers to meet. This incidental piece of dialogue raises a question that lies at the heart of *The Third Man*. What are the mirrors, the images, through which we recognize—or more importantly, misrecognize—"ourselves" in the process of subject constitution? As Holly walks into a café the camera follows his point of view as we see a rather lengthy close-up of his book, its cover a lurid depiction of a cowboy—perhaps the iconic figure of American masculinity—with a blazing six-gun in his hand. Later in the same scene, an almost comically direct visual link is made between Holly's all-too-American "mirror" and the European "mirror" of fascism. If the iconography of the American Western provides an instantly recognizable hypermasculine model, then the analogous icon of fascist masculinity might be that of the ubiquitously represented figure of the Führer himself. As Holly and his companion—the homosexually coded Baron Kurz—leave the café, the Baron makes genial conversation: "I'm so glad to have met you, the master of suspense. Such a good cover, I think." As he speaks the Baron holds up the book, its cover at head height between himself and Holly. It temporarily obscures another pedestrian walking toward them. As the pedestrian gets closer to the camera, and walks between the two men, the cover of the book is displaced by his face, which bears the immediately recognizable stigmata of Hitler, by way of Charlie Chaplin—the black eyes, the lock of hair, and, most importantly, the toothbrush moustache. The face of this Chaplinesque parody of Hitler is made spatially interchangeable with that of the "Oklahoma Kid," who has in turn been transplanted to Vienna. Holly's "cover"—his naturalized masculine identity—has been "blown." Holly recognizes himself in his American mirror, just as we, the spectator, recognize its displacement into a second mirror, and suspect that both recognitions originate in the same specular structure. Fascism, in turn, is filtered through the lens of Hollywood, returning as the trace of Charlie Chaplin's antifascist masterpiece. The spiral of masculine identities circles once more to American popular culture—pulp fiction and Hollywood cinema—in the face of the cowboy with his blazing six-gun. *The Third Man* continuously foregrounds its interrogation of masculine subjectivity as it is constructed within multiple contexts, from Nazism to Hollywood. The film invites us, as spectators, to find a series of broken mirrors in the rubble; what we discover upon looking into them is the dubious machinery of our own subject constitution.

The Third Man inscribes identity, masculine identity in particular, within a playful and irreverent cascade of images and codes drawn from Hollywood, from fiction and popular culture. If one of the mirrors for Holly is the "Kid" of the American West—the masculine icon with whom he literally comes face-to-face as he attempts to enter the foreign, fatally ambiguous world of postwar Vienna—then the city itself, with its rubble mounds and the remaining baroque streetscapes juxtaposed in chaotic promiscuity, presents for our excavation the trauma of broken subjectivity. Reed repeatedly encloses scenes of rubble and collapse within elegant frames, emphasizing their importance by supplying us with surrogate viewers to eye these compositions, as in a scene in which Holly, waiting for the appearance of Harry Lime, looks out a café window onto a dark square bordered by the incomplete facades of baroque buildings. Holly—whose moral code

Figure 2.2 *The Third Man*: "A good cover:" The Lone Rider of Santa Fe meets The Great Dictator.

and utter isolation are encapsulated by the title of one of his books, "The Lone Rider of Santa Fe"—brings his lonely "holy faith," his straightforward belief in unitary identity, to the epistemological simplicity of his search for "truth."[19] He is our surrogate, naively approaching the mystery of this world of "noir," in which the only illumination is the occasional beam of blinding light, not truth at all but a theatrical trick, the "limelight" to which Harry Lime refers and for which, perhaps, he is named. If the first "mirror"—the cover of "The Oklahoma Kid"—ironically presents for our misrecognition, through the surrogate of Holly, a self with unity and unproblematized masculinity, then the cityscape shows up brokenness, with the only possibility for coherence a frankly performative one.

The entire city of Vienna, as envisioned in this film, is a stage. We are provided at every turn with performers and audiences, as the city becomes a theater. The inherent theatricality of baroque architecture is exploited by the director as it provides the setting for a denaturalized, performative identity. The "mystery" that is the focus of the film, which Holly as the Western sheriff proposes to solve so that order can be restored, is gradually revealed to us as a staged performance. The putative death of Harry Lime, first understood as an accident and then as a murder, turns out to have been a play, complete with valedictory dialogue from the dying man. The apparent destruction of the individual subject—sudden death in a traffic accident—is artificial performance, no more a "natural reality" than its constitution. Visual echoes of the stage set abound in *The Third Man*. Windows repeatedly become theater boxes, as legions of observers contemplate the scenes taking place in the streets below. Lighting—an intense, dramatic chiaroscuro—is used throughout to heighten the sense of theater. The dark shadows of the nighttime city are broken by unexpected explosions of light, as in the illumination from a suddenly opened window that reveals the face of the supposedly dead and buried Harry Lime, who smiles in wry and seductive amusement, as if commenting on this melodramatic device. In another key moment of "theater," soldiers and policemen are arranged in darkness around and above an empty square, waiting breathlessly for Harry's appearance on this stage; they are both actors in the drama and an audience transfixed by the moment of suspense, so familiar to us as film spectators. An ominous shadow appears as the apprehension increases. The tension is finally broken by the appearance of an elderly balloon seller, a figure out of carnival and comedy, who will not be got rid of until he has made a sale, and who, as the zither plays a cheerful waltz, leaves a delicate little white balloon in the massive hand of a tough British sergeant. This is a typically sly and self-reflexive acknowledgement of the film's own artifice. The genres have been mixed up, and the wrong character has been cued; someone from an entirely different movie has walked into the scene.[20]

In *The Third Man*, the interplay of spectatorship and spectacle, of exhibition and surveillance, contributes to the denaturalization of subjectivity, pointing up the charade, the elements of masculine "drag" that are always present in film. These elements are sometimes literalized, as in the figure of the Oklahoma Kid, or suggested, as in the contrast between the rugged fatigues of Sgt. Payne (himself a huge fan of Holly's pulp Westerns, caught up in the same specular model) and the little balloon tethered to his massive hand. It is significant that *The Third Man* focuses its denaturalizing "limelight" on masculine identity, specifically. The only female character of any importance in the film—Anna, Harry's former lover whom Holly desires—has a very underwritten role and seems to exist primarily as a triangulating device, a conduit, and a "cover" for the intense homoerotic desire that characterizes the relationship between Harry and Holly. It is the ideological imperative of masculinity—in both pre- and postwar Vienna and in American popular culture—that is under scrutiny here.[21]

After Lime's all too overdetermined "resurrection" from the dead, the only sustained meeting between the two men takes place on a Ferris wheel.[22] Identity is split and multiplied as "the lone rider of the holy faith" confronts his double, the charming and cynical sociopath. The intense, eroticized link between the two men is brought into focus, its triangulation and displacement demonstrated as Harry idly writes the name Anna within a heart on the fogged window. Holly obstinately, even desperately, clings to his version of naturalized heterosexual masculinity, his misrecognition of himself in the "cover" of his novel. However, the specular idyll that he initially, perhaps, envisioned in Vienna with Harry is now shattered. Harry abandons Holly too, by exploding his fantasy and, most importantly, by forcing him to confront the failure inherent in the specular structure, the emptiness out of which an illusion of stable, unitary subjectivity is provisionally constructed. In response to Holly's suggestion that he turn himself in to buy Anna's freedom, Harry sardonically replies: "It's a far, far, better thing that I do than I have ever done, the limelight, the fall of the curtain, oh no." In evoking Charles Dickens' *A Tale of Two Cities*, in which one man nobly sacrifices his life by substituting himself for an identical other, his "mirror image," Harry both makes explicit and mocks the specular process that Holly seeks to enact. Instead of offering Holly a reflection that renaturalizes, however illusorily, his own cherished identity, Harry calls the whole process into question, offering a view of subjectivity as wholly performative, a theatrical act with a hackneyed script. He exposes the dubious machinery of subject constitution and casts, with a raised eyebrow and an ironic smile, an unforgiving "limelight" on its functioning. There is no "natural" self, no unproblematized masculinity, only a series of quotations and imitations.

The Ferris wheel is directly juxtaposed to rubble at the beginning of the sequence, in a confusing moment in which cinematic continuity appears to falter. The wheel itself is perhaps, a complex visual joke; Reed's camera underscores the wheel's abstract beauty, lingering on the elegant pattern of crisscrossing girders. Its circularity—indeed, its ocularity—suggests with sly irony both the closed loop of specular subjectivity within which Holly moves and the void at its center: at one point, the empty wheel frames Holly as he waits. The rubble and the amusement park are in some sense "equivalent," as they comment on the meeting that is about to occur. The Ferris wheel, despite its severe beauty, represents the excessive world of the carnival, the same milieu from which the balloon seller comes. The balloon seller is a disruptive figure, who instigates a moment of distanciation by suddenly confusing genres, making visible the system of conventions that govern both representation and the "misrecognitions" that it invites, while simultaneously denaturalizing masculinity by presenting us with contradictory signifiers—the delicate balloon and the hard-boiled soldier. Carnival is a universe in which performance and spectatorship are paramount, in which convention is stood on its head, and reversals are frequent. The Prater wheel, therefore, is the perfect setting for Harry's own act of distanciation, his exposure of the performative, his explanation of identity as a phantom of the "limelight." As the wheel circles, the illumination and background of the scene are constantly shifting, as shadows and beams of light flicker across the faces of the two men. Our view of the world changes dizzyingly—we alternately see it far below and defamiliarized, the human figures described by Harry as "dots," or close and familiar. Light and shadow are the "currency" of film—here, the basic building blocks of cinematic representation are forced into our awareness as they are fragmented, a sort of rubble of signification.

This failed specular romance, the offering and shattering of possible mirrors, brings us, the film's spectators, face to face with our own ache and longing, our own drama of desire. The constitutive wound, the painful rupture of plenitude and fullness that is at the basis of subjectivity, draws us back again and again, as we seek out spectacle and long for analgesia, the "cure" for what ails us. Reed and Greene invite us, along with Holly, to confront—in a typical blend of tragedy and dark comedy—the impossibility of this "cure." Harry, in interrupting the erotic exchange of admiring glances, the mutually jubilant "misrecognition" that Holly has come to Vienna hoping for, has "stolen" from him—and, by extension, from all of us—the only "medicine" that might help. Penicillin, the new wonder drug, is another symbolic focus for this tantalizing and ultimately shattered hope. Harry's great crime—the reason he is a fugitive and has had to disappear by staging his death—has been to steal this scarce and vital substance, adulterating it with water. When Calloway, the British major, decides to destroy Holly's illusions about Harry for good, he stages a casual "errand" in which he accompanies Holly to a children's hospital ward. As Holly walks around the ward, looking at the maimed and helpless children who would have been cured if Harry had not adulterated the penicillin supply, the camera does not show us the victims themselves. Instead of seeing the children, we look at displaced representations of them: as Holly looks down into a crib, we see attached to its railings a teddy bear, also "looking" down at the child in the bed. The simultaneous poignancy and ridiculousness of the teddy bears scattered about the ward is characteristic of the way Reed sets up the scene as a whole: the silent sisters who nurse the children in a moving display of tender devotion wear headdresses that are visually preposterous, making them look improbably like ships in full sail.

The indirect, displaced representation of suffering paradoxically throws into relief—again, perhaps, into the "limelight"—the pain that we, as much as Holly, bring to this moment. It is as if we, the spectators, cannot be expected to directly confront the agony caused by the failure of a "cure." The suffering of the children is our own suffering, as well as the suffering of Holly: we are all, symbolically, Harry's victims. After Calloway has staged his little drama for Holly's benefit, and has convinced him finally to give up on his "romance" with Harry, he talks about Holly's book: "I didn't know there were snake charmers in Texas." With this line, Calloway is acknowledging his role as manipulator; Holly is an easy mark. Calloway is also talking about the hypnotic nature of both spectatorship and specularity. When Holly turns away from Harry, he is averting his gaze from that particular mirror, but not from the principle of specularity itself. He is still, like us, "charmed:" he will never leave "Texas," the symbolic territory of mirrors. "Texas," as the primary locus of the American Western myth constructed by Hollywood and pulp fiction, functions here as verbal shorthand for the whole system of subject constitution that has broken down so irretrievably in the Vienna of *The Third Man*. "Texas" is not only the land of the cowboy, but also the land of the "Oklahoma Kid" in his hypermasculine drag; its "cover" extends over the territory of fascist masculinity also.

For us, too, the "charm" of spectacle will never fade; the scopophilic desire that brings us to seek our pleasure in the movie theater, to rapturously "misrecognize" ourselves in the mirrors on screen, still compels us. If we approach cinema in search of healing, however, it is only the impossibility of a "cure" that ultimately confronts us. We are hypnotized and enchanted, fully engaged by the "snake charmer" of cinema. However, while inviting our pleasure, this film also forces us to contemplate the apparatus that produces it. As *The Third Man* places us in the postwar rubble, it interrogates the ideological ramifications of our fascination with spectacle. Using the vocabulary of film noir, with its many stylistic allusions to German expressionism, the film ties together the "mirrors" of postwar American popular culture and German fascism and situates itself within the debate about what sorts of subjectivities and representations can exist in the postfascist universe. In the context of its unique historical moment, it asks us to consider the instability and provisionality of the selfhoods available to us. All of us, as spectators, as "broken" subjects, can only hope to navigate the ruins of subjectivity. In *A Foreign Affair* and *The Third Man*—films made almost simultaneously in the ruined capitals of Nazism—the fascist city so memorably and chillingly envisioned by Speer and the hypermasculine Nazi subject immortalized by Riefenstahl return as trace and echo. The ghosts of masculinities past again walk the city streets and, improbably but perhaps inevitably, step straight through the looking glass and become one with the reflection in our more familiar mirrors. The cowboy, the American soldier, and the slightly tarnished film-noir hero merge with their Nazi counterparts.

Chapter 3
The Web of Spectacle

Bernardo Bertolucci's *La strategia del ragno* (1970) is indeed a stratagem, ensnaring us within a busy web of ambiguous seductions. The film takes us to a small, historic Renaissance city in northern Italy, stunning our senses with its beauty; this intense aesthetic pleasure is, characteristically, a snare that Bertolucci gradually tightens until we, the spectators, are struggling uncomfortably in a trap woven from what we can only recognize as the silken strands of our own scopophilic satisfaction. The beautiful town of Tara is the setting for an encounter between the "past"—the fascist Italy of 1936—and the "present"—Italy in 1968—in which familiar epistemological categories lie in ruins. "Tara" as a name is highly overdetermined, itself a complex web, meshing multiple strands of cultural, political, historical, and artistic references. Its perfectly preserved historic cityscape, in which physical destruction is glimpsed only briefly, presents, like the overtly visible ruins of Rossellini's *Paisà*, an insistent question: how does postwar Italy rebuild, relive, renarrate, and recinematize the Italy of Mussolini? Rather than the rubble we see in Rossellini's film and in Helma Sanders-Brahms' *Deutschland bleiche Mutter*, or the traces of a vaporized city in Resnais' *Hiroshima mon amour*, Bertolucci gives us a historiography of perfect preservation, a surreal suspension of destruction, an unchanging physical environment in which the monumentalization of a certain vision of "the past" masks a crisis of epistemology and subjectivity just as acute as the one realized in the other directors' ruined streets. In the town's unchanging streetscape, which has looked much the same for 400 years, we meet people who appear physically not to have aged since the 1930s. Time in Tara is out of joint: it passes unpredictably, inconsistently or, in many instances, not at all. Influences from the world of 1968 dissipate and disappear—a sleek modern train may bring the film's protagonist to Tara's fascist-era train station, but before he can leave by the same means, the tracks are submerged in vegetation, and change and movement are converted into stasis. Life in the Tara of 1968 is predicated on a monolithic, literally monumental mode of interaction with its fascist history, a mode that subsumes and nullifies any challenges or differentiation. The film's protagonist, Athos Magnani, arriving in the town for the first time, discovers that he is, in fact, already subsumed into its static, marmoreal historiography, a crucial element within this signifying system. There is nothing new under the sun of Tara, and Athos' features turn out to be identical to those of its most famous citizen, the father he never knew, also named Athos Magnani, who is preserved in a sculpture in the main piazza. Young Athos is greeted with the words "uguale, uguale" ("the same, the same")—his living flesh is the same as the stone image of the antifascist hero, and he, in his very existence, incarnates Tara's mythology of itself.

The doubled body of Athos, father and son identical across time and facing each other in flesh and monumental marble, brings us to the core of Bertolucci's polemic in *La strategia del ragno*. The town of Tara in 1968 clings stubbornly to, and has even organized itself around, the myth of Athos père, its resistance hero: the son is a perfect mirror of his fossilized father, reflecting only sameness. We see an exchange of glances between the past and the present in which the two are rendered identical and interchangeable. Difference of all kinds, including sexual, temporal, and semiotic differences, is rigorously banished. When a character in the film—a child asked to procure American cigarettes—proudly answers, "niente esteri" ("esteri" refers to foreign cigarettes, but this sentence is also roughly translatable as "nothing from the outside"), the ostensibly casual statement resonates, a manifesto for Tara's determination to protect its monolithic construction of its fascist past. Tara, as becomes increasingly clear, is a specular paradise. It is a circular exchange of glances, a closed economy of signification, which no outside element can disrupt. Anything from the world beyond is either blocked—literally stopped in its tracks, like the train—or seamlessly incorporated, again literally, as the corporeal body of Athos fils is legible only to the extent that it is "uguale, uguale," incarnating a familiar signifier.

Bertolucci's polemic in *La strategia del ragno* is an accusation of equivalence—like young and old Athos, the fascist era and postwar constructions of the fascist body politic have grown from the same flesh in each other's image: "uguale, uguale." *La strategia del ragno* can be read as an intervention in the long and still ongoing debate within postwar Italian culture about the place of fascism in Italian history and national identity.[1] If fascism itself, like Nazism, was, as many theorists have maintained, predicated on a specular system that attempted to eliminate difference, it is possible to see postwar attempts to come to terms with it as adopting many of the same strategies. Soon after the war's end, the philosopher Benedetto Croce, a towering figure in Italian intellectual life throughout the first half of the twentieth century—so influential, in fact, as to have been nicknamed "the lay pope"—famously "explained" fascism as a brief aberration in the true trajectory of Italian history, a history that he understood as an unbroken arc reaching from the Risorgimento to the Resistance, a striving toward "liberty."[2] The political convenience of this formulation is obvious: the connections between fascism and the liberal nationalist regimes and philosophy from which it, arguably, originated are completely obscured; divorced from its connections to the past, fascism also casts no shadow on the future. Croce described the twenty-plus years of fascist rule as a "parenthesis," or even as the result of an alien "virus," infecting the otherwise healthy body politic. According to the Crocean model, therefore, fascism itself embodies the disruptive alterity, the threat of which has been eliminated with the restoration of "health," with, to extend this rather suspect metaphor, the resistance as the therapeutic agent that has eliminated the pathology. The year 1968, shortly before the release of *La strategia del ragno*, was, of course, a pivotal year in Italian intellectual and political life; the second generation after fascism, the "sons" of the resistance, began to stage an Oedipal rebellion against their mythologized fathers, and from this point the Crocean orthodoxy with regard to fascism was challenged.[3] Historians including, most famously, Renzo de Felice, alter the terms of the discussion by rethinking the history of the fascist *ventennio*. Bertolucci, with this film, enters polemically into the debate.

In *La strategia del ragno*, the fascist and postfascist body politic, and the fascist and postfascist body in the literal sense, are represented as seamlessly one, in an apparent answer to the Crocean metaphor. The film appropriates Croce's corporeal metaphor, but subverts it; Bertolucci is deeply concerned with how bodies signify, deploying the body in a fashion that destabilizes Croce's hegemonic formulation. If, for Croce and many liberal postwar intellectuals, there is a clear distinction between "health"—the ostensibly salubrious state of Italy before and after the fascist "ventennio"—and the pathologized but temporally limited eruption of fascism, in Bertolucci's film, the reverse is true. Tara, the fascist and postfascist town, in which the action of the film takes place, is, in both periods—to the extent that they can be separated at all, always a problematic issue in this film—a world from which all forms of alterity are categorically banished. Indeed, categories themselves are banished. This specular universe has progressed even beyond the point of needing to insist stridently on the absolute "otherness" of a marked term—as, for example, Nazism did with the Jews—to a state in which the fantasy of the exclusion of alterity seems to have stabilized, and no longer must be insisted upon, at least not consciously. This enduring specular structure, based on a fear of the narcissistic wound any acknowledgment of difference creates, allows for no change and is identical in 1936 and 1968. The danger of the eruption of an "other" that might endanger the specular oneness and plenitude ostensibly offered by both the fascist and postwar iterations of Tara appears to have been eliminated. This potential loss has ostensibly been averted by a strategy—one of the strategies, perhaps, of the film's title—of removing the very concept of categorization, with its implied possibility of more than one category, of difference.

One of the ways in which the possibility of difference as a disruptive element is eliminated is by the cancellation of sexual difference. The world of Tara can be read as founded on a psychic, political, and historical analgesia. It embraces, however illusorily, the specular plenitude of the Lacanian Imaginary; the very concept of sexual difference, a reminder of our trauma as we were torn from Imaginary fullness and unity, is a threat to this analgesic economy. Bertolucci approaches his excision of difference almost playfully. By using the name Athos he is posing the absurd possibility of a realm in which the feminine does not exist. The name "Athos" is a crucial part of the web of references and echoes in which *La strategia del ragno* ensnares the spectator: this name, and that of the town of Tara itself, are strands in Bertolucci's symbolic and semiotic skein, woven using signifiers that are often highly overdetermined and that compress multiple semiotic operations into single term. One of the many things that the word, "Athos" invokes is the absence of sexual difference: it is the name of a mountaintop monastery in Greece in which no female of any species, whether woman, cow, or hen, was allowed to set foot. It is a medieval example of misogyny gone mad. In *La strategia del ragno*, the name is symbolic of the fear of those for whom any admission of difference would threaten the specular structure, the closed semiotic system, on which their universe is based.

The improbable absence of women in the Tara of 1968 is marked. It is significant that Draifa, the mistress of Athos the father and the film's only important female character, does not live in Tara. Draifa—who bears another highly overdetermined name—lives outside the town: visiting her involves a long walk or a bicycle ride.[4] In an early sequence, as Athos fils walks into Tara for the first time, women are present: we hear their voices conversing and exclaiming, and we see a middle-aged woman seated in a kitchen chair in front of her doorway, in a fashion typical of small Italian towns. It is as if sexual difference only exists before the web that is Tara has fully ensnared Athos fils. As he continues his walk into the town, the visual and acoustic presence in the streets of Tara of the literal feminine—actual women and girls—fades, and the soundtrack supplies an alternative. We hear the quavering voice of an old man singing "quand'ero piccina, piccina..." ("when I was very small [feminine ending]").[5] This nonsensical statement—an old man claming the identity of a young girl—introduces the crisis of classification that Tara embodies. The literal feminine does not exist here because of the threat that difference poses to Tara's specular world; instead, its elderly male inhabitants return in song to the narcissistic wound that difference inevitably creates, insisting, as an analgesic strategy, on eliding and denying it.

Repression of difference is evidenced in absurd statements concerning identity in both its meanings—sameness and a differential mode of subject constitution. As Athos walks toward his first encounter with his father's image, in which he becomes a perfect mirror reflecting back only sameness and disallowing possible difference, we see that postwar Tara is indeed predicated on a specular structure strikingly similar to that of the fascist era. Athos' uncanny mirroring literalizes the narcissistic structure already foundational both to Tara and to fascism; alterity of all kinds is banished and sameness rules. Sexual difference is, perhaps, the most crucial area in which this strategy operates; gender and sexual difference as organizing principles have vanished in the epistemological abyss that is Tara. Gender, when it is an issue at all, is frequently undecidable—as shown in a long and unresolved discussion about the sex of a rabbit, which ultimately remains undetermined. In Tara, sexual difference ("é maschio!" "Ma, é femmina!") cannot be signified any better for rabbits than for people—here Bertolucci gives us some comic cross-species slippage reminiscent of the monks of Mt. Athos. These arguments about determining sex consist of meaningless assertions that are instantly contradicted with no resolution possible. It is as if the very question is an impossible one. All questions of difference bleed into each other and all are elided in the same way. Another discussion of difference, equally confounding, occurs when Draifa's servant, whom Athos had taken to be a boy, sits painting his nails at the kitchen table, Athos rather plaintively asks: "ma che razza di bambino sei?" ("But what type of boy are you?") The child responds with the classic unmasking gesture of the transvestite performer, in reverse—he/she removes a hat to reveal long hair. In discovering that a person with whom he has interacted as a member of one gender is a member of the other, Athos demonstrates a confusion that is emblematic of the quandary that is so essential to the web of *La strategia del ragno*. Tara is in a permanent state of epistemological collapse: it is an enclave in which difference exists only as potential contamination, the pathologized element that might come from the outside to rupture the ceaseless and seamless circulation of the specular gaze. The statement, "niente esteri" perfectly expresses the unchanged nature of Tara from 1938 to 1968, echoing both the fascist insistence on the plenitude of purity and the Crocean formulation of fascism itself as the rupturing, contaminating element.

Tara is a paradise of the imaginary, rigidly excluding any acknowledgment of the painful wounds that are part of all subject constitution. The outsider to the town, Athos fils, recognizes himself in the physical representation of Athos père—a stone bust the town is about to dedicate—and realizes that his body is completely identical to his father's, completely substitutable for it: the constant commentary that greets his arrival is "uguale, uguale;" "the same, the same."[6] If we, too, as spectators are to achieve "sameness," to anesthetize the wound to a narcissistic structure that the presence of alterity constantly irritates, we too must "misrecognize" ourselves on screen, entering into the kind of specular exchange of glances that characterizes both the fascist and the postfascist, or even the Crocean, universe. Bertolucci's project in this film, therefore, is intensely critical here of both fascism and postfascist society, and, by extension, perhaps the project of film in general in its invitation to the spectator. By foregrounding spectatorship as it does, *La strategia del ragno* appears to be attempting a paradoxical, even contradictory, effect. The film invites us in, providing the avenue of substitution and offering us narcissistic bliss, at the same time unmasking this very process, forcing a critical revaluation as it demands that we notice and interrogate our own scopophilic desire.

Spectacle and the pleasure it provides are closely associated with fascist film and as such were sometimes viewed by postwar artists, in a Brechtian or even a Crocean context, as tainted; neorealism was, in the immediate postwar period, articulated partly as a reaction against the aesthetic of spectacle.[7] Rather than banishing spectacle from his films, Bertolucci chooses to foreground it as a deliberate choice, to explore its pleasures, and to interrogate its complex psychic and political meanings. If the structure of substitution invites us to seek a series of mirrors, as do Bertolucci's characters, it also invites us "in" in other ways. Our presence as spectators is always invoked, coded into this film as a necessary element as we see events unfold as spectacle, in a denaturalized context, following the conventions of opera, theater, adventure films, rather than anything we might be tempted to confuse with "real life," always a suspect category at best. Bertolucci brings us again and again to the contemplation of spectacle. We are offered the role of coproducers, interchangeable with the actors on screen, orchestrating a sort of theatrical, operatic, or, by extension, filmic identity, a subjectivity of spectacle, that attempts a reentry into the narcissistic, specular paradise of the Imaginary, even as it, ultimately, insists upon the futility of that attempt. Athos père, like Fassbinder's faded fascist movie star, Veronika Voss, appears to be engaged in a constant dialogue with his own image, constituting himself as a creature of stage and aria, and of the silver screen, in a stylized performance of masculinity, always in costume as he poses and dances in his dashing and much commented on "giacca a l'Inglese," the safari-style jacket of a 1930s adventure hero, and perhaps, of the white (ironically Anglicized) hunter of fascist colonial fantasy.

Bertolucci presents Athos as having an identity so mobile, inhabiting so many incompatible contexts simultaneously (including, of course, the logical impossibility of two people, father and son, occupying the same body at different temporal moments) that he is always to be found on both sides of the mirror, substitutable between positions, simultaneously subject and object, self and other, origin and reflection. The body of Athos, in its infinite mobility as a signifier, points toward the fluidity that characterizes all epistemic systems in *La strategia del ragno*. Bertolucci cycles through an ever-changing series of narrative and discursive frameworks, never allowing the film to come to rest within any one particular context. We see the figure of Athos—already, as a single body and name split between two different subjects, representing a profound challenge to any notion of subjectivity as unitary or whole—as a signifier situated within several different and seemingly incompatible systems. Athos, ever malleable despite an attempt by the citizens of Tara to fix his image in marble, is constant only in his shape-shifting quality as he slips and slides through a veritable avalanche of contexts.

Bertolucci's sources are literary, cinematic, musical, and architectural. Perhaps the most suggestive element in the cascade of discursive allusions within which we are submerged throughout *La strategia del ragno* is Bertolucci's repeated reference to the "Dreyfus affair," the political scandal that preoccupied fin de siècle Europe. The postfascist Tara of 1968, already blurring in unsettling ways with the fascist world of 1936, must also, therefore, be understood within the context of 1898, the year Emile Zola published his famous letter about the Dreyfus case, which began with the words "J'accuse!" *La strategia del ragno* can be read as polemic in the same vein as Zola's intervention. The film, on one level, is Bertolucci's own bitter and polemical "j'accuse" directed at the hypocrisy and lies of postfascist Italy: it is an accusation pointing directly at the comfortable but dubious mythology of antifascism on which postwar society was built. The historical figure of Dreyfus perfectly embodies the contradiction and moral ambiguity at the center of *La strategia del ragno*. Dreyfus was, like Athos père, perceived as a hero and a traitor, both sanctified and vilified. The Dreyfus affair forced France, and Europe more generally, to confront the corruption and prejudice upon which its glorified ideals of militarism and masculinity were based. In Italy in 1968, a similar reevaluation is beginning, and Bertolucci is placing himself at the center of that dialogue.[8] *La strategia del ragno* mounts a complex attack on contemporary Italian approaches toward the past. In the 1960s, the historiographic battle lines were drawn between those who, like Renzo de Felice, were considered by their opponents to be "apologists" for fascism, arguing that it—initially at least—enjoyed a broad popular consensus and that Mussolini was a genuine, if flawed, political visionary, and those for whom the only tenable position was consistently to refute all claims that Mussolini's regime ever had any legitimacy of any kind, and to exalt the antifascist struggle. Bertolucci positions himself in opposition to both points of view.

La strategia del ragno, like *Il conformista* and *Novecento*, Bertolucci's other films set during the *ventennio*, is, without question, antifascist. Bertolucci strongly condemns the fascist regime and those who were complicit with it. However, in *La strategia del ragno*, he treats antifascism and the resistance with considerably more skepticism than in the other films, directly questioning cherished mythology. The town of Tara, in its isolated, improbably preserved perfection, represents in microcosm the oversimplifications and willful blindness with which postwar Italian society had attempted to address the ambiguous residues of fascism. As Athos fils learns in his first hours in Tara, time has "stopped" there; so too has any process of confronting the more complicated legacies of the fascist regime. The town of Tara, by making Athos senior a hero of the antifascist resistance, naming streets, squares, and social halls after him and placing his statue in the piazza, has literally concretized a mythology of its own history. It has done away with the messy realities of complicity and collaboration in favor of sanitized myth. Athos' statue meets our eye with a blind, marmoreal stare directed straight into the camera and straight into the eye of the living Athos, who, as we are repeatedly told, is both physically identical and, in the rigid historiography of Tara, required to be symbolically equivalent to his fossilized father.[9] The phrase repeatedly used to describe Athos fils, "uguale, uguale," refers as much to young Athos' position in the circulation of images, history, and memory in Tara as to his physiognomy. The statue and the living flesh come face to face on screen, as Bertolucci imprints on celluloid his own contribution to the fraught postwar historiography of fascism. In focusing so skeptically on the concretized representation of the myth of Tara's antifascism, Bertolucci also casts a rather cynical eye on his own project of representing "history:" the traces of the past on celluloid are necessarily subject to skeptical self-scrutiny.

The choreography of young Athos' arrival in Tara and his first "meeting" with his marmoreal father points clearly toward the debate about historiography and masculinity that is so central to *La strategia del ragno*. As Athos fils descends from the gleaming modern train that has brought him to the "home" he has never seen, he is accompanied by a man in the white uniform of the modern Italian Navy. The sailor moves with an exaggerated military bearing; marching in a straight line along an empty boulevard and executing a pointlessly precise ninety-degree turn, he sits on a bench and exclaims "Tara!" We follow his gesture and see what young Athos sees: the picturesque Renaissance town in the middle distance, perfectly framed beyond a field of lush corn. The theatricality of the sailor's utterance, "introducing" his companion to history-as-spectacle, which opens a series of confrontations with a fossilized, static, ostensibly unambiguous past, is presented by Bertolucci in a way that foregrounds its rhetorical elements. The sailor's immaculate military perfection, along with his bizarrely rigid body posture, points to a style of performative masculinity that is especially relevant to the film's consideration of fascism. However, it is worth noting that the sailor is not in fact a fascist figure; rather, he is the only other person who arrives from the universe outside Tara, the world in which time moves forward at a normal pace. He represents the postfascist state of the 1960s: evidently, Bertolucci seems to argue, the exaggerated, robotic militarism is still a viable stylization of masculine identity. The sailor, therefore, introduces the continuities between fascist and postfascist male subjectivities posited with such devastating insistence in the film. He is young Athos' first interlocutor, and his first "double," in a film in which male characters seem able to substitute endlessly for each other. (The sailor is about the same age as Athos fils—in fact, he is the only other young man we see in Tara. He arrives with Athos and is running for the train as Athos ties to escape later in the film: it seems that the sailor, unlike either Athos, can actually leave.) The rigid, white-clad sailor, presumably a native of Tara who is home on leave, is a harbinger of the rigid, fossilized "hero," the stone father whom Athos fils will presently encounter.

The sailor's theatricality, the air of an impresario with which he utters the word "Tara," begins a series of allusions, a complex matrix of cultural references within which Bertolucci embeds his analysis. "Tara," obviously, is a reference to Victor Fleming's 1939 Hollywood film, *Gone with the Wind*.[10] It is the name of Scarlett O'Hara's family mansion, itself named for the home of the mythical kings of Ireland, and represents the lost way of life of the antebellum American south; nostalgia for Tara, and for the ugly economy based on racism and slavery, drives the story of that film, and perhaps is partially responsible for its enduring popularity.[11] The racist subtext of *Gone with the Wind* is certainly relevant to a consideration of Italian fascism in 1936, when the country was reclaiming its "rightful" empire through a series of colonial wars.[12] The Duce's culture industry learned from Hollywood and used myth and carefully calculated historiography to legitimize its claim to Italy's "fourth shore" in Africa.[13] Bertolucci's reference to *Gone with the Wind*, that classic of revisionist historiography, arguably implicates also the Italian film industry, which in the 1930s superseded Hollywood sales in Italy, previously a very reliable market for the American studios.[14] Historical revisionism was a specialty of the Italian culture industry under fascism. Films such as Gallone's *Scipione l'Africano*, probably the most well known of the monumental historical dramas produced during the fascist period, presented a mythic version of the Roman Empire designed to justify Mussolini's colonial aspirations. (*Scipione l'Africano* was released in 1937, two years before *Gone with the Wind*, and one year after Bertolucci set the fictional death of Athos père; Italian armies completed their conquest of Ethiopia in the summer of 1936.) Manipulated nostalgia and revisionist historiography during the fascist *ventennio* were not limited to cinema—the urban landscape was reconfigured as set design when the fascist regime rebuilt the center of Rome to create military parade routes with ancient monuments strategically in the background.[15] The cityscapes of Italy, therefore, must also be read as "textual" constructs. In making the physical environment of Tara—gorgeously shot by Vittorio Storaro—so vitally important in *La strategia del ragno*, Bertolucci is continuing and commenting on the fascist manipulation of historic cityscapes as symbolic currency.

Bertolucci's first carefully framed shot of Tara in the middle distance, shown to us at the same time as Athos fils sees it following the sailor's orchestration of his (and our) gaze, demands, therefore, to be read in several contexts. In showing us the perfectly preserved Renaissance town of Sabbioneta, where the film was shot, Bertolucci invites consideration of history as managed spectacle.[16] Athos Jr. is not merely looking; he—and, Bertolucci states, we—gaze in ways that are insistently problematized and denaturalized. Our presence as spectators is coded in from the first moments of the film. With the sailor's flourish, the first of a series of self-reflexive gestures, a persistent mise en abîme effect, essential to *La strategia del ragno*, is initiated. The impresario-like gesture with which this scene is presented to us, and the linking of the protagonist's gaze to our own, connects the "history" that we are about to see—the film's depiction of events during the fascist *ventennio*—with a chain of different iterations of "history-as-spectacle," from the urban-planning-as-theater of the ducal Gonzaga family (who built Sabionetta and its famous Renaissance theater) to Hollywood to Mussolini, and places *La strategia del ragno* itself squarely within this dubious lineage. The scene the sailor "introduces" is also ravishingly beautiful, a jewel-like Renaissance city-in-miniature, its campanile and rooftops richly colored against the dark green corn: aesthetic pleasure, our desire and gratification as spectators, is invoked and subjected to skeptical consideration in this opening sequence. In *La strategia del ragno*, the act of looking is always, itself, looked at.

As Athos *fils* leaves the sailor behind and continues his walk into the town of Tara, approaching the various memorializations in stone of Athos *père* with which the town appears generously furnished, *La strategia del ragno* maintains its disorienting focus on looking, spectatorship, and spectacle. Knowledge and vision are insistently problematized as we, like the protagonist we are watching, are introduced to the landscape of the film.[17] Athos walks up the middle of an almost empty street; there is a break in continuity as the camera cuts to Athos' a new position, and comes briefly to rest on his back as he stands still, seemingly transfixed, staring at a wall of rusticated stone blocks; the camera dollies forward, in a disorienting movement, until the back of Athos' head takes up most of the screen. However, we have still not been shown what it is that has so insistently caught his attention; indeed, it seems there is nothing there besides the surface of the wall. Bertolucci's camera cuts suddenly to what momentarily seems to be nonsensical dark block lettering against a white background, and pans rapidly across it from right to left, in a movement opposite to that which our eye "wants" to make, which would be to read the inscription from left to right; we must therefore read the words retrospectively, conferring intelligibility on them in a counterintuitive fashion.[18] The inscription reads: *Via Athos Magnani*. Both young Athos and we, the spectators, are introduced to the central problem of the film: the question of how to "write" and understand the relation of the present, the Italy of 1968, to the fascist past is presented in a way that underlines Bertolucci's distrust of easy intelligibility. The sign at which young Athos is so enigmatically staring contains his own name—someone who has arrived in Tara as, apparently, a more-or-less-viable postfascist subject—as well as being an element in the hagiography of a putative antifascist hero; we encounter both in a disorienting blur, only seeing the whole sign after the camera cuts away to a long shot of Athos crossing the empty piazza.

As Athos walks further into Tara, this central quandary is restated in a comic interlude, typical of the sudden shifts of tone and register that characterize Bertolucci's treatment of fascism and historiography in *La strategia del ragno*. In what is, perhaps, a tongue-in-cheek reference to Italian neorealist cinema, Bertolucci shows us two old men, with the seamed, lined faces of people who have worked hard all their lives, sitting in one of the shadowy colonnades that line the streets of Tara. This sequence is shot in a style reminiscent of the classic neorealist idiom, with an unmoving camera framing all of the characters in the same shot, allowing them to move through the space within the frame; as in many neorealist films, there is an effect of depth of field, of space on several planes, with Athos in the foreground, the two men in the middle space, and a window opening to the outdoors between and behind them. Athos stops to ask for directions to a hotel: the encounter starts reasonably enough, with one of the old men telling him to "turn right, and then left." Chaos erupts, however, when the other man intervenes angrily, and the two begin shouting contradictory directions, until the conversation collapses into a cacophony of cries of "left" and "right." Athos walks away as the shouting continues, commenting dryly: "When you've agreed, I'll stop by again."

If neorealism was, among other things, a declaration of the new directions taken by Italian culture after the fall of fascism, the sly introduction here of a familiar neorealist trope is suggestive. The old men of *La strategia del ragno* seem like a cliché, with their weathered "peasant" faces and their regional dialect; indeed, they are almost parodic figures.[19] Their appearance at the beginning of the film represents a critique—however affectionate—of the attempts by Italian filmmakers of the immediate postwar period to create an antifascist cinematic idiom. Neorealism defined itself, in part, in opposition to the familiar genres for which the cinema of the fascist era was best known: grand military dramas, often historical, and escapist high-society romantic comedies. This extremely influential cinematic movement represented, both to Italy itself and to the world at large, the country's success in leaving fascist culture behind and creating an innovative, politically informed, more "authentic" view of Italy than that afforded by the Duce's visions.[20] However, Bertolucci is complicating this issue considerably by placing *La strategia del ragno* in dialogue with neorealism. The nonsensical debate of the old men, their shouts of "left" and "right," can be read as a ridiculous political allegory, matching, perhaps, the "ridiculousness" of Italian politics and government in the years since the war. Bertolucci is, unquestionably, committed to a politically engaged cinema; however, *La strategia del ragno* strenuously refuses familiar forms of political rhetoric.[21] Neorealism, in its self-conscious assumption of the mantle of a postwar, antifascist national cinema, made certain aesthetic statements that were also, necessarily, a political rhetoric. In giving us this scene of old men who might have stepped out of a neorealist film, Bertolucci affectionately lampoons the "old men" of the previous generation, the great neorealist directors of the immediate postwar period.[22] The simplistic political imperatives, the Manichean political divisions of "left" and "right" that were so essential to the struggle against fascism are also, perhaps, seen here as a lingering echo of the Manichean world view of fascism itself. In this film—in contrast, perhaps, to *Il conformista* or, especially, *Novecento*—facile claims of "left" or "right" are profoundly ironized.

If the neorealist filmmakers, the "old men" of the antifascist generation, claimed a clear political position, Bertolucci, in *La strategia del ragno,* has assumed a much more ambiguous stance toward the politics and aesthetics of cinema. Young Athos' dialogue with the two old men occurs as he unsuccessfully attempts to orient himself in his environment, seeking guidance for his navigation of Tara: instead of a useful template for navigation, what he is given is a nonsensical, though passionately articulated, set of directions. Later, after Athos has found his way to Draifa's villa and is retuning in the dark to Tara, he finds the old men still arguing, their dialect now almost fully incomprehensible. Bertolucci gives us a long shot of Athos walking toward the camera down the colonnade, the linear space illuminated by occasional lamps, the movement shown in a single lengthy take. He passes silently between the men, who are shouting and shaking their fingers at each other—they separate briefly for Athos to pass between them, but pay him no attention: their absurdly impassioned argument continuing as he walks away. The tone of this scene is ruefully comic, and perhaps somewhat elegiac. Athos has indeed come back, as he promised them earlier, but has gained nothing: their oversimplified, binary argument about political direction has degenerated into an incomprehensible shouting match. If the marmoreal, monumentalized figure of Athos the father embodies the heroic myth of the Resistance, the fossilization of postwar historiography, the two old men, perhaps, symbolically incarnate the "corpus" of neorealism in *La strategia del ragno*. Neorealism is acknowledged here as a basic part of the environment, encountered early and repeatedly, given material form in the faces and voices of the indomitable, deluded old men of Tara. It is important, impossible to ignore, and perhaps even beloved. However, as a political strategy it is superannuated and even absurd; the old men shout their contradictory imperatives, their cries of "left" and "right" echoing through empty streets in a town where time has stopped.

Bertolucci repeatedly returns to the "look" of neorealism in *La strategia del ragno*, acknowledging it as an aesthetic forerunner even as he proceeds to depart decisively from it. His choice of "Magnani" as the last name of his doubled protagonist is another example of the overdetermined naming that is so important in this film. Like the words "Athos" and "Tara," "Magnani" has important cultural and historical echoes. The great actress, Anna Magnani was, after the release of Rossellini's *Roma, città aperta* in 1945, the figure most associated with Italian cinema in the postwar period, especially neorealist film. She was, in fact, so well known and beloved, so closely associated with national identity, that she was sometimes referred to as "the face of Italy."[23] The shadow of Anna Magnani, therefore, and with her Rossellini's invention of a new postfascist film style, are encoded into *La strategia del ragno* from the moment that young Athos reads his own name on the street sign. Bertolucci presents the Tara into which young Athos enters at the beginning of the film as saturated with neorealism. Many later scenes also employ a characteristic depth of focus reminiscent of neorealism, including long takes, and a relatively stationary camera. Bertolucci also tends to frame dialogue in a more or less stable two shot instead of cross-cutting; he often shows something else going on in the background and action happening in several planes, as when he shows Draifa and young Athos sitting at a table eating and talking, with a garden, in which a servant moves in and out of the shot, framed in a window behind and between them. He also, in depicting the citizens of Tara, employs nonprofessional actors playing familiar popular figures, or in some cases "themselves," a common neorealist practice.

However, Bertolucci also departs radically from a neorealist "look," stepping into a style much more characteristic of the European avant garde of the 1960s, with jump cuts and other techniques designed to disorient and defamiliarize, and frequent breaking of continuity and diegesis. This deliberate disorientation is especially marked in the flashback scenes, in which we jump from past to present and back again, from father to son. In these scenes, time is manipulated in ways that underline Bertolucci's departure from neorealist tenets. Far from the attempt to achieve an effect that experientially resembles "real time"—often discussed but only occasionally attempted in practice by neorealist filmmakers—Bertolucci consistently undercuts any sense of temporal coherence.[24] The temporal disorientation so essential to this film is intensified by the fact that most of the characters, including Draifa and old Athos' coconspirators, are depicted in both time periods by the same actors, with no evident change in age. We are given no temporal signposts to enable us to understand what we are seeing: time here fails as an epistemological category. In one striking scene, Bertolucci cuts between the two Athoses, father and son, both characters shown in headlong flight as they run away from the same men through the same woods. This sequence is edited so that the action appears continuous; however, we see that the actor Giulio Broglia, who plays both the young and the old Athos, is dressed differently as the film cuts back and forth between the two characters. The difference in clothing—we see old Athos' signature safari jacket and red scarf and his son's nondescript attire—is all that signals the temporal shift.

Bertolucci, therefore, presents time as a contested element in *La strategia del ragno*; the incoherence of temporality mirrors the deliberately incoherent juxtaposition of different film styles. Throughout the film, the handling of time signals that the director is both acknowledging and reproducing the stylistic signatures of neorealism, and moving away from them in favor of a new film praxis that, as part of its raison d'être, problematizes the relationship of cinematic representation and "reality," however defined, as an external object. As an Italian director in the 1960s dealing with fascism and the antifascist resistance, Bertolucci must necessarily engage in some sort of dialogue with neorealism: it is, inescapably, foundational. The "ghosts" of neorealism are always present in *La strategia del ragno*, returning to haunt the screen in much the same way that Athos père returns, incorporated within the son he never met ("uguale, uguale") despite all the efforts of young Athos to distinguish himself from his father. The image of the two Athoses, sutured together as they run through the woods, mirrors Bertolucci's own complicated "mirroring" of neorealism. Instead of reflecting only sameness in relation to his cinematic ancestor, as the doubling of Athos does, the director performs a complex ballet of similarity and differentiation, homage and rebellion. It is a filial process, with all the complexity and ambivalence that that implies.

In *La strategia del ragno*, operatic performance serves a mirror in which the protagonist tries desperately to "misrecognize" image for self, erasing the distinction between subject and object, canceling out exteriority and, therefore, alterity. The logic of substitution holds sway as old Athos literally substitutes his own body for that of the Duce as the ultimate victim of a murder he himself has plotted and then betrayed, which takes place at the high point of a performance of Verdi's *Rigoletto* in the town's sumptuous, perfectly preserved Renaissance opera house.[25] The story of *La strategia del ragno* obviously bears important similarities to *Rigoletto*, in another instance of the economy of substitution and exchange so characteristic of this film. Film and opera are equivalent, "uguale, uguale," substituting for each other, and we, the film viewers in the theater, are also the audience in the opera house as we watch a double staging of the operatic spectacle. Like *Rigoletto*, *La strategia del ragno* turns on a murder in which a new victim replaces the intended one, with a complex series of substitutions, mirrorings, and misrecognitions taking place.[26] Athos père, in the flashback scenes to 1936, is shown in his role as the local antifascist provocateur, orchestrating a series of dramatic spectacles that are harmless and often rather silly, as when he dances defiantly and mockingly to "Giovinezza," the fascist anthem, at a local festival. In organizing his ultimate, triumphant spectacle, the murder of Mussolini—who is scheduled to visit Tara and attend a performance of *Rigoletto* in the opera house—Athos inserts himself into Verdi's opera through a complex series of substitutions. Initially, he replaces the Duca of *Rigoletto* with the Duce, Benito Mussolini.[27] Ultimately, Athos substitutes himself for the Duce and arranges to die in his stead, making himself into a hero murdered by the fascists and recasting his political assassination as political martyrdom.

Athos père completes his operatic orchestration of events by inserting himself as a substitute martyr into other iconic preexisting narratives.

The allusions to Verdi continue as Athos arranges to be given a series of supernatural "warnings' similar to those given by the witches in Verdi's opera, *Macbeth*. Verdi, whose name (the letters standing for "Vittorio Emanuele, Re D'Italia") was the code chanted by patriotic crowds at opera performances to express their desire to unify Italy under the kings of Savoy during the Risorgimento, is referenced repeatedly by Bertolucci precisely for his status as national patriotic and cultural icon: the irony, and the challenge to Croce-style historical narrative, is unmistakable. Athos' orchestration also encompasses references to *Giulio Cesare*, presumably both the Handel opera and, as is the case with *Macbeth*, the Shakespeare play, with messages of impending death slipped to the hero by a mysterious black clad figure, "modernized" by Athos into a motorcycle messenger. This initiates the narrative that blossoms into heavily plotted complication before it is ultimately resimplified, compressed into the inscription on the statue encountered by Athos' son in "modern" Tara: *eroe vigliaccamente assasinato dal piombo fascista* ("hero murdered in a cowardly way by fascist lead"). Old Athos' construction of his own martyrdom encompasses a ridiculous excess of incident, an absurdly lavish use of cultural references and melodramatic symbolism.

Bertolucci employs this excess of allusion to clearly identify both of old Athos' plots—the initial plan to assassinate Mussolini and the later choreography of his own murder—as precisely that: plots. The histrionics of historiography are on full display, as operatic as the performance of *Rigoletto* on the stage. The stories offered as historical reality, which comprise Tara's narrative of its past in the fascist era, mirror almost exactly the stories of the opera stage. They—like the film's two protagonists who oscillate between flesh and marble, between past and present, exchanging positions constantly—are substitutable for each other, "uguale, uguale." This similarity resembles, in its turn, the complex mirroring action, the ambivalent filial resemblances and rebellions, which instate the dialogue with neorealism as cinematic ancestor; historiography as codified, aestheticized performance in the grand operatic manner is echoed and interrogated, skeptically and perhaps again affectionately, in *La strategia del ragno*. Athos père, after several false starts concerning the attempt to murder the Duce, ultimately choreographs the narrative of his own death to harmonize with *Rigoletto*, dying to the accompaniment of a full orchestra. That the tragic death in the opera—which generates Verdi's famous "Maledizione," which we hear sung repeatedly in the film—is the result of a series of absurd errors and identity substitutions adds another layer of absurdity as we contemplate Athos' grandiose demise, itself founded on mistakes, subterfuge, and a substitution: Athos and the Duce are "uguale, uguale," both ridiculous "heroes" with an unfortunate tendency to linger on in marble.

A phrase that seems to haunt *La strategia del ragno* is spoken by Draifa during her first encounter with Athos *fils*. When asked if there was ever an official inquest into the death of Athos *père*, Draifa responds with a statement that befits her name: "una presa in giro c'è stata:" "there was a joke/hoax." The trial of Dreyfus, her namesake and her father's hero, was a joke, a pointless and predetermined exercise; so was the inquiry into Athos' murder. The use of the phrase is suggestive of more, however, than just another similarity, another example of the logic of "uguale, uguale" that pervades this world of resemblances. *Una presa in giro* is a set phrase, a common "dead" metaphor, perhaps no longer thought of primarily as figurative language; it is analogous to the English expression "pulling one's leg," which has a similar meaning, and is similarly seen as a set semantic unit and not as an active metaphor. It is another overdetermined speech act, a verbal "joke" that, like the names of many of Bertolucci's characters, opens up several different contexts and possible interpretations. A "giro" is a turn or a tour: it implies duration and movement. In a sense, the phrase "una presa in giro" describes *La strategia del ragno* as a film, and can be read as a key to unlock or decode the larger stratagem in which Bertolucci ensnares his audience. This film indeed "takes" (the verb *prendere*) us on a tour, a movement through the landscape of postwar Italy's engagement with its fascist past. Bertolucci keeps pulling our leg, offering an array of narratives and cinematic styles, only to undercut each of them. One meaning of the verb *girare*—to which the noun *giro* correlates—is to film, to shoot footage; the film camera is referred to as a *macchina di presa*. The movie camera is itself, therefore, *una presa in giro*.

The grand "joke" that is at the heart of *La strategia del ragno*, then, is that we are unable to settle into any one cinematic idiom or field of reference, but must oscillate dizzyingly among wildly different approaches, unable to come to rest in one style of constructing reality, or indeed to assume any "reality" at all. This deliberate production of perplexity, this exercise in bafflement, produces in the audience a mirroring of the incomprehension and disorientation of Athos Jr. as he wanders through possible realities, again creating a relation of similarity, making the audience and the protagonist "uguale, uguale." It also captures in microcosm Bertolucci's stratagem throughout the film as a whole, the web in which he continually ensnares us. Bertolucci's affectionate consideration of his cinematic ancestors, the great neorealist directors of the 1940s who attempted to create a distinctive antifascist and postfascist Italian art form, is one part of the fragmented territory we traverse, as is our confrontation with the fossilized, marmoreal face of antifascism and the enshrined memory of the resistance memorialized in the streets of Tara. As we see Athos Jr. take his slow, repeated *giri*, his tours through the city, filmed in a disorienting combination of neorealist-style long takes (a take is *una presa*) and deep focus using a relatively stationary camera and lengthy tracking shots versus the apparently incompatible new wave cinematic arsenal of jump-cuts, dizzying zooms, unexplained flashbacks, and continuity breaks, the *presa in giro* becomes evident. *La strategia del ragno*, as part of its strategy of bafflement, takes us on a "tour" of Italian history that seems almost Crocean in its approach, ranging from the Renaissance (the theater and the cityscape of Tara) to the Risorgimento (the use of Verdi's name as the coded symbol of national unity) to fascism and the resistance. This *giro*, our tour, can only be captured on film, imprinted on celluloid within the turning, the *giro*, of the movie camera. As Bertolucci foregrounds the complex processes of historiography, exploring its political and aesthetic implications, it becomes clear that we, the audience, are both coproducers and the victims of the "joke." The original inquiry into the death of Athos Sr.— the generating event of the mythology through which Tara, a recognizable if bizarrely off-kilter microcosm of postwar Italy, defines itself—was, as Draifa informs us, a fascist canard, a meaningless exercise with a predetermined result. Now we are once more, in this film, returning to the events of life in fascist Italy through the literal *presa in giro* of the movie camera. As the camera takes us on a tour through Tara, historiography itself is the self-reflexive focus.

The inhabitants of Tara resignify the spaces of their historic city by placing at its center, literally, the face and name of Athos Magnani; the perfectly preserved Renaissance history embodied by Tara is rewritten as the town transforms itself into a memorial to the (spurious) hero of the antifascist resistance.[28] This resignification attempts, unsuccessfully, to elide all ambiguity or contestation: when Athos junior enters the town of Tara, introduced to it by the gesture of the sailor/impresario, he is entering a space in which the possible meanings of the past, the potential historiographies, have ostensibly been reduced to one. The contested spaces of history have been drastically simplified, made monologic and monumental. The postfascist streets and piazzas of Tara—as well as its "official" cultural spaces, ranging from grand opera house to youth club—present a singular, monologic version of historical "reality;" all competing versions and voices are silenced. In this, of course, the body politic of the modern town is identical, "uguale, uguale," to that of the fascist era. Throughout *La strategia del ragno*, Bertolucci foregrounds acts of historiography, analyzing the ways in which they are mediated, and the consequences and implications of that mediation.[29] Historiography is highlighted as an all-pervasive activity, one that gives meaning to the very spaces we inhabit, and both structures and is structured by all our epistemological assumptions, whether we are conscious of them or not. Bertolucci presents his own work as sharing this essential attribute: it is clear that this film is also a highly self-aware act of historiography. In this, *La strategia del ragno* itself can be described by the phrase that returns as a leitmotif in the film; it, too, is "uguale, uguale," a mirror.

CHAPTER 4
THE ATOMIZED SUBJECT

Alain Resnais' *Hiroshima mon amour* and Helma Sanders-Brahms' *Deutschland bleiche Mutter* speak to us from the ruins, inhabiting a condition of absolute destruction and placing us at an epistemological "ground zero." The two films form part of a transnational dialogue that cuts across the boundaries of national cinema and language. Though they may appear, on the surface, to have little in common—they were made over twenty years apart (1959 and 1980, respectively) in different countries and at very different moments in the history of cinema—they share an important preoccupation, which invites consideration of them together. They both take as their central project the dissolution of epistemological categories, the very demarcations and boundaries that would appear, so undeniably, to relegate them to entirely different historical periods and to different national and linguistic fields. Both perform an operation of archeology, excavating—decades later—the epicenter, both literal and symbolic, of destruction; they turn over the scattered rubble, exposing its unweathered surfaces and returning us to the scene of crisis.

In Hiroshima and Berlin—cities that have, in Marguerite Duras' unforgettable image, risen into the air and returned to ground as ash and rubble—the past persists as "specter," a presence paradoxically made more insistent by absence. It is legible in scattered physical remnants, or in the photographic negatives emblazoned onto stone by the literally inconceivable light of the atom bomb, a trace that is more compelling than any "real" flesh and blood. Both films insistently problematize any concept of knowledge or the perceiving subject by presenting us with subjectivity as shattered, split, and multiplied; in both, the subject emerges as inseparable from any possible object that can be "known," and the slippage between subject and object is a defining condition. In each case, spectatorship is both foregrounded and denaturalized, functioning as the vehicle by which the collapsed epistemologies and subjectivities are considered. Temporal delineations disappear as the boundaries between past and present are repeatedly crossed. Linear causality is ruptured: any conventions or assumptions governing temporal or causal relationships—the very existence of the categories of past and present—collapse and "history," like unitary subjectivity, is a casualty of war. Historiography, therefore, is a major concern of both directors. Rather than knowledge, based on assumptions of transparency or perceptible "reality," "history" becomes a matter of mediation. Both directors engage in innovative cinematography, and the unsettling manipulation of the conventions of narrative and genre, to dislocate past and present.

Several of the directors discussed in *Cinema After Fascism* have deliberately unsettled the category of "the document," most notably Roberto Rossellini and Billy Wilder. However, to both Sanders-Brahms and Resnais, a profound and audacious attack on the boundaries and limits of the documentary form is essential. Both challenge the distinction between "truth" and "fiction," dismantling the codes of the documentary and penetrating the borders of the form, refusing to respect its epistemologically "privileged" status among cinematic genres. Sanders-Brahms, for example, gives us literal dialogue between "reality" and "fiction:" a figure from a famous documentary of postwar Berlin—a homeless child in the rubble—is intercut with, and speaks to, the protagonist of her feature film, their conversation sutured "seamlessly" together in shot/countershot.[1] Resnais presents unmarked shifts between historical documentary footage, contemporary photographs of the destruction mounted on a museum wall, a Japanese feature film made shortly after the bombing, "fake" documentary, and the film-within-a-film that we "see" being shot, all of which—like his innovative unmarked flashbacks—he uses to rupture the flow and continuity of his narrative, producing a thoroughly indigestible text, impossible to process in conventional ways.

Both *Hiroshima mon amour* and *Deutschland bleiche Mutter* somatize their dismantling of epistemological boundaries, inscribing the process on the bodies of their female protagonists. In the half-paralyzed face of Sanders-Brahms' Lene, there is no coherence between the parts, no wholeness or unity; her face becomes, like the film, "cut," sutured, and pieced together so that any construction of integrity, whether of the subject of or the (illusory) "reality" we see on screen, is denaturalized. Lene continues to inhabit the rubble—the broken remnants of the unitary subject—long after the literal destruction has been cleaned up. The nameless Frenchwoman of *Hiroshima mon amour* also physically incarnates the collapse of epistemology: the boundaries separating her body from the world are breached as she tears at the wall of the cellar in which she is imprisoned, marking them with her blood and incorporating them, literally, into her body as she eats pieces of the wall. It seems fitting, therefore, to place *Hiroshima mon amour* and *Deutschland bleiche*

Mutter in dialogue with each other, eschewing demarcations of national cinema, scholarly field, or traditional historiography in order to consider them together.

In the synopsis that accompanies her screenplay for *Hiroshima mon amour*, Marguerite Duras states: "Nothing is 'given' at Hiroshima. Every gesture, every word takes on an aura of meaning that transcends its literal meaning" (9). This is a description of the film's central project. In *Hiroshima mon amour*, the "literal" is always superseded; meaning is not unified or singular, but is multiplied and fragmented. Meanings here are by definition excessive of any single context, ripped away from their original matrices and inserted into new ones. Each conversation, event, or object in the film carries with it the trace and echo of other conversations, events and objects. Resnais makes innovative use of the flashback to accomplish this: we look at a man's hand in the "present," and it is displaced by the trace of another—long dead—man's hand. The past persists into the present, just as the ghostly images burned into existence by the atomic blast persist in modern Hiroshima; linear time and temporal contexts collapse.[2] As spectators of *Hiroshima mon amour*, we are left to negotiate this confusing field of excess, slippage, and echo. We ourselves are part of the system of displacement that reigns in the film.[3] Resnais and Duras focus extensively on looking, whether in the contemplation of a museum exhibit or watching a film being shot. We are watching a film about people watching the making of a film—our own gaze as spectators is multiplied many times and becomes the focus of our contemplation. Our scopophilic desire becomes a central focus as Resnais, in a distinctly uncomfortable fashion, forces us to confront our voyeuristic investment. The first shot of *Hiroshima mon amour* places us uneasily in the position of voyeur and conflates the horror of the atom bomb and the erotic charge of a sexual encounter. In our first sight of the intertwined bodies of the film's two protagonists, we initially see the sweat beading their skin as, possibly, the symptom of irradiated bodies—we realize only gradually that this is not the case.[4] The scenes of the lovers in bed, therefore, carry the trace of the atom bomb, just as the many scenes of looking carry the trace of our own spectatorship. What we "see," ultimately, is our own gaze.

Hiroshima mon amour, like many of the other films discussed above, presents the spectator with a crisis of epistemology. Duras and Resnais give us a universe in which everything is in flux, and instability, slippage, and displacement are the only structuring principles. Duras, through the voice of the female protagonist, describes the universe that contains the shattered city of Hiroshima as follows: "Chaos [*désordre*] will prevail. A whole city will be raised from the earth and fall back as ashes" (24). Even the physical realm itself has no solidity or stability. In the destroyed city, we inhabit, once again, a world of literal and metaphoric rubble, in which all preexisting structures have been destroyed, destructured, reduced to their randomly scatted elements (or, in the case of Hiroshima, partly vaporized); any structures that may replace them are provisional by definition, ad hoc constructions built out of the debris, that will never be able to claim the authority or permanence of their predecessors. Resnais forces both his characters and the film spectator to negotiate an epistemological wasteland; knowledge, truth, history, temporality, and subjectivity are all constantly destabilized, represented as reconstructed arbitrarily from rubble and always on the verge of collapsing once again. *Hiroshima mon amour,* therefore, questions not only the possibility of any kind of ultimate knowledge—negating any "truth" that is not provisional and unstable— but also undercuts any assumption of a unified subject who is in a position to "know" anything. Subjectivity in the film is a deeply problematic concept: the self is presented to us as a collection of fragments, displacements, and disunities. We, the film's spectators, are necessarily drawn into this spiral of slippage, substitution, and fragmentation, discomfiting though it may prove to be.

The main characters of *Hiroshima mon amour*—a Frenchwoman and a Japanese man, both unnamed in the film—circle obsessively around the issues of memory, vision, and knowledge. Like Rossellini in the opening of and ending segments of *Paisà* (in which we see the landscape of flow of the Sicilian lava fields and the riparian world of the Po Valley segment) and Sanders-Brahms, who opens *Deutschland bleiche Mutter* with a shot of the watery reflection of a swastika flag, Resnais chooses to confront the audience with the limitations of vision from the first moments of the film. After the credits, the film opens with a confusing shot of intertwined bodies in a darkened room. At first it is extremely difficult to identify what we are looking at: there is a period of ambiguity before we realize that we are in fact looking at a (whole and healthy) human body. It takes even longer to identify the body part: an arm and shoulder. Duras, in the screenplay of *Hiroshima mon amour,* describes the desired shot as follows: "All we see are these shoulders, cut off [*coupée*] from the body at the height of the head and hips" (15). Our first sight of a human body, therefore, is deliberately fragmented, cut into pieces, like the celluloid of the film. The first moments of *Hiroshima mon amour* create uncertainty and disorientation in the spectator; they prevent us from approaching the film with any sense of mastery. The fragmentation of the bodies on screen and the darkness of the shot match the fragmented quality of our own experience as viewers, the deliberate refusal by Resnais and Duras to allow any comfortable "knowledge," even to the extent of identifying what we see before us on the screen. The first line of dialogue follows: a male voice, speaking in measured tones. Duras characterizes the desired emotional affect as "flat and calm, as if reciting:" "You saw nothing in Hiroshima. Nothing" (15). These words could be addressed as much to us as spectators as to the speaker's conversational partner within the film's diegesis. We are being warned that we too will share in the epistemological crisis soon to erupt in the film as a whole. We have come to see a film called "Hiroshima," which deals with real "history," but we will "see"—that is, "know"—"nothing." However much we may wish for knowledge, truths built upon a stable epistemological edifice, we are, and will be, given only obscurity and fragmentation. The film here is questioning its own visual project—even as we look at the images on the screen, our gaze itself is problematized. "Knowledge" is not an option; eventually, yet again, we will have to settle for spectacle.

The initial dialogue between the protagonists is, perhaps, a struggle between two competing epistemological attitudes that would appear at first to be irreconcilable. The male character repeats his flatly negative, emotionless statements as the woman contradicts him: "I saw *everything. Everything*" (15). As the woman continues to assert what she has "seen"—the hospital that treated the victims of the atomic bomb—a montage of views of a hospital appears on screen. Here, the audience is also "seeing" what the woman describes, while listening to the man as he evenly maintains that we have seen "nothing."[5] We, the audience, want to "believe" this visual experience—which is also, of course, emotionally powerful, the images of human suffering inviting our identification and compassion—but this desire is constantly undercut by the man's continuing flat negation. Again, the effect is one of disorientation and uncertainty. The woman goes on to describe having seen the museum of Hiroshima, and once again a montage sequence showing the exhibits of the museum appears on screen, paralleling our gaze with hers as she insists on what she has seen despite his denials. A museum occupies an apparently privileged epistemological position: it is the place where "truths" are catalogued and arranged so that we can "know" them. The very existence of the museum is an assertion of the viability of a stable epistemology. By referring to the museum so insistently, repeatedly citing her multiple visits—"four times at the museum in Hiroshima" (17)— the woman would appear to be affirming this stance. However, as she continues, the emphasis shifts from the idea of the museum as source of epistemological certainty to a discussion of the people who are looking at the exhibits: "I saw the people walking around. The people walk around, lost in thought, among the photographs, the reconstructions..." (17). Three different gazes are brought together in her description of the museum: the woman's remembered gaze, the gaze of the museum goers we see in the montage that fills the screen as she is speaking, and our own gaze as we, along with the museum's patrons, stare numbly at the photographs and exhibits of the destruction of Hiroshima. In the course of this initial conversation, the woman moves from an assertion of the stability and trustworthiness of her gaze, with an emphasis on its result, an unproblematized statement of what has been seen and the belief that complete knowledge can be attained, to a consideration of the process of looking. From the first moments of *Hiroshima mon amour*, therefore, the central epistemological question of the film is laid out for us: how and what can we "know," through the epistemological instrument of the gaze. As the woman, in her somewhat disjointed speech, moves from looking for certainties and mastery to looking at looking, spectatorship becomes a central focus. As the film continues, Resnais and Duras will return repeatedly to a consideration of these two positions.

A pivotal scene in *Hiroshima mon amour*, in which many of the film's central concerns and questions are embedded, takes place at the beginning of the second section. The female protagonist stands on the rooftop balcony outside her hotel room. She is wearing a Japanese style kimono and holds in her hand a delicate china cup. She is relaxed and smiling, notably graceful and poised, her body position almost classical in its contraposto. She is looking down at a street in Hiroshima, where a group of bicyclists is passing. Her attitude is of enjoyment, confidence, and mastery. This is one moment in the film in which we see the Frenchwoman occupying such a position, however transient or illusory. As she looks down from her position of mastery, above the citizens and streets of the city, the woman's gaze is unproblematized, a rare occurrence in the film. It is the serene, confident look of a subject that can define itself securely in opposition to the object of its gaze. We share in this gaze through a series of point of view shots; we, too, are invited to take up this enviable posture. Characteristically, however, Resnais and Duras set up this possibility only to undercut it. As the Frenchwoman turns to look at her Japanese lover, we see her silhouetted in the doorway, her whole and unfragmented body beautifully framed in an elegantly composed shot. This shot calls attention to its own harmony and beauty: the framing is deliberately conspicuous, the composition noticeable. The beauty, wholeness, and balance in this shot are meant to be noticed and are in stark contrast to the opening shots of *Hiroshima mon amour*, in which the intertwined bodies of the protagonists are visually cut up into segments—fragmented virtually to the point of unrecognizability. Almost immediately, however, this pleasing unity is shattered, and the apparently stable self is presented as fragmented and in flux. We follow the woman's gaze as she looks at the outstretched hand and arm of her sleeping lover. At this point, the film's first flashback occurs: in place of the lover's arm, twitching gently in sleep, we see suddenly ("brutalement" [43], in Duras' words) the writhing hand and arm of a man who is terribly injured—or, as we later discover, dying. A woman—the protagonist—is frantically kissing his bloody face. The flashback is very brief and profoundly disconcerting in its violence and emotional power; there is no explanation—the audience is left to try to make sense of what we have been shown. The camera then returns to the figure of the woman framed in the doorway; the resonance of this shot has changed, however. The woman's gaze—in which we share—has ceased to be a reliable instrument of epistemological certainty, but it leads instead to its collapse. The woman's gaze constitutes her in two different times, two different places: temporal unity and linearity are no longer operative, and time has become a fluid category. "Past" and "present" intermingle freely and unpredictably.

The sudden flashback also ruptures the diegesis of the film. Although there is a diegetic explanation, as we eventually discover, within the context of the Frenchwoman's "story" of Nevers, the immediate effect is, once again, disconcerting. We don't initially have the information we need to "fit" the flashback into the film's diegesis—on the contrary, it seems to come out of nowhere, without warning or explanation. In addition, Resnais' disconcerting approach to flashbacks, ignoring the codes usually employed, deliberately creates confusion and disorientation, breaking through our pleasurable investment in "believing" the diegetic universe of the film. If we are invited to identify through the earlier use of point of view shots in this scene, the flashback sequence pushes us back again. Equally importantly, this entire sequence calls attention to the artifactuality of what we are watching. If the diegetic universe of the film is ruptured, we cannot dwell comfortably within its illusion; *Hiroshima mon amour*, therefore, continually foregrounds itself as medium.

The female protagonist of *Hiroshima mon amour* is in Japan to act in a film. Before she and her Japanese lover leave the hotel room, she dresses in her costume—an old-fashioned white nurse's uniform, with a large red cross on the cap.[6] The uniform suggests the authority of "science," the positivist regimes of knowledge and certainty that are so insistently called into question throughout the film. It symbolizes, perhaps, the "ancien régime" of Enlightenment epistemology that Resnais and Duras are attempting to overthrow. The revolutionary nature of their project is suggested—with, possibly, a touch of self-deprecating humor—when the male protagonist explains why he speaks such excellent French: "That's why. To read about the French Revolution" (34). Once again, in the scenes of the film being shot in Hiroshima, *Hiroshima mon amour* draws us, its spectators, into a self-reflexive dialogue that deepens the epistemological crisis that is already operative: the emphasis on the process of filming functions as a distanciation technique, once more breaking the diegetic illusion—yet again, we are reminded that we are watching a film.

As we see the recreations of Hiroshima immediately after the atom bomb, we are confronted with the machinery by which "history" is produced. We see extras being made up as bomb "victims," their wounds and burned skin carefully applied by technicians. The result is, of course, virtually identical to the scenes that we have already been shown of exhibits from the museum devoted to the "real" Hiroshima. As Resnais' protagonists interact within the Hiroshima movie set, we alternately watch them watching and watch with them in a series of point of view sequences. We see the Frenchwoman and the Japanese man moving among the "victims;" we see cameramen, make up artists, extras milling around. Duras suggests that this artificial construction of "history" is par for the course in Hiroshima: "We gather that they have just finished shooting an enlightening film on Peace at Hiroshima. ...A crowd passes along the square where they have just been shooting the film. The crowd is indifferent. Except for a few children, no one looks, they are used to seeing films being shot at Hiroshima" (39). This slightly cynical statement is suggestive: nobody knows better than the inhabitants of Hiroshima, who have become an international symbol, that all "history," whether filmed or not, is mediated and manipulated. They themselves are permanently a spectacle, the distinction between their "real" experience and the fictive recreations of it having disappeared almost completely. The filming sequences in *Hiroshima mon amour* emphasize again that the boundaries between "history" as "fact" and "fiction," between past and present, have been breached. History has become spectacle, and the past—as recreations of the burned and wounded bodies of 1945—intermingles with the present in the streets of Hiroshima, just as they do when Resnais plunges us into unsignaled flashbacks.

When the male protagonist approaches the Frenchwoman on the movie location, having tracked her down, he finds her asleep, stretched on the ground in her nurse's uniform, her cap and hair in disarray. For a moment, she looks dead; her position, the suggestion of a corpse, creates a visual connection both to the Hiroshima victims and to the figure of her dying German lover, whom we have briefly glimpsed in flashback. Immediately following, after the man's intense gaze has literally awoken the woman (again, the act of looking is foregrounded), we see the two lovers against the background of a series of placards carried by extras in the film that is being shot. "Two workers—carrying an enlarged photograph from the picture *The Children of Hiroshima* showing a dead mother and a child crying in the smoking ruins of Hiroshima—pass between them. They don't look at the photograph" (40). Throughout *Hiroshima mon amour*, the Frenchwoman's story is paralleled to the story of the bombing victims of Hiroshima. Her suffering, her symbolic death in the cellar at Nevers, and this second death as she sleeps at the movie location are, through these placards, directly linked to all the dead of Hiroshima. Characteristically, however, Duras informs us that even the "documentary" evidence of the photograph, ostensibly the most transparent and least mediated version of history, actually comes to us through many layers of mediation, including the prism of two separate films. We are invited to contemplate both a city and a person in a state of dissolution—any reconstruction from "the ashes" is tenuous at best in both cases.

The woman's madness, the dissolution of self, is linked symbolically to the destruction caused by the atom bomb, to the situation of a city reduced to rubble and partly vaporized. She and her lover are in his house, where she has begun to give him an inkling of what happened to her in Nevers. The story is told to us also through flashbacks, which are initially just as confusing as the one at the beginning of Part II. As the woman tells her lover that the man in Nevers was not French but German, we see a brief, dark medium long shot, through an open doorway, of a shadowy figure in what appears to be Wehrmacht uniform crossing a courtyard. The grainy shot has the feel, almost, of documentary footage. If the photographs we have seen earlier, both in the museum (where history is presented as fact) and the movie location (history as spectacle), are used to undermine the epistemological distinction between "fact" and "fiction," then this brief shot, with its quotation of the authoritative genre of the documentary film embedded diegetically in the "memory" of a woman we know to have been mentally unstable, also appears deliberately provocative. Again, Resnais and Duras are casting doubt on familiar epistemological assumptions: a documentary film is no more privileged than the fragmentary memories of a former madwoman. As the story continues, the flashbacks become lengthier, but no less disorienting: scenes of countryside rush past as if we were traveling at speed. We continue to shift back and forth between present and past without a clear contextualization, or any delineation between the two.

After the lovers leave the Japanese man's house, they go to a restaurant by a river. As they pass through the city, we see people, individually and in groups, standing and looking out at a wide river. Duras describes the scene this way: "Night falls over Hiroshima, leaving long trails of light... sometimes people along the muddy banks watch the tide rising slowly" (53).

The lyricism of Duras' description, which is matched by Resnais' beautifully scenic, panoramic shots, are aesthetically pleasing at the same time as they function as another distanciation device, denaturalizing the action that follows. The river, in its boundarilessness and fluidity, mirrors the dissolution of so many of the epistemological categories that are undercut throughout *Hiroshima mon amour*: knowledge can no more be grasped than water. The phrase "longues traînées lumineuses" is suggestive: the "long, luminous traces" of light as night falls on the river bring to mind the play of darkness and light on the screen, film itself as long, luminous traces of light. Duras describes the setting as follows: "Those seated at the back of the café don't see the banks of the river, but only the river itself. The mouth of the river is only vaguely outlined. There Hiroshima ends and the Pacific begins" (53).[7] The scenery here again comments on the structure of trace and echo, substitution, slippage, and fluidity that underlies *Hiroshima mon amour*. This riverscape, as seen from the restaurant's windows, is literally boundariless; it has no beginning or end, no stable contours that we can see, and blends into the vast waters of the Pacific. The "imprecision," as Duras characterizes it, is precisely this: the collapse, symbolized by the fluid riverscape, of epistemological structures. The river estuary here has the same symbolic function as the rubble of the bombed city. It is within sight of the river at Hiroshima, as wavery reflections of light on water play across the faces of the actors, that we will begin to understand the echoes and traces, "les trainees," of the past within the present as the Frenchwoman tells her story.

Duras goes on to make a rather remarkable statement about what occurs in this riverside café: "A miracle has occurred. What miracle? The resurrection of Nevers" (53). It is in this setting—with its collapse of spatial distinctions, the invisibility of boundaries between land and river, the intermingling of river and ocean and sky—that the "miracle" of the rupture of linear time, of divisions between past and present, the "resurgence" of the past, can take place. The Frenchwoman begins her account by describing the Loire river, in terms that are similar to Duras' description—confirmed by vision—of the river at Hiroshima. The Loire—the woman's "native" river—is defined by "its irregular course and its sand bars" (54). Hiroshima and Nevers are the "same" place, both defined, paradoxically, by the symbolic unsustainability of definitions. The riparine landscape, with its hazards to navigation, mirrors the epistemological hazards that by now are so familiar. In addition, we discover later that, in Hiroshima, other temporal distinctions are also undermined. There appears to be no boundary between night and day, as the Frenchwoman observes with delight: "I love that...cities where there are always people awake, day or night…" (70). In the unique environment of Hiroshima, a city that has been blasted into literal and symbolic ash by the atom bomb and where even nature shares the characteristics of rubble, a complex ballet of memory and forgetting, of traces, echoes, substitutions, and displacements, can be enacted.

As the man and woman talk, more epistemological delineations rupture. The man verbally assumes the identity of the dead German lover, speaking in the German's "voice" as he responds to the Frenchwoman's story.[8] (He has, of course, already been a substitute for the German, physically rather than verbally, as his sleeping body, merging with the German's dying one in the first flashback, becomes the trace of the past.) This semantic substitution starts at the beginning of the café sequence, immediately after the discussion of the Loire, and continues intermittently throughout: "'When you are in the cellar, am I dead?' 'You are dead…'" (54). The man, therefore, is no longer a securely unitary self but suffers the multiplication and fragmentation of his subjectivity. As the woman describes her period of madness—the ultimate dissolution of self—he chooses to follow her, allowing himself to become a "broken" subject and, in addition, embodying in his selfhood the trace of the past, which has now fully erupted into the present as we lurch back and forth between flashbacks of Nevers and the café in Hiroshima.

As the woman describes and remembers her experiences, Resnais brings us back to scenes of the cellar in Nevers, the site of the woman's madness and her confinement. The cellar, which would initially appear to be the diametric opposite of a boundariless river—it is, in fact, the Frenchwoman's prison, a place of impregnable walls that cut her off definitively from the outside world—paradoxically becomes, itself, a symbol of the rupture of epistemological categories. The cellar is a place in which temporal boundaries dissolve: there is no distinction between summer and winter. As the woman describes this, she immediately follows it with a mention of the Loire river: "In Nevers, the cellars are cold, both summer and winter. The city is built along a river called the Loire" (53). In this statement, the cellar and the river are brought together, their juxtaposition emphasizing the ways in which they, unexpectedly, are directly parallel in their symbolic function. In one of the most striking flashback images in *Hiroshima mon amour*, we are shown that the walls of the cellar are not the solid, unrupturable boundaries we might expect. Duras, in her appendix to the published screenplay, describes it as follows: "For lack of something better, saltpeter can be eaten. The salt of the stones. Riva eats the walls…she is in a universe of walls. A man's memory is in these walls, one with the stone, the earth, the air" (96).[9]

Figure 4.1 *Hiroshima mon amour*: the Frenchwoman consumes the cellar wall.

The phrase "a universe of walls" might initially suggest, again, a universe in which boundaries are unbreached, delineations—whether physical or conceptual—absolute; however, these walls are breached by memory, their substance symbolically broken down, their solid stone incorporating also the fluidity of the past. Through the woman's act of eating, she takes the cellar walls into her body, merging them with herself. Several epistemological categories collapse in the cellar flashback sequences in *Hiroshima mon amour*. The woman is visited in her confinement by a cat, whose interaction with her is described by Duras as follows: "The cat's eyes and Riva's eyes look alike and stare at each other...there is nothing else in the cellar except a single stare, the stare of the cat-Riva" (98). The Frenchwoman has, symbolically, "merged" with the cat: they have become one entity, a "chat-Riva." Here, there is no distinction between an animal and a human being—this conceptual boundary has been ruptured, leaving us, again, with an epistemological paradox. Finally, the essential distinction between life and death itself falls away: they become meaningless categories. We have already seen the living body of the Japanese man stand in or substitute for the body of the dead German soldier; we have also heard the living man speak in the "voice" of the dead one, offering himself again as a stand-in, this time verbally, continuing to embody the trace of the past, of Nevers in Hiroshima. As the woman continues to describe her experiences in the cellar she, too, symbolically offers her own living body as analogous to her German lover's dead one: "I can say that I couldn't feel the slightest difference between this dead body and mine. All I could find between this body and mine were similarities" (65). The "wall" between life and death has symbolically collapsed, ceased to function as a partition or boundary, like the walls of the cellar itself. Death and life intermingle, as do flesh and stone. The woman also collapses gender difference: the relationship between her female body and the German's male one is defined by likeness—"resemblance"—rather than difference. Up to now, we have had male standing in for male, the body of one heterosexual love object displacing the other. Here, however, the "wall" between male and female also collapses, subsiding into the disorderly pile of epistemological rubble at our feet.

The sequences, central to *Hiroshima mon amour*, in which we are thrown back and forth between the café in Hiroshima and the cellar in Nevers, represent the point in the film, therefore, in which the ongoing epistemological crisis finds its fullest expression. The Frenchwoman's madness, the rupturing of her subjectivity and its collapse into symbolic rubble, is multiplied, mirrored, and echoed on many different levels. The boundarilessness, fluidity, and displacement that are the only structuring principles in the universe of the film are also what define the woman's selfhood. If the Loire and Hiroshima rivers have become established as metonymic terms for this epistemological dissolution, then Duras makes very explicit the ways in which the woman's subjectivity has come to resemble them, in its fluidity and "disorder:" "The rivers also still flow as if nothing had happened. The Loire. Riva's eyes flow like the Loire, but *directed by pain*, amid this confusion" (95; Duras' emphasis). The Frenchwoman's eyes "flow;" her subjectivity is fluid, shifting, boundariless, like the Loire itself. If her subjectivity can be said to have any structure, it is one that is entirely different from any that we know, a unique subjectivity built out of her suffering. It is directed, structured— Duras' word is *ordonné*—through pain into the opposite of structure: the translation renders this destructured state as "confusion;" Duras calls it *ce désordre* (Duras, 134).[10] The Frenchwoman's selfhood may have been reconfigured, or "ordered" anew, but the configuration that comes into being as the result of her suffering is one of slippage and "disorder:" she no longer fulfills the criteria of unitary subjectivity. The trace of woman's collapsed subjectivity is expressed in everything that surrounds her, just as she herself echoes and mirrors walls, rivers, and cat, in a boundariless commingling, her world without stable delineation of time or seasons, gender, or even life.

The cities of Hiroshima and Nevers, the two settings of *Hiroshima mon amour*, have become metonymic terms for the epistemological crisis that is at the heart of the film. Duras and Resnais draw strong parallels between the dissolution of the woman's subjectivity and the destruction visited upon Hiroshima by the atomic bomb. The collapse of the stable subject disrupts any possibility of mastery or of "knowledge" in the conventional sense; this "broken" subject is itself the trace and echo of the ruptured and disrupted universe emblematized by Hiroshima and, ultimately, Nevers. The Frenchwoman, in an interior monologue near the end of the film, brings them together once again: "Nevers that I'd forgotten, I'd like to see you again tonight. Every night for months on end I set you on fire, while my body was aflame with his memory" (78). "Aflame"—Duras' word is *incendié*, burned—is an important symbolic choice here: it refers to the massive firestorm caused by the detonation of the bomb in Hiroshima. Near the beginning of the film, in the first bedroom sequence, we have heard the woman's description of this "history," the burning of Hiroshima: "I was hot at Peace Square. Ten thousand degrees at Peace Square. I know it. The temperature of the sun at Peace Square" (17). In this statement, the woman places herself at the center of the conflagration, at ground zero: "I was hot in Peace Square." In symbolically subjecting her protagonist to this very overdetermined heat, Duras directly equates the rupture of the self and the immolation of Hiroshima. In the statement near the end of the film, not only are Hiroshima and the woman's body equated as *incendié*, reduced to ash, but Nevers is also brought into the equation as it, too, is subject to the same firestorm. "Memory," the persistent trace of the present in the past, the continued presence of the absent and the dead, is the "fire" that "vaporizes" subjectivity and epistemology.

The famous final lines of dialogue in *Hiroshima mon amour* again foreground this equivalence. The woman says: "Hi-ro-shi-ma. Hi-ro-shi-ma. That's your name." The man replies: "That's my name. Yes. Your name is Nevers. Ne-vers-in-France" (83). Duras' specification of a staccato pronunciation for the names of the cities—articulated in the film in a flat, antinaturalistic mode, as if the two protagonists were somehow in a trance—is telling here. They are no longer just place names, even very overdetermined ones. By removing these two words from "natural" or "everyday" language, by denaturalizing them, Duras and Resnais are, in a sense, marking them as excessive of their original context. Duras and Resnais show us the ways in which the words "Hiroshima" and "Nevers" have become metonymic constructs, both displacing and standing in for the complex dance of slippage, displacement, echo, and trace that characterizes the epistemological project of the film. Hiroshima is the vaporized city that has, in Duras' memorable image, been lifted off the earth and fallen again as ashes, with its riverscape that has no boundaries that we can see. Nevers is a town on the boundariless Loire, in which subjectivity becomes as random and fluid as the river itself. Both, in their states of dissolution, represent the rupture of any stable identity, the collapse of models of subjectivity. The self is fragmented and scattered, reduced metaphorically to ash and rubble, burnt, even vaporized. The trace of history and of subjectivity remains, like the ghostly images burned into being by the bomb or as piles of rubble containing the disheveled, randomly scattered elements of what once existed. We, as spectators, are caught in the ongoing epistemological crisis, confronted repeatedly with the limits of vision and the impossibility of "knowledge." We must recognize "ourselves," our own fragmented subjectivity. Any attempt we may make to attain unity or mastery, however illusory that might prove ultimately to be, is immediately undercut. We, too, inhabit Hiroshima and Nevers.

Duras' statement, "nothing is given in Hiroshima," could also apply to Germany as we encounter it in *Deutschland bleiche Mutter*: Helma Sanders-Brahms also refuses to present us with an epistemologically stable world. Her film, again, questions such fundamental concepts as subjectivity, history, and truth, deconstructing such oppositions as past and present, truth and fiction, subjectivity and objectivity, and public and private spheres. An interrogation and defamiliarization of "history" is an essential part of the project of the film: it is highly aware of its own acts of historiography, continually foregrounding this process. "History," the retrospective construction of a "past," is presented to us as an almost arbitrary structure, and as such subject to constant revision, reconfiguration, and rewriting. History is envisioned in *Deutschland bleiche Mutter* as a textual construct, a work of narrative, subject to the rules of narrative rather than of "fact." "The past" has no autonomous existence, or at least none that we have access to: the idea of "truth," any stable conception of "the way things really were," has been deprivileged or removed.

The first shot in *Deutschland bleiche Mutter* is a lengthy take of the wavering reflection of a swastika in the water of a lake. The reflected image is broken by a rowboat passing across it, and the camera lifts to show two men in the boat, whistling and calling to a woman walking. The shot of a reflected swastika—the icon of Nazism, functioning here to situate the diegesis of the film historically, making the action in the scene that follows comprehensible—problematizes historiography, foregrounding mediation, construction, representation.[11] It underlines the fact that what we are watching is not "the past," but instead an artifact, a film about the past. The swastika in the water is like the picture on the screen, both flickering images of moving light and color, and both mediated images: the swastika—which aggressively occupies the territory of the screen, a provocative image with which to begin a film with "Deutschland" in its title—is doubly a representation, a picture of a reflection, the image of an image. The presence of two men in the boat also foregrounds the film's problematization of history as representation, as mediated, constructed: the men are spectators, looking, watching, in much the same way we are, as the spectators of this film. The men's gaze is perhaps voyeuristic, or transgressive, since there is a somewhat aggressive eroticization of the woman at whom they are looking, who disdainfully ignores their calls. The two men (Hans—as we later learn—who will become the father of the narrator of the film, and his Nazi friend, Ulrich) watch a brief, self-contained, wordless sequence of events. The woman—Lene, who will become Hans' wife and the narrator's mother—is attacked by a German Shepherd (that most overdetermined of canine breeds, a matched set with the swastika) belonging to some men in military uniform; she resists but does not cry out. The men proceed to interpret what they see: Ulrich posits the unknown Lene as a "true German woman" because of her courage in remaining silent when attacked (by a "true German dog"?). Hans and Ulrich are in a physically separated space, a different zone, from Lene—they are on the water and she is on land—and at a considerable distance from her and do not intervene in the action in any way. Their distance and separation from the action, as well as their passivity and voyeuristic, eroticized pleasure in the tableau before them, reinforce the similarity of their position to ours as spectators.

Not only, therefore, is awareness of the medium—of the construction and representation of this "history"—built into the opening sequence of *Deutschland bleiche Mutter*, but our own presence as spectators is also coded in: the spectator is an essential element in this process, a coproducer of meaning, a participant in any historiography in which the film might be engaged. Any expectation of truth on our part, then, of unmediated access to the past, or the idea that we are unproblematically watching a "true story" (which the autobiographical elements in the film, as well as the extensive use of documentary footage, might encourage) is doubly problematized. This history—as artifact, as story and narrative, as construction—is subject to rewriting by both the producer and the receiver. The presence at the beginning of the film of the two men, as spectators and "writers" of a narrative, introduces another very important problematic: the idea of woman as spectacle, as construction of the male gaze, as imagistic. Sanders-Brahms, in the course of the film, plays with female subjectivity, undercutting, through techniques like masquerade and multiplication, the familiar (in both senses of the word) construction of woman as image and spectacle that she deliberately sets up at the beginning by reproducing, within the diegesis of the film, the relationship between image and spectator on which this construction is based.[12] Sanders-Brahms deliberately evokes it as a necessary part, perhaps, of any reflection on cinematic historiographies. She makes almost playful use of it, linking it at the opening sequence of the film to powerful images of domination, like the swastika and the dog. This evocation of the concept of the "male gaze" is so highly overdetermined that—even as we react emotionally to the sight of swastika and the attack of the vicious dog—we are forced to notice it as carrying a heavy symbolic freight. This sequence, then, works to denaturalize the process of spectatorship at the same time as it invites us to participate in its pleasures.

Any construction of the gaze as linked in a simplistic fashion to power and gender is, in this sequence, defamiliarized and revealed as much too simple. At the same time, this sequence informs us that the film will, indeed, consider the link between spectatorship, power, and gender in more complex ways. The gaze of the woman as spectator, as well as spectacle to be gazed upon, subject as well as object, becomes central; the female subject emerges as mobile and multiply configured, as simple binary constructions of gender break down—including those based on feminist readings of the unidirectional axis of the male gaze. We are invited to consider our own gaze as we observe the gaze of the men at the lakeside "theater;" for them, the spectacle they have seen and the narrative they have "written" points to some useful and stable (to us, perhaps, chilling) reassurances concerning the concepts of power, nation, and gender, a truth about "the German woman." As the process of spectatorship is denaturalized, our gaze brings us to the opposite of this reassurance: any constructions brought into being by our scopophilic desire, by our own visual hunger, consumption, and pleasure, are necessarily "written in water." Again, as in *Paisà* and *Hiroshima mon amour*, water fills the screen; this environment of ripple and flow, of wavering reflections, turns out to be yet another epistemological "wilderness," a place that resists boundaries and problematizes vision, denaturalizing any process of constructing reality. This watery beginning sets the stage for the epistemological questioning that dominates the film as a whole. In the water of the lake, or in the rubble of the destroyed city, nothing is "given."

Deutschland bleiche Mutter deals with material that is, at least on the surface, presented to us as autobiographical, as true to lived experience, as "real." The voice-over in the film, the speaking "I" introduced to us as the grown-up Anna who is present as a child in the second and third sections of the film, could be taken as reinforcing the perception of the film as a "true story," the story of the film-maker's own parents and childhood—though this privileged status is double-edged, also inviting dismissal of the text as too subjectively personal, too lacking in "objectivity," to be of use as a credible act of historiography. Obviously, this concept of autobiographical material is deeply problematic. But it appears that the film, at least early in the history of its reception, was often discussed according to this paradigm of fidelity or lack thereof to a knowable "true experience."[13] Once again, however, this epistemological expectation, this paradigmatic construction of what constitutes useful "history," is introduced only to be undercut and deconstructed. Sanders-Brahms attacks—somewhat playfully, perhaps— the oppositions between fact and fiction, subjectivity and objectivity, truth and discourse, until they become meaningless terms.[14]

The voice-over that structures *Deutschland bleiche Mutter*, while it on one level emphasizes the film's autobiographical content and thus would seem to reinforce a claim for the privileged status of "truth," also functions to call attention to the film as artifact, undercutting any possibility that it might be approached as unmediated reality.[15] In fact, the narrator—the "I" that is the persona both for the daughter represented within the diegesis of the film and for the extradiegetic figure of the director—frequently comments on the ways in which she has altered reality, has rewritten experience for the purposes of narrative, for what she refers to as the "story." For example, as we are introduced to the cast of characters, the narrator begins to tell the story of Lene's sister and then corrects herself: "But this is your love story, my mother and father." This statement underlines, again, the constructedness of what we are seeing: this "story" has an author and is governed by the rules of narrative. There are many other instances in which the voice-over is used to interrupt the illusionary realism of the film. It is remarkable that, as McCormick states, *Deutschland bleiche Mutter* was criticized for being "realistic," and "illusionary," by "antirealists" who consider "realism inherently bourgeois and depoliticized" (194). It was also, again, attacked for being too "subjective," not historically "accurate" enough. It seems that the "personal" and "subjective" autobiographical approach that Sanders-Brahms adopts, the voice-over by a character who, albeit as her child self, is diegetically present in the film, automatically signals to many that the film is making a claim to be "true." Therefore, according to some critics, that should be rejected as bourgeois and reactionary; to others, it seems that the film's value should be determined by whether or not it manages to be "objective." The voice-over's double function, then, is to set up an expectation—that the director is identical to the character of Anna in the film, and that is therefore her own "real" experience, a "true" story, though perhaps a "subjective" one—and to act as a distanciation device, undercutting these very expectations.[16] The irreconcilable—and perhaps playful—doubleness of this approach, and its contradictory imperatives are, again, epistemologically challenging: nothing is "given" in Hiroshima or Germany.

The privileged epistemological status of "the document" is another construction destabilized in *Deutschland bleiche Mutter*, as it is in *Hiroshima mon amour.* Sanders-Brahms undercuts the audience's expectations about knowledge and reality through her use of documentary footage. Documents, especially photographic ones, do not, supposedly, "lie:" the "documentary" has traditionally been assumed to transcend its own nature as artifactual medium, to give the present access to the past. A film taken from an American bomber of a German city on fire or a film of Berlin women clearing out rubble (both of which Sanders-Brahms incorporates into her film) are privileged representations of "reality"—it is clear, from the opinions of many of the critics of the film, that this idea of reality still persists in the context within which Sanders-Brahms was working. The documentary footage, like the voice-over, therefore, serves the double function of setting up such an expectation, playing into a construction of the "fact" as privileged only to undercut it. There are several ways in which Sanders-Brahms undermines the concept of authenticity as it relates to the documentary. She, at times, weaves documentary footage into the film so that the audience is, at least momentarily, unsure whether we are looking at the "real" Berlin or at Sanders-Brahms' reconstruction of it—an example of this is a scene in which documentary footage of "Trümmerfrauen" at work blends into a shot of Lene and Anna clearing out rubble with a group of other women. The "document" and the "reconstruction" are juxtaposed in such a way so as to fool the spectator into thinking that both are documentary footage, until we notice the face of Eva Mattes (the actress who plays Lene) in the crowd. At another point, Sanders-Brahms completely erases the boundary between the document and the feature film. Documentary footage of a young child searching for his family in the ruined city is crosscut with shots of Lene so that it appears that the boy is conversing with her, replying to her questions: they seem to interact in the same space, the same plane, reciprocally, in shot/countershot. Like Duras and Resnais, therefore, Sanders-Brahms comments directly on the function of the document, particularly the photograph and archival footage. Both *Hiroshima mon amour* and *Deutschland bleiche Mutter* use the epistemologically privileged status of the document to, paradoxically, undermine the subject/object split on which such constructions depend.

The deconstruction of epistemological assumptions, the depriviliging of documentary as bearing a less-mediated relationship to "reality" than feature film, is obviously a challenge to historiographic constructs.[17] The disconcerting effect of this is central to Sanders-Brahms' strategy. In establishing a dialogue between the past and the present—literally, in the case of the conversation with a long-vanished little boy, and the many instances of direct address by the voice-over narrator to Hans and Lene—she is emphasizing again that the past does not have an authentic, hermetic existence. She codes in our participation as constructors and interlocutors of "the past," through the deconstruction of the boundaries between "historical reality" and "fiction." The use of documentary is also, like the voice-over, a classic distanciation device, breaking down the naturalistic illusion of the film, exposing it as artifact and construction.[18] The boundaries between fact and fiction, document and story, reality and illusion (and the hermetic cinematic illusionism that, by its very self-sufficiency and completeness, is coded as reality) have been "intruded on," rendered permeable, and the foundations of these constructions have been undermined.

Yet another important way in which any expectation of truth or un-mediated reality is undermined, and a process of distanciation occurs, is through the use of narrative and fairy-tale elements.[19] The most striking use of these elements is the very long sequence in which Lene recites the Grimm fairy tale, "The Robber Bridegroom," while on screen we see her carrying the toddler, Anna, for days or weeks through a war-torn, almost deserted, landscape. There are some connections, if fairly abstract ones, between the fairy tale and the on-screen action; for example, in the fairy tale, the bride lays a trail of ashes, and on screen we see Lene and Anna entering an abandoned building that has tall smokestacks and large ovens, reminiscent, as Kaes, McCormick, and Bammer all point out, of a cre-matorium. The general effect, however, is one of disconnection and es-trangement. There are other traditional fairy tale elements in the film, which cumulatively have an effect of breaking the self-contained, natu-ralistic illusionism of the film in much the same way, paradoxically, as the documentary footage does, even though documentary and fairy tale are at opposite ends of the spectrum of reality/truth versus fiction as it is tradi-tionally constructed. By making fairy tale and documentary structurally equivalent, Sanders-Brahms is, again, deconstructing this dichotomy.

The fairy-tale elements in *Deutschland bleiche Mutter* also work toward denaturalizing femininity, foregrounding the constructed, even the textual or discursive, nature of the feminine. This is, I would argue, another central project of the film and goes hand in hand with the deconstruction of famil-iar epistemologies and historiographies: Sanders-Brahms undermines both at their foundations, leaving them tumbled and fragmented. The openly textual interruptions, or eruptions, into the film deal with archetypal con-structions of "woman:" the Grimm fairy tale and Bertolt Brecht's poem entitled "Germany, Pale Mother" with which the film begins. Sanders-Brahms has been criticized for an essentializing gender, of adopting more or less uncritically the allegory expressed in the Brecht poem—woman as eternal mother and as land/nation.[20] However, Sanders-Brahms' use of this allegory can be read precisely as a critique of such essentialist construc-tions of woman.[21] Such prominent use of a Brecht poem seems to demand at least the possibility of reading these textual irruptions as a classically

"Brechtian" element. The Brecht poem is projected onto the screen as text and is at the same time read in voice-over by Brecht's daughter, Hannah Hiob. Hiob's reading is striking for its flatness and monotony, its strained and awkward declamatory tone. In a sense, the reading also functions as a distanciation technique. If the allegorical figure of Woman is effective because of its emotional power, Sanders-Brahms' use of it empties it of emotional content. The poem appears as decontextualized, disinvested, estranged textuality. It is of central importance in the film—it provides, after all, the title—but, in its strangeness and unvarnished textuality, it is not an invitation to unquestioningly adopt the essentialist allegory of the Mother/Land, but instead to denaturalize femininity by foregounding it as textual construct. The use of the Brecht poem only problematizes the category of Woman, and the ideal of Mother, rather than asserting them as essentialist categories. The poem and the narration of "The Robber Bridegroom" do not participate in any way in the fiction of the film; they interrupt the cinematic illusion, erupt into the film as raw text. The spectator is forced to consider the Mother/Land trope, femininity as it appears in fairy tales, the category of woman itself, as textual constructs and to "read" all of *Deutschland bleiche Mutter* in this context.

Sanders-Brahms' film was criticized extensively for being "subjective;" yet, like Resnais and Duras, she uses her "subjective" approach as tactic to overwhelm distinctions between the self and the outside world, between the subject and the object. She floods each into the other until the boundary between them becomes as fluid as the river at Hiroshima, or the lake that is the "theater" of the film's opening excursion into self-reflexive historiography. Duras' Frenchwoman incorporates the walls of a cellar into her body, literally consuming this solid, linear boundary; in eating the walls, she erases herself as an epistemological subject that is constructed in opposition to an outside object. The object, symbolically, becomes subject and vice versa throughout *Hiroshima mon amour.* Sanders-Brahms' protagonist also incarnates a challenge to the subject/object split within her body. She develops Bell's palsy, making her face into a "wall," her flesh incorporating a visible boundary with no function, the effect of which is distinctly uncanny. Lene incorporates into her body the principle of boundary and division itself: it becomes her physical being. The split in Lene's features is often read as representing the split "motherland" of Germany after the war, or other splits related to gender, the family, and public versus private spheres: these readings all participate in the assumption that there is some sort of allegorical relationship between Lene's physical pathology and her social, cultural, or political environment. It can be argued, then, that Lene has "consumed" the condition of the outside world, absorbing it into herself. However, the apparent allegory itself, paradoxically, challenges allegory.

Once more, then, we see a woman's physicality challenging binary constructions and rupturing the ostensibly stable epistemological structures that depend on a distinction between the subject and an object outside the self. Lene has inhabited a world of rubble, in which no boundaries, no stable edifices, exist. In a provisionally "rebuilt" society after the war, one whose edifices—most obviously the concept of national identity, but also gender and the family—can never be entirely renaturalized, she incorporates the substance and apparent structures of the outside world into her body, "becoming" the object outside the self and simultaneously maintaining her position as subject. In this, Lene resembles the Frenchwoman in Resnais' film who, in her cellar near the Loire River and in the redeposited ashes of Hiroshima, has traversed various lines and oppositions that represent stable epistemological structures. Duras/Resnais and Sanders-Brahms have both reconfigured the subject, removing its capacity to be defined in relation to an object: in so doing, they have disputed historiographies based on the privileges of the document and of "the past" as a knowable entity.

CHAPTER 5

THE PASSION OF VERONIKA VOSS

Rainer Werner Fassbinder's trio of films set in the early years of the Federal Republic of Germany—*Die Ehe der Maria Braun* (1979), *Lola* (1981), and *Die Sehnsucht der Veronika Voss* (1982)—places us in the ruins of fascism. In addition to physical ruin—which is certainly present, especially in *Maria Braun*—Fassbinder's films explore the intangible but no less excruciating ruin of subjectivity. Indeed, it could be said that the project of these films is to create ruin as well as to document it. Fassbinder's Bundesrepublik Deutschland (BRD) trilogy constitutes a disconcerting act of historiography: he is meditating on the relationship of his present (the late 1970s and early 1980s) to the multiple "pasts" it has retrospectively constituted—Germany in both the fascist era and the postwar years. Fassbinder "ruins" conventional temporal divisions, refusing to respect any boundaries or demarcations between fascist Germany and the nation that was its successor as he examines the persistence of structures of desire and power. To this damaged historiography is added the ruination of desire and spectatorship. The subject is constituted both as a phantasm of spectacle (a creature of smoke and mirrors) and as an obsessive spectator, with scopophilia as the ruling desire. The self can never be naturalized when its unstable architecture is so obvious: its inadequacy is excruciating. As representation in Fassbinder's films circles obsessively around the site of its own constitutive collapse, so too does subjectivity, returning ceaselessly to the moment of its rupture. The subject is provisionally brought into being, defined by desire, seeking the fantasy of plenitude, as it reenacts, in its turn, the scene of its failure. It is to the screen that we turn to seek analgesia, relief from the pain of our ruined subjectivity. Fassbinder's films appear to take this nonliteral ruin as their project as well as their object: they destabilize and denaturalize familiar epistemological structures and the machinery of subject constitution. With the BRD trilogy, Fassbinder seems to enter into a constitutive abyss in which epistemology and, hence, knowledge or representation are fragmented and incoherent, and the only possible subjectivity is a frankly performative one. This creates a paradox that is an ethical and aesthetic necessity: the only imperative of representation is to fail *as* representation.

Die Ehe der Maria Braun begins and ends with literal ruin: physical destruction frames the film and is a crucial part of the mise-en-scène. The film, taking us from Maria's marriage under a rain of bombs in a collapsing registry office to her death in a gas explosion that shatters her house, presents subjectivity as ruptured, symbolically in ruins like the literal ruin that acts as frame. *Maria Braun* parallels the "miracle" of the reconstruction of the Federal Republic of Germany from the rubble of the Third Reich with the equally miraculous construction of a new subjectivity. Like most miracles, however, this one does not stand up to close scrutiny. At the beginning of the film, behind the credits, there is a long, straightforward shot of a portrait of Adolf Hitler hanging on the wall of the registry office in which Maria is attempting to be married. Fassbinder opens with an iconic representation of the Nazi past, one that provides a crucial clue to the unstable, "jerry-built," always-already-collapsing subjectivity that is at the center of his vision of postwar Germany. In the psychic economy of the Nazi state, Hitler seemingly promised an unproblematic, unitary subjectivity. The iconic figure of Hitler is essential to the mechanism of narcissistic identification. Fassbinder shows us Nazism, through the image of Hitler, as offering a way to deny the trauma of subjectivity, providing a specular universe in which the inevitable wound of separation is anesthetized within a fantasy economy from which all traces of alterity—any reminders of difference, with its ceaseless salting of the wound—are ruthlessly banished, "vernichtet" with the body of the dead Jew of the Final Solution. Yet, this "Endlösung" failed to finally bury the threat to a specular subject. The portrait of Hitler at the opening of the film, therefore, with its vanished promise of narcissistic, specular plenitude emphasizes the bankruptcy of the postwar subject. Alterity has arrived with a vengeance. The former models of subjectivity lie in the rubble with the portrait of the Führer; the narcissistic wound is open and bleeding.

In Fassbinder's *Die Sehnsucht der Veronika Voss* (1982), spectatorship and analgesia are closely linked.[1] Pain is a crucial and excruciating element in this film; the desire or longing of the title is, perhaps, the desire for freedom from pain, the longing for analgesia. When Frau Dr. Katz dispenses, in her all-white clinic, doses of morphine to her wealthy and addicted patients, it is to alleviate an undefined, and perhaps indefinable, but still agonizing ache. When asked if the pain experienced by her patients is "real," or if the "condition" is curable, Dr. Katz's reply is ambiguous. The pain that is so indeterminate yet so central to all the action in *Veronika Voss* is not "curable" precisely because it is part of the constitution of both subjectivity and spectatorship.

The film, from its opening moments, invites us to contemplate our own "Sehnsucht," the compelling longing and desire—our own need, perhaps, to anesthetize the traumatic wounds—with which we approach the image on the screen. Our presence as spectators is "coded in" to the screen image, the distinction between spectator and spectacle virtually erased, from the first scene of the film. In a kind of mise en abîme, we watch the film's protagonist—an actress past her prime—sitting in a darkened movie theater watching herself perform a snippet of melodrama in which a drug-addicted actress gazes at the morphine she desperately needs, and speaks a line that will be repeated later in this film; we enter into a kind of infinite loop of possible subject positions in which all the options—audience, actress, fictive character, "real" person, tormented addict, dedicated film consumer—are all interchangeable. To complicate matters further, Fassbinder includes his own image in this scene, both as one of "us"—an audience surrogate—and as part of the spectacle, as he leans forward with a slightly sinister geniality in the seat behind Veronika, contemplating the movie screen. Both Veronika and Fassbinder himself appear, simultaneously, as integral to the spectacle and as its absorbed consumers. Like Veronika, we gaze upon ourselves; we seek, once more, to misrecognize the unitary subject, gratifyingly whole and unwounded. Even as we approach the screen seeking analgesia, however, this opening scene, in its foregrounding of this very desire, serves notice that no analgesia will be forthcoming. Fassbinder does not offer us a seamless diegesis to which we can surrender; rather, he repeatedly opens gaps in that diegesis, exposing the film as artifact and more or less arbitrary construction, highlighting it as representation, and forcing us to contemplate the fissures in the images that we see. Like Veronika, seeking to exchange a glance of recognition with her own image on screen, we long for completeness, for a narcissistic unity in which there is no distinction between subject and object, self and other. Ultimately, however, neither director offers us any satisfaction of our desire; instead, they both bring us repeatedly to the scene of its failure and of our loss.

The first words of dialogue in *Die Sehnsucht der Veronika Voss* are, characteristically, mediated twice, as part of the film within a film with which Fassbinder opens. A woman on the screen within a screen, spotlighted in intense chiaroscuro, only her face illuminated, says: "Help me, help me. I can't stand the pain. The pain. It's tearing me apart. Have mercy." This statement signifies in several systems simultaneously: it is the plea of a desperate woman in morphine withdrawal within two diegetic worlds, the two films, which are both, at this point, unfamiliar to us. In a sense, neither film is yet privileged: we don't know what the relationship between them will be. The opening statement is also of intense interest to surrogates who are both within and outside these diegeses: the audience on screen, the presumed audience watching the Fassbinder film, and the director's representation of himself, which may or may not be readable as such by any given audience member. This statement of pain is presented—within, as it were, quotation marks—using conventional elements from melodrama that both heighten the emotional impact of the words and dilute it, acting as a defamiliarization device. The complex mise en abîme within which this opening sequence is contextualized, and the obtrusive use of distinctive, stylistic elements associated with a particular film genre, put us on notice that one of the main things with which this film concerns itself is the nature of film itself.[2] A statement of intense pain, of unbearable need, both introduces and suffuses the obsessively self-referential circling at the core of *Die Sehnsucht der Veronika Voss*. Fassbinder asks us to look at ourselves looking at cinema, to consider all the elements of its representation, through a lens flooded from the outset by pain and longing. Pain is the condition by which we see; it is as foundational to this film as the lighting, itself a major element in Fassbinder's self-referential spiral.

After the elegant, retro-chic 1950s-style credits—which appear to be raised letters lit from above, casting shadows on a blank background—Fassbinder gives us a shot of the movie theater from the back, over the heads of an anonymous, and rather sparse, audience. The action on the theater screen—a long shot of a long shot—is initially difficult to follow. We see two figures struggling: one dressed in white and the other in black. The shadows of the credit sequence are echoed by a large, cross-shaped shadow looming behind the two figures, dominating the space. This almost absurdly overdetermined symbol is diegetically inexplicable in terms of the action that we see on the screen-within-a-screen. Only later do we realize that it is the shadow of a mock-up of a mullioned window on the mock-up of the sound-stage that Fassbinder has erected on his own sound stage; he has the director of his fictional melodrama echoing—shadowing—his own distinctive propensity for obtrusively mediated shots, filmed through windows, railings, in mirrors or through glass, a propensity that is characteristically evident in *Die Sehnsucht der Veronika Voss*.

In many ways this giant cross in shadow is a fitting opening for this film; it suggests a strategy of excessive signification, a semiotic flooding of the screen with an immoderate, undisciplined profusion of possible meanings, refusing ultimately to privilege any one semantic context or approach. One area of indeterminacy specifically relates to the history of cinema: like Bernardo Bertolucci, Billy Wilder, and Carol Reed, Fassbinder never allows us to come to rest comfortably in any one cinematic style or idiom, keeping us teetering uneasily on the border between film genres, from noir thriller to 1930s melodrama to Sirk-like 1950s-style high romance.[3]

Just as important are the shadows and echoes of history of a different type: the film is full of shadows and "ghosts" of all kinds, from a past that the present cannot leave behind, despite its best efforts. If Bertolucci's *La strategia del ragno* is a challenge to the prevailing Italian discourse about fascism and the resistance, then Fassbinder's film also enters into the debate about historiography in Germany. In the Germany of Adenauer, the period depicted in *Veronika Voss*, the Nazi past is rigorously excluded from discussion; Fassbinder's work was an important part of the retrospective engagement with Nazism that began in the early 1980s.[4] The character of Veronika, with her faded Nazi-era glamour, epitomizes the return of an unwished-for but still alluring past, one that exerts a strong hold on the world of the present.[5]

The shadow of the cross, therefore, like the shadow in the credits, opens *Veronika Voss* with an intimation of the many shadows haunting this film. By shadowing his opening scene with the symbol of Christianity, Fassbinder is letting us know that religious discourse and imagery are major contexts within which the symbolic language of the film must be understood. In a sense, all explanatory or teleological narratives are equivalent in the economy of the film: Christianity emerges as one of many discursive matrixes, in uneasy dialogue with Nazism and with the messy amalgam that is postwar democratic society. Fassbinder's use of Christianity as a major symbolic matrix for the film is characteristically transgressive, often aggressive, and always highly ironic; it is also associated with a wide and contradictory variety of affective responses, ranging from scathing contempt to compassion. The appearance of the large cross (which relative to the human figures on the screen would be just the right size for a crucifixion) signals the true nature of the excruciating fiction of *Die Sehnsucht der Veronika Voss*. In the broadest sense, this film is about resurrection, albeit with a distinctly dark twist: Veronika, the Nazi-era film star, and the world of Nazi culture that she represents have risen from the grave and are walking, alarmingly but perhaps inevitably, through the streets and cultural spaces of postwar Munich.[6] As a revenant, she is singularly unsettling: her presence in the postwar city evokes longings, desires, and allegiances that would be better kept dead and buried.

The opening sequence of *Die Sehnsucht der Veronika Voss*, in which the cross first appears, is built around Veronika's encounter with her image on screen, as is a later scene in a jewelry store. The precarious relationship between image and reality—and "reality" is always a slippery concept at best—is announced from the beginning as a central problematic of the film. The film's title, and the name of its protagonist, establish Fassbinder's preoccupation with the nature of the image and places this preoccupation within a discursive context based, once more—ambivalently and ironically, as always—on Christianity. The name "Veronika" refers, itself, to the events surrounding Christ's suffering and death. It was the name of the woman who, in the gospel accounts of the crucifixion, wiped the sweat from Christ's brow with a cloth, which then bore the image of his face.[7] This supposedly authentic cloth—interpreted, like the shroud of Turin, as a sort of super-icon, an image that bore a direct, rather than a mimetic relation to the body of Christ, of divine, or at least miraculous, origin—subsequently became a well-known devotional relic, known as the sudarium.[8] This vernicle—a medieval term, the name of the saint later being transmuted into a noun describing this kind of image—is uniquely privileged: it is indexical in the purest sense. The image that it carries originates from the bodily presence of the person it represents; there is literally no separation between image and referent because the image is composed of the physical substance of what it depicts. The vernicle is materiality directly transmuted into image, with no gap or mediation between reality and representation. It is highly suggestive that Fassbinder incorporates this echo, the complex metaphor of the vernicle, into the title of *Die Sehnsucht der Veronika Voss*. Like the sudarium, Fassbinder's title bears a trace: it is about the longing for the perfect image, one that would seamlessly join representation and reality, overcoming the inevitable loss, the sadness and mourning, experienced because the image inevitably fails to satisfy this desire. The longing of the title, therefore, as well as the longings overtly present in the film's story—for example, the cravings of drug addiction or the desire of a former start to reexperience the fame of her heyday—also can be read as the longing that cinema awakens, and the analgesia that it appears to offer but fails to deliver. The longing of Veronika is to perfectly embody her name, to become a vernicle. Her desire is to overcome the split between subject and object, to recognize herself perfectly in the image as mirror, experiencing perfect identity between the two; she wishes to see herself and her image as, to use Bertolucci's phrase, "uguale, uguale." The identity Veronika longs for, the eternal goal of her perpetually failing comeback, is in fact the identity between image and reality, the seamless unity of flesh and icon.

Veronika is recognized as she moves within the city by a select few. Those who know her—as evident in a chance encounter in a jeweler's shop—respond with a surreally fierce and almost frightening loyalty and, paradoxically, a deeply peremptory deference: it is as if, in being recognized as a resurrected presence and figuratively asked "quo vadis," it is Veronika herself, the Christ stand-in, rather than any version of Peter, who is sent back to her torment, to be crucified anew. Veronika's body, apparently unaltered, matches in the flesh a treasured photograph of her in her heyday and is a sign of the possibility of a larger resurrection, a return to an earlier time, that of the Nazi period. Instead of having her resurrected status confirmed by having a finger thrust, by a doubting St. Thomas, into her wound, she is presented with a photographic portrait of herself as an UFA star, reinterpellated into that role in by a sinister admirer who has no doubts at all. If anything, the roles are reversed: it is Veronika who doubts or—like Christ—wishes to escape, and her interlocutor who aggressively enforces her status as revenant, the incarnation of the destroyed past reappearing alive in the present.

In the scene in the jeweler's shop, Veronika is running a scam: she is returning for cash a brooch she has demanded that Robert Krohn pay for. Ultimately, it is recognition that allows her scam to succeed, giving her money for the drugs that she so desperately needs. However, it is clear that, much as she desires fame and recognition, it is double edged. Her image, with which she comes literally face-to-face once more in this scene, is a sign that exerts a peremptory force.[9] Much of the scene with the jewelry store owner, an ardent admirer of her earlier work who steps in to facilitate Veronika's transaction, is shot from below, through the glass of the jewelry display case that also serves as a counter. It is a very unsettling angle, and it creates a disorienting, subtly disquieting effect that is typical of Fassbinder's work. The shot distorts space, placing the body of Veronika on the same plane and in the same scale as the objects in the display case; the jewelry seems massively enlarged, suspended around Veronika's head and face. We see Veronika's body from the knees up, clad in an elegant fur coat; the edge of the counter forms a visible line that appears to cut right across her throat. Her head is surrounded by necklaces, giving the effect of chains. They perfectly frame her face so that she seems to be looking through a perforated screen; one necklace, a chain with heavy, thick links, appears to lead away from her neck like a dog's leash. As the store owner (played, in another interesting twist, by Fassbinder's mother, Lilo Pempeit, the revenant, perhaps from his personal past) recognizes her, saying Veronika's name, she moves into the shot, until she is standing next to Veronika with her face partially obscured by the chains that frame the other woman's features. The shop owner says: "You remember, don't you? 1944, I think, in Berlin." She walks out of the shot. We see Veronika, through the glass panes, turn her head, which still appears cut off at the neck by the line of the counter, and look out of the space of the shot to her left. Near her left shoulder, just below the line of her gaze, the clamp that holds the panes of the counter together seems to float; it forms a cross. Veronika, looking at what we later realize is her picture, says, "yes, I remember." She proceeds to correct the dates—it was 1943, not 1944—and seems transfixed as the shopkeeper says: "I remember it as if it were yesterday."

Figure 5.1 *Die Sehnsucht der Veronika Voss*: Veronika seen through the display case.

The photograph seems to offer almost unmediated access to the past—it transmutes 1943 into "yesterday" and, by its very presence erases the boundary between past and present. The image and its wielder, the shop owner, seem to possess all the agency in this sequence, and Veronika is merely reactive, as she backs across the shop pursued by her photograph. If, in other scenes, Veronika appears to be more or less in control of the production of herself as image, here the image is a trap.[10] She is confronted with a vision of herself that she both desires deeply and fears: she incarnates the image, as icon made flesh. There is no distinction between image and reality here, between representation and original, or between present and past. The portrait is one of the few things the shopkeeper has recovered from the rubble of Nazi-era Munich—it embodies loss and, at the same time, the return of that which has been lost. The lost object reappears without curing in any way the pain of the original loss—if anything, it intensifies it. The photograph seems to dictate Veronika's identity, constructing reality rather than reflecting or representing it. It exerts a peremptory force, from which Veronika retreats, but cannot escape.

In the distorted space of the shot through the display case, flanked by the metal clamp that forms a cross at her left shoulder, Veronika is given to us in the full regalia, both tongue in cheek and tragic, of her sacrificial role. The cross that appeared in the first sequence, presiding over Veronika's encounter with her own image in the movie theater, reemerges here to contextualize this second meeting with herself as symbol, as icon of a past that is worshipped and longed for, and always about to merge with the present. The references to the movements and interactions of the resurrected Christ that appear throughout *Die Sehnsucht der Veronika Voss* are very evident in this scene. The cross, as perhaps the most overdetermined signifier possible, a sign within which multiple meanings can be compressed, is singularly appropriate as a metaphor for the suffering we see so often in this film. As we discover later, through Robert Krohn's conversations with the chillingly dispassionate Dr. Katz in her bleached white clinic, what Veronika and Dr. Katz's other patients experience is pain, pure and simple. This pain, according to her physician, is without determinable cause—it is neither psychic nor physical—but is "real" because it is experienced as such. From the first sequence of the film—the movie theater scene—it is evident that confronting her own image causes Veronika intense pain. We see her in the theater, sitting in front of Fassbinder who is an apparently enthralled spectator, appearing to suffer physically at the sight of herself. She closes her eyes in pain. As she sits with her eyes closed, she hears "herself" say, on the old soundtrack, "I will give you everything I possess, everything I am…Everything." Here, Veronika (or at least, the image of Veronika— again, the complex relationship between image and reality is established early as a major focus of the film as a whole) declares herself as sacrificial. After receiving the drug (and muttering a guttural "Danke" as the needle penetrates her body), she says, "I have nothing to offer you but my death." (Her "danke" has distinct erotic overtones: for Fassbinder, characteristically, the passion of Veronika Voss is sexual and masochistic as well as biblical.) This statement, again offering her suffering as sacrificial, her death given to and for someone else, is greeted by the needle-wielding doctor with a cynical: "thank you. Cheap gifts like this I can do without."

Veronika emerges here as a notably debased Christ figure: her agony and death are a worthless gift. In fact, the film she is shooting in the flashback is called "Insidious Poison;" poison is, of course, "Gift" in German. This bilingual pun in the title of the film-within-a-film captures the essence of the film that we are watching. Fassbinder's own insidious strategy in creating a metadiscourse about cinema as part of its (slightly) more overt discourse about history, guilt, and repression is a decidedly mixed gift. Veronika, as our representative, gives "everything" in exchange for analgesia, the surge of release, however fleeting, provided by morphine. As we see "ourselves" sitting in the movie theater as an absorbed audience—along, of course, with the director as avid cinema fan—we are, perhaps, making a similar bargain: we also desperately desire analgesia. An attempt to reconfigure the conditions of subjectivity to heal the wound that Veronika, as icon and sacrifice, embodies for us is what brings us to the theater, and we are willing to surrender to the insidious gifts of cinema to attain it.

The doctor's dismissive line in the melodrama is spoken as a sound bridge, as Fassbinder cuts away from the scene in the theater to another disorienting, uncontextualized image: we are confronted with a wall of lights, blinding in their intensity, through which we can barely make out Veronika. Like Bertolucci, Sanders-Brahms, and Resnais, Fassbinder flashes back and forward in time without providing signposts for the audience—we are always disoriented temporally, as we try to follow these films that focus in large part on the thorny relationship between past and present. It is only as we hear a voice calling "cut!" and another calling the title of the film and the number of the take that we realize that we are seeing a flashback to the earlier life of the woman we have seen on screen twice over. The number of takes—five—is low: this prewar Veronika does not need to work to achieve perfect authenticity. We are returning, in this first flashback, to her moment of wholeness, now irrecoverably lost, in which there was no gap between image and reality, but an easy, inevitable seamlessness. The contrast to the scene we see her shoot in the post-Nazi world, in which she goes through take after take, muffing her lines and unable even to simulate the appropriate emotion, is marked. In this first flashback, we see the presence of everything that Veronika, in the aftermath of Nazism, has lost. She has acclaim, love—an attentive screenwriter husband—and perfect lighting. Everything in her life, whether in her public or private worlds, contributes to making her the perfect creature for celluloid.

The mediated selfhood that defined Veronika in the fascist past contained no lies: her life on screen and in the flesh were one. The nimbus of light that surrounded her, and displayed her to ideal advantage, was arranged for her, following her almost automatically—she did not have to choreograph an imperfect simulacrum of it by having faintly contemptuous waiters turn off lamps and light candles, as she does in the later scenes. What has been lost, then, is clear: the postwar Veronika has fallen out of a quasi-Edenic feeling of unity and wholeness into the experience of herself as imperfect, fractured, and divided subject. Her fall from an illusory unity—it was, after all, merely a studio simulation of a self—and her ill-fated attempts to return to this earlier state are cast in terms of cinema. Both Veronika's prewar completeness, and her damaged post-lapsarian, post-Nazi self are explored through the metaphor of film. She turns to film to assuage the pain of the loss of specular unity; we do the same thing, as we watch her watching the film within a film. In this, she is our proxy and our sacrifice. It is to the movie theater and to the film set that she comes to look for lost Edens, and they both let her down: she closes her eyes in enormous pain as a spectator of her past glory, and the failed attempt to shoot a movie scene leads to her collapse, writhing on the floor in pain, until she can get a shot of morphine.

Veronika's suffering, her *Leidenschaft*, is absolute and irredeemable. Rather than any kind of redemption—a notion both ridiculous and poignant, repellent and alluring, as is Veronika herself—torment and resurrection, passion and sacrifice in *Die Sehnsucht der Veronika Voss* lead only to repetition. There is no story that will redeem the past in the present or resignify the relationship between the two. The concept of expiation is at the heart of the narrative of Christianity; here, suffering as redemptive is a concept raised by the presence of Christian imagery from the first moments of the film. Its treatment, however, is very much tongue in cheek: Veronika is a distinctly unlikely Christ-figure. As Veronika commits suicide in her locked room at Dr. Katz's clinic, we hear church bells and a blessing in Latin on the radio. By giving us death on Easter Sunday, Fassbinder again casts Veronika in the Christ role, but with a distinct difference. Rather than dying on Good Friday and being resurrected on Easter, Veronika offers a compressed version of the two states. Her death and resurrection are equivalent because she is already the embodiment of both: she was already dead, as incarnation of the lost past, and already resurrected, as revenant. She has inhabited and unsettled the living world after her symbolic death for much longer than the crucified Christ's brief visitations to his disciples in Christian mythology. Fassbinder does suggest—in a typically ambiguous and ambivalent way—that Veronika's agony is sacrificial: she suffers as a representative of a Germany in which present and past ceaselessly bleed into each other. Her image is both a catalyst and a sign of that bleeding: whether imprinted on celluloid and projected on screen or reproduced and framed as a photograph, it acts almost as a solvent to dissolve the boundary between past and present.

We are not in any way, however, offered Veronika's suffering as redemptive of the crimes of Nazism: that would be altogether too simple an analogy for this highly complex film. In fact, her addiction and torment are multifaceted and polysemic. Veronika's agony, and her craving for the analgesia provided by morphine, can be read in multiple contexts. The cross that looms so obtrusively at the beginning of the film, and returns again to gloss Veronika's second encounter with her own image, is simultaneously a red herring and absolutely crucial to this excruciating story: it is an announcement of the strategy of rhetorical and semiotic excess, the messy profusion of signifiers and interpretive matrixes in which no single term or context prevails. The ambiguity of this sign suits the ambivalence with which Fassbinder seems to view his protagonist. His approach to her and her suffering is contradictory, both scathingly cynical and deeply compassionate. The film's title points to Veronika's longings, her unsatisfiable desires; these can be defined, at least in part, as due to the pain caused by the wounds of difference and subjectivization, the disjunction between image and referent, subject and object. In this, she fulfills the part of a sacrificial being: she distills the narcissistic, melancholic psychic formations with which postwar Germany approaches loss, the loss of the specular structures that tended to shape subjectivity in the Nazi era.[11] Veronika's pain is unhealable because it is representative of foundational structures of the self. Fassbinder gives us an off-kilter passion play, a story of sacrificial death, of unbearable suffering and (dubious) resurrection, the passion of Veronika Voss.

If the distinction between subject and object is at the core of any acceptance of difference, of the realization of alterity, we see in *Veronika Voss* a style of subjectivity in which there is no gap, however illusory, between self and other. The aching wound of difference is barely bandaged over, as Veronika seeks always to return to this narcissistic paradise, to a state in which there is no separation of self and other, As both Elsaesser and Silverman have pointed out, she is always in the act of seeing herself; whether there is a screen in front of her or not, she perpetually contemplates her own image, conceiving of herself as a creature composed of light and shadow, commenting on the lighting wherever she is, and adjusting it to maximum advantage.[12] She seeks to literally occupy the roles of subject and object simultaneously, eliminating the difference between them and, therefore, difference itself. As in *Die Ehe der Maria Braun*, in which the image of Hitler in the opening shot suggests the lost specular fantasy represented by the fascist state, Fassbinder turns again in *Veronika Voss* to the Nazi past to suggest the longed for world that Veronika is trying to regain.[13] As Alice Kuzniar points out, she represents continuity with fascism as she attempts to live in the 1950s as she did on the UFA screen, provoking among the fans who recognize her a nostalgia for fascism. One of the pieces of information that Robert Krohn, the reporter who is Veronika's lover and the film's male protagonist, uncovers in his cursory "investigation" of her life is her status as a Nazi screen icon—we hear that there was talk of an affair with Goebbels.

The change that has occurred by 1955, when the film is set, is painfully evident in a scene in which Veronika is shooting a small part in a new film, a considerable comedown in status. (To add insult to injury, she is cast as the mother of the romantic lead.) The script calls for tears, which Veronika cannot produce. She bemoans the fact that in the old days she could always feel the appropriate emotion and cry when required. Then, there was no distinction between her subjective experience of emotion and the representation of emotion in her image; her self—the subject—and the image of herself that she produced and surveyed—the object—formed an organic whole. In the postfascist world, this becomes problematic, even as she continually tries to reenact the wholeness. Eventually, rather than submit to the indignity of a glycerin tear applied by the makeup department, a vulgar simulacrum of the unity that was once so effortless, she collapses and is returned to the tender care of Dr. Katz for her analgesic "treatment." The irony here is clear; the nature of her pain, for which she needs morphine, is signaled by her inability to embody, by crying for the camera, the image of pain—and the management of her own image is Veronika's constant fixation, both on and off camera, whether the image is imprinted on celluloid or merely on the retinas of others. Self and image, subject and object are no longer seamless; in fact, they are in conflict. Only Dr. Katz's needle can anesthetize the trauma of this rupture.

The site of the anesthetizing treatments, Dr. Katz's clinic, appears to be a place in which difference has been eradicated. This is signaled by Fassbinder's use of whiteness, a lack of color that is both absolute and appalling. Elsaesser refers to *Die Sehnsucht der Veronika Voss* as a "film blanc," playing on the idea of film noir, a genre to which, along with several others, Fassbinder is clearly referring. Indeed, whiteness suffuses the film as Fassbinder pushes the black and white in which he has chosen to work to its extreme, making the stark, blinding lack of color—an absence that becomes a dominating presence—an essential element. In the clinic, there are not even shadows: they disappear in blinding whiteness. It is interesting that there is a figure who might appear to represent both racial and sexual difference—a black male American soldier, played by Günther Kaufmann, one of Fassbinder's long-term lovers—whose dark skin and uniform provide the most noticeable nonwhite elements in several scenes. He poses no real threat to the economy of sameness, however. Rather than being disruptive, his blackness serves to reinforce the extreme whiteness that surrounds him. This character's diegetic function is never made clear: he might, it seems, be employed packaging and delivering morphine. Perhaps, along with the country and Western music that plays ceaselessly on the clinic's radio, he is there primarily as a symbolic representative of America, of the international culture of spectacle to which Veronika refers in a flashback to her heyday, when we see her state her intention to make films for the American "dream factory." Hollywood too, Fassbinder suggests, invites us to engage in the sort of specular dialogue in which we, like Veronika, can try to regain our shattered narcissistic paradise, to anesthetize our wounds; it offers, like Dr. Katz, the hope of analgesia. Fassbinder, however, strips away even the mirage of pain-free bliss, confronting us both with the intensity of our trauma, and the impossibility of achieving our desire. We hope to misrecognize ourselves, yearn to find in that reflected mutual glance our fantasy of plenitude, unity, and mastery, but we find ourselves staring instead into the abyss of our failure as stable subjects. As the cloying country and Western soundtrack we hear in the clinic informs us, we have "sold [our] soul to the company store:" we are addicted to the illusory analgesia offered to us by cinema, and willingly in thrall to the "dream machine." We step through the ruins of the specular edifice, in a complex dance of spectacle and substitution, finding only fissure and fragmentation, the unhealable wound for which no analgesia is possible.

The male protagonist of *Die Sehnsucht der Veronika Voss*, the sports reporter Robert Krohn, has a relationship to Germany's Nazi past that is no less complex than that of Veronika. Robert's work seems to raise past specters, traces of vanished times and people, with some frequency, despite its ostensibly apolitical and unintellectual nature. A nimbus of history—the trace of losses and victories, crimes and attempted rationalizations, often emerging in seemingly trivial contexts—seems to surround Robert. He is younger than Veronika; although we never find out his exact age, he is presumably too young to have been complicit, as an adult, to the crimes of the Nazi regime. However, if Robert is in his 30s in 1955, as he appears to be, he would have been a young adult, and presumably of military age, during the war; the specifics of his past are not revealed in the film but there is definitely some ambiguity. Certainly no hint emerges of his hobnobbing with the Nazi elite, as Veronika is rumored to have done. Robert appears, however, to be as profoundly defined by the loss of a deeply desired past as Veronika, although perhaps his lost Eden is more inchoate than hers.

A naturalized masculine subjectivity seems to be among the primary losses for Robert. He lingers morosely and ineffectually on the fringes of a potentially hypermasculine world, the sports field, that could conceivably offer a masculine identity matching the one on offer in the mythologies of Nazi society, but is ultimately only a pale substitute for the requisite battlefield. "Loss" and "losing" are words that seem especially associated with him, that come up often around him, as do their opposites, "triumph" and "victory." Robert's job as a sports reporter brings him into a world in which winning and losing are clearly defined; sport—and, of course, its association with the Nazi regime—is part of the context in which the character of Robert must be read. A colleague at his office at the newspaper, Grete, makes fun of him for the simplicity of his black-and-white universe of winners and losers, expressing surprise that he should be interested in a figure associated with the arts like Veronika Voss, of interest only to "culture vultures." However, this apparent clarity begins to take on an almost parodic quality as the concepts of victory and loss develop complex and contradictory meanings. Later in the same conversation, Robert says to Grete, describing Veronika: "she belongs among the losers." Robert identifies loss as what defines the appeal of Veronika: she carries loss with her, trailing the vestiges of everything she has been and represented, and that has been lost. Robert's fascination with her seems to be centered on how she handles the problematic of loss: by her existence as revenant, the past returning to the present, she embodies both loss and its denial. In this sense, she is a consummate melancholic figure: if the lost object is incorporated into the self, if there is no separation between subject and object, then the object can never be truly lost, never truly belong to the past. This melancholic structure is the essence, perhaps, of Veronika's strange appeal; it makes her the perfect object of desire for a man who is suffused by unacknowledged loss.

Robert's first extended conversation with Veronika takes place at a restaurant called "Privileg;" it is an ornate courtyard space with dramatic sightlines, the space in which Veronika most explicitly "directs" herself as image, rearranging the lighting and proclaiming herself as a creature of celluloid, "a woman of light and shadows." If, for Veronika, this encounter represents the opportunity to attempt to overcome the gap between image and representation, between subject and object, and to live up to her name by becoming in truth a "vernicle," for Robert it offers a chance to escape loss. Veronika offers him, quite explicitly, a new "mirror" within which to (mis)recognize himself: this is to be his "privilege." She invites him into the circle of light she orchestrates for herself, offers to envelop him in her aura as a celluloid creature—she will make him into the leading man she deserves. Characteristically, the hapless Robert initially appears confused by Veronika's attention, her invitation to him to look at her and help bring her back into being in a state in which she is absolutely congruent with her image. The script that she attempts to ventriloquize through Robert is one that appears to deny, or even to defeat, loss. Veronika begins her attempt to provide an appropriate character for Robert by asking him about his work, stating what appears to be both a sexual and an epistemological credo: "You're a sports reporter. That must be exciting. . . . People who fight are always exciting. Victories are exciting. Defeats . . ." (She leaves the last word hanging, with a blank expression on her face.) Veronika's words are an epistemological statement, in that she is evoking a world without the knowledge of loss: loss, and the related word defeat, here become a highly mobile term, sliding through a range of meanings, trailing echoes of different contexts.

Fassbinder's selection of terminology for this crucial piece of dialogue is suggestive. He uses *kämpfen*—to fight, or struggle—which is clearly not a neutral choice, or one that can be limited to one meaning or context: Hitler's manifesto, *Mein Kampf,* comes immediately to mind, especially given Veronika's Nazi past. Victory and glorious struggle—with a unambiguous element of Nazi-flavored eroticism mixed in—are the only reality; defeat cannot even be used in a sentence, but is left suspended, bereft of syntactical context and disavowed. (The word used is *Niederlagen*, a noun based in metaphor: to be below.) Fassbinder also invokes another highly overdetermined word: *Siegen* (victories). One might be surprised to hear

Siegen in this context—the word more commonly associated with sport, at least as a verb, is *gewinnen*, which does not drag along quite the same trail of associations. *Siegen* is a word very closely linked with militarism and nationalism throughout German history, and especially with the language of Nazi Germany. Even more, perhaps, than *Kampf, Sieg* is a word that is universally recognized, even by non-German speakers, as an essential element in the rhetoric of Nazism, as in the all-too-familiar (and cinematically beloved) phrase *Sieg heil!* When Veronika says, in the next sentence, "tell me about your victories" ("Erzähl mir von Ihren Siegen"), she is literally scripting dialogue for Robert and inviting him to enter into a very specific kind of narrative. Robert, hapless as always, misses his cue, and steps back from this opportunity, saying: "My life's pretty humdrum. No victories, no defeats, anymore." The word "anymore" is interesting here, however: it places Robert's statement in a temporal context, suggesting that the root of his problems are, like Veronika's, connected to the relationship between past and present, to history and memory.

This disavowal, though apparently oblivious, seems to be the beginning of Robert's deep fascination with Veronika; he may be late in taking up her offer, but it has deep power for him. She is offering him a role—again, literally—in her world, and analgesia is part of the package. While he may not need to seek out the needle of the good Dr. Katz, he can attempt to escape his melancholic life, in which he is reacting to some inchoate loss but unable, like Veronika, to separate himself from what is lost to allow, in psychoanalytic terms, genuine mourning. He has constructed his life around a pallid recreation of the struggles and victories of Germany's past, the glorious *Kampf* and *Sieg* invoked in Veronika's invitation. Instead of the battlefield, he inhabits the soccer field; instead of experiencing a great love, he shares his bed with a woman with whom he, as he informs Veronika, "gets along." Robert's work is a sad simulacrum of what might have been past glory. As a sports reporter, he is peripheral even to this colorless, bloodless reproduction of war—an observer, not a participant in the "struggle." He doesn't move away from this unsatisfying reenactment; instead, he returns to reminders of the loss.

Veronika is clearly presenting Robert with a rescripting of his rather tattered masculinity as part of the analgesia package. Their first encounter, when he comes upon her weeping in the rain after she has walked out of the movie theater showing her film, begins with a scripted masculine gallantry that involves direct citation of very specific past models. He offers the soaking wet Veronika the protection of his umbrella: she in turn offers him lines from a familiar and preexisting dialogue, acting as ventriloquist and making him her dummy. (This seems to be a chronic position for Robert.) She says, smiling, and he repeats, smiling back, the phrase "Schirm und

Schutz," literally translatable as "umbrella and protection." Robert here is given another Robert, Robert Schumann, to cite and hence become: the phrase is a quote from Schumann's song, "O Freund, mein Schirm, mein Schutz."[14] Schumann evidently wrote this song as a love offering to his wife, Clara; Fassbinder is referring here, therefore, to one of the most mythologized love stories of German culture, with Robert Krohn cast as the great composer and lover. By introducing herself to Robert by offering him this role and ventriloquizing these words through him—as well as by appearing to regard his job as a sports reporter as the epitome of masculine struggle, the equivalent of glorious war—she offers him a mirror in which he can gaze on himself gazing on her; it allows him to see himself, to paraphrase Virginia Woolf's sardonic summary of one of the intangible benefits of masculinity, reflected at twice his natural size.

Veronika also reintroduces into Robert's life the possibility of a more "satisfying" performance of gender difference—that is, one in which the pain that any kind of difference at all, the rupture in narcissistic wholeness and unity that difference represents, is repressed. This is a specular structure in which he can gaze on her as a perfect image. The "vernicle," which overcomes the gap between representation and reality, replicates the specular structure and the melancholy of wounded narcissism that psychoanalytic critics like the Mitscherlichs would argue is foundational to structures of loss in post-Nazi Germany. Robert should play the archetypal male—the "Sieger" rather than the eternal "Verlierer"—and gaze on Veronika, because of course every perfect image requires a qualified audience: the "vernicle" is only miraculous if it has appropriate worshippers. Robert's role is to abet Veronika in her desire to become the image perfected, as essence and representation united, and to help stabilize her inherently precarious achievement of this goal.

Robert is clearly frustrated—inchoately, as always—with his existence as a bad copy, with his world of pale simulacra and imperfect imitations of some kind of essential masculine identity. The illusion of a seamless subjectivity, the overcoming of loss at the core of the self, is what Veronika promises to him and, perhaps, the origin of his obsession with her. She will be the perfect image, and he will be the perfect spectator, confirming both her and himself with his gaze, looking at her as she looks at herself. Gender difference, then, is reinscribed and renaturalized through a process in which the pain of difference is repressed. This allows Robert, perhaps, to stop dimly sensing that he is a bad copy of that compelling (if illusory) figure, the "natural" masculine subject, and produces a more successful gender performance by both the male and the female. The Nazi specular economy created a structure of subjectivity in which difference was denied—"vernichtet," like the reviled Jew, and the gender or sexual "deviant." The interplay of gazes between Robert and Veronika accomplishes a targeted analgesia. The painkilling effects of morphine may be more direct, but this interpersonal exchange alleviates a similar agony. Like morphine, however, it offers only fleeting relief; the structures it creates are inherently unstable and must be repeatedly reinscribed.

Contained within the details of Robert's comings and goings as a sports reporter is, arguably, a microcosm of German history. These references appear in an almost offhand way, slipped in with the sly casualness characteristic of the embedded discourse about Germany's past in many of Fassbinder's films. Fassbinder was an ardent sports fan, especially of soccer, and sports appear repeatedly in his films.[15] (An especially well-known example occurs at the end of *Die Ehe der Maria Braun*; the radio broadcast of the World Cup championship won by the Federal Republic of Germany in 1954 blares on the soundtrack throughout the final scene, juxtaposed with Maria's ambiguous suicide or accidental death. After the explosion, Fassbinder shows us, with devastating irony, the rubble of Maria's luxurious villa, as the radio screams: "Deutschland ist Weltmeister!" "Germany is world champion."[16]) Fassbinder uses soccer in *Die Sehnsucht der Veronika Voss* in a similar way, as part of his complex exploration of issues of national identity. Both Robert's identity as a German in the post-Nazi society and his masculinity seem to be negotiated in his relationship to his job. The repeated mention of the 1860 soccer team from Munich, which seems to be Robert's primary "beat," is suggestive. The team is referred to in several conversations, and its stadium is the destination to which Robert heads at the end of the film, after Veronika's death—we hear him instructing the taxi driver to take him there. The 1860 team, from both Robert's and Fassbinder's home city, has an illustrious past, having been founded in the eponymous year and won several national championships.[17] Obviously, by these repeated references, which also name the decade in which Germany came into being as a united nation, Fassbinder is invoking Germany's imperial past—the team now known as TSV München 1860 rose shortly before Bismark's united Germany and remained an important presence on the national scene through the twentieth century. After the appropriation and reorganization of national sports teams as part of the propaganda efforts of the Third Reich, the team did well throughout the 1930s and gained a national championship in 1941. München 1860 was one of the cultural institutions—and there were many, whether athletic, corporate, or artistic—that flourished both in the Nazi era and in postwar Germany.

Fassbinder uses the team, therefore, as one more way to explore the persistence of the past into the present. Robert is just as much an agent by which the past steps into the present as Veronika; like Veronika, he is a dedicated consumer of mediated images, film, and still photographs—as are we, the audience, and Fassbinder as director, constituted as we are as scopophilic consumers in the opening film within a film, which colors everything that follows. Fassbinder shows us a framed portrait in connection with Robert, just as he does with Veronika: behind Robert's chair in the newspaper office hangs, somewhat precariously, a photograph that is approximately the size and shape of the one with which Veronika is confronted at the jewelry store. Instead, however, of being, as far as we can tell, an image of Robert himself—as, of course, the picture in the jewelry store is a head shot of Veronika herself—it is a portrait of a smiling, uniformed soccer player, appearing to resemble Fritz Walter, a star captain for TSV München 1860 after the war, who also played for the team in the 1930s. As Robert moves behind his desk to sit down, his head blocks our view of the photograph: it becomes, momentarily, a framed "head shot" of him. This image, a direct parallel to the one that confronts Veronika in the jewelry store, demonstrates, perhaps, that Robert engages in a similar re-cognition. He knows again his past, and the past of Germany, which reasserts itself through an image, an apparently unimportant piece of the mise-en-scène that echoes the publicity portrait that we have seen as icon and object of worship, and that unites past and present through and for Veronika.

The TSV München 1860 team also epitomizes in other ways the palimpsest—the interpenetration of layers in which the past is never truly absent—that characterizes postwar Germany, and gives added resonance to Fassbinder's exploration of this topic. In 1972, the official home of the team was moved from the old "Sechsiger Stadion" to the new Olympic Stadium—Fassbinder, as a Munich-based soccer fan, would presumably have been familiar with both. The Olympic Stadium was built for the 1972 Olympics, an event that was supposed to supersede in both national and international memory the 1936 Olympics. Rather than erasing the memory of the 1936 games, of course, the 1972 games reinforced it, as the venue for the terrorist attack on Israeli athletes, a new mass murder of Jews on German soil. The 1936 games were universally acknowledged as a triumph of Nazi propaganda (with the memorable exception of Jesse Owens' performance). They also represent an important moment in the history of cinema, through the brilliant filmmaking of Leni Riefenstahl's *Olympia*. By referring indirectly to the Olympics, therefore, Fassbinder is also invoking the dubious history of film and its success as the medium of choice for fascism.[18] The 1860 team, with its move to the Olympic Stadium, also opens up the memory of Nazism and war through its physical location— again, this would presumably have been familiar to German audiences. The new stadium, and its accompanying Olympic village with a park and lake, were built on a site used to store the debris from the wartime destruction of Munich. The rubble—mountains of material from collapsed buildings that were assumed also to contain body parts—was turned into a literal mountain, a central feature of the park. This "Trümmerberg," or "rubble mountain" overlooks the Olympic venues and, at least at one point, had a cross at its summit memorializing the unknown citizens of Munich probably interred within it.

Sports and film are indelibly connected by their shared function as highly successful propaganda tools deployed by fascism: in this sense, Robert, though he writes about sports in the 1950s, is the equivalent of Veronika, the walking embodiment of Nazism in the postwar world. If Veronika herself is a revenant, a creature from the past haunting the present, her swan song, "Memories Are Made of This"—here a self-description that captures her symbolic incarnation of the past—could also be used to describe soccer as it is deployed in *Die Sehnsucht der Veronika Voss*. The sport becomes, symbolically, a bridge between past and present, an occasion for temporal slippage and the interpenetration of different time periods. Sports also are intimately associated with spectatorship—and it is important to remember that Robert's role on the soccer field, that simulation of glorious *Kampf* and *Sieg*, is not as participant or actor, but as spectator and mediator. Spectator sports and the Nazi cinema—with its calculated deployment of spectatorship for political ends, to encourage the creation of the necessary styles of subjectivity—are inextricably entwined through the ghost of Riefenstahl and her archetypal *Olympia* films, arguably the origin of modern sports photography and very influential (though frequently disavowed) for filmmakers of all stripes. Veronika—a character Fassbinder has stated was loosely based on the Nazi-era film star Sybille Schmitz, whose postwar life had a trajectory much like that depicted in the film—also echoes Riefenstahl, a screen diva as an actress as well as one of the most influential directors, especially of documentary, in the history of cinema. She, too, was rumored to have had affairs with high-ranking Nazi ministers and spent her postwar years attempting to disavow, or at least distract attention from, her active complicity with the fascist regime. (Riefenstahl, unlike the fictional Veronika and the historical Schmitz, had the dubious fortune to survive through the end of the twentieth century, rather than suffering an early and glamorously tragic death.) The trace of Riefenstahl and the 1936 Olympics, then, enters the film through a complex temporal slippage, echoed in the 1860 soccer team that leads us back to Bismarck and Hitler, and forward to the modern Olympic Stadium in Munich, and from there to the murder of Jews (notwithstanding the important differences between Palestinian terrorists and Nazism) and the Final Solution, and finally to the rubble that dominated the urban landscapes of Germany after the war. Robert still inhabits that rubble.

The relationship between Robert and Veronika could be read as "Schutz und Schirm" for both, a pact to protect each other from the pain of loss, the loss that is both deeply personal and generalizable, paradigmatic of the situation of postwar Germany. The deal seems to include a more stable gender identity for both, the illusion, again, of a seamless, unfractured, "natural" subjectivity—one of the things, perhaps, that has been left behind in the rubble of the destruction of the Third Reich. We initially see Robert as dominated by strong female characters of a very "modern" type, independent and tough working women who feel free to ridicule and infantilize him. Grete, his colleague, can joke easily about drinking and sex and affects a world-weary cynicism with her rumpled clothing. Her teasing of Robert has a sharp edge, a friendly contempt. Fassbinder shoots the scene between them in a way that emphasizes the chaos of the newspaper office in which it is set: the camerawork is highly mobile, even disorienting, with much evidence of Fassbinder's predilection for shots through screening objects, often glass (dirty, in this case), that have the effect of denaturalizing space. There is action happening on several planes as people keep moving in and out of the shot, figures blocking our view and opening it up again in what appears to be random patterns, with unrelated sounds and conversations impinging on the soundtrack. The elements of the mise-en-scène for this sequence strongly suggest film noir, with bands of light and shade from Venetian blinds striping the walls, a blur of cigarette smoke, and moving shadows from ceiling fans swinging across the screen.

This scene's unmistakable quotation from a dominant postwar film genre (and an iconically American one at that) emphasizes that Robert, as a postwar male, is a denaturalized subject both in his national and in his gender identities. He is surrounded by signifiers that do not "fit" him, with cinematic elements that confuse us, and a visual framework drawn from a very specific cinematic context that is imported to Germany and, perhaps, demonstrates the absence of any viable German national culture in the 1950s. When we see Robert interacting with his girlfriend, Henriette—also strong, cynical, and rumpled—he is again contextualized by signifiers that suggest a bankrupt German culture. Henriette discovers a poem that Robert has been writing on his typewriter and snatches it away over his protests, teasing and laughing at him in an infantilizing way. (He, in response, behaves like a sulky child.) As well as being a warrior manqué—relegated to the fields of sport rather than the fields of battle— Robert turns out to be an artist manqué. The poem, which appears on the screen in a close-up of the sheet of paper, seems to be about memory and the past. In fact, although Robert appears to be the author of the poem (he tells Henriette: "I told you not to read my poetry!"), it turns out to be plagiarized. Whether the plagiarism is committed by Robert within the film's diegesis—which would make him a fraud, and also a poetic prophet—or the poem is simply appropriated extradiegetically by Fassbinder to make a point about language, literature, and history is not clear. The poem is a slightly rearranged version of one published in 1966 by Günter Eich, a well-known German poet strongly identified with the immediate postwar period; it is about the problematic nature of memory, the bleakness of postwar subjectivity, and the persistence of Nazi tropes.[19] As a "writer," Robert seems to enter into the world of the arts that Veronika inhabits, making him unexpectedly a "culture vulture," and suggesting depths that are invisible to others—at least, to Grete who has teased him about his lack of interest in anything less simplistic than sports. (Given the ineffectuality of Robert as a character, however, it seems that his subjective "depths" might, in fact, be rather shallow, as are Veronika's.)

The presence of the Eich poem at this point in the film, at a moment in which Robert is clearly thinking about Veronika—he has a letter from her in front of him, which he attempts at first to conceal from Henriette—serves to place his longing for her within the context of very specific postwar literary and artistic dialogues. Günter Eich is most identified with a moment in German poetry in which the national literature, in the aftermath of Nazism, was conceived of as standing at "zero hour." (Rossellini, obviously, appropriated this metaphor for the title of *Germania, anno zero*: 1946 is the "zero year.") The contamination of German literature—indeed, of the entire edifice of German culture—was thought of as complete: German writers, it was argued, should remove themselves as much as possible from the historical past of their national culture and literature.[20] Poets such as Eich were careful not to claim any status other than a provisional one for their work; they consciously avoided any temptation to reerect any sort of edifice of German culture. Writing of this type was often referred to as *Trümmerliteratur*, or "rubble literature." Robert, then—ventriloquizing Eich—is writing, figuratively, from the rubble. This poem, as employed by Fassbinder, is a *De Profundis* of sorts; rather, however, than being a cry from the depths of a tortured individual subjectivity—which in Robert's case are rather difficult to locate—it emerges from the depths of a bankrupt national culture. As Robert stands in the rubble, there is no uncontaminated way to return to the historical, prefascist German culture, and there is no viable model for a new postwar national culture. When Robert, then, encounters Veronika—this alluring UFA star, the incarnation of past Nazi cinema—he is looking at her from a position in which nothing has emerged to replace a destroyed Nazi culture. It is precisely because of this bankruptcy that the revenant from the past, walking the postwar city, exerts such power. In his citation of Eich, Fassbinder is invoking—perhaps with both sympathy and somewhat cynical amusement—a moment when German culture thought of itself as standing at "zero." This characteristic moment of intertextual play underlines the symbolic bankruptcy with which Fassbinder's characters are confronted. The use of the Eich poem emphasizes that we are all—characters, spectators, director—at *Stunde Null*: any preexisting structures, whether political, cultural, or artistic, are in ruins around us. This rubble is omnipresent, influencing everything we do, but cannot be rebuilt into any coherent edifice. It can only reappear as an eternally absent presence, pervasive but always lost; it reemerges as specter, as trace and echo. The desire created by temporal slippage, by this reemergence of the past to fill the void of the empty present, is the "longing" that haunts and animates *Die Sehnsucht der Veronika Voss*.

AFTERWORD

In *Heidegger and "the Jews,"* Jean-François Lyotard addresses the crisis of epistemology and representation after "the disaster," interrogating the collapse of what he calls "the architectonics of reason:" "It is impossible to build anything whatsoever from or on this debris. All one can do is thread one's way through it, slip and slide through the ruins, listen to the complaints that emanate from them." Citing Walter Benjamin and Theodore Adorno, Lyotard continues: "Philosophy as architecture is ruined, but a writing of the ruins, micrologies, graffiti can still be done" (43). In *Cinema After Fascism*, it has been my project to, as Lyotard suggests, "slip and slide" through some of the epistemological ruin, to explore the "graffiti," the always provisional, chaotic, and profoundly self-reflexive ways in which desire and subjectivity are inscribed in the universe of epistemological ruin that we, the postwar, postfascist, and post-Holocaust film spectator must negotiate. My discussion in *Cinema After Fascism* has focused detailed attention on a few films, attempting both to engage them closely on a textual level and to situate them in dialogue with each other and with a complex spectrum of ideological, historiographic, or aesthetic discourses. In this afterword, I would like to consider some of the broader meanings implicit in the title *Cinema After Fascism*. The title refers most obviously to chronology: the films discussed here were made after the fall of fascism and, more importantly, they all construct their own aesthetic and political vision as defined in essential ways by "coming after." In the ruins—always both literal and symbolic—of fascism, naturalized subjectivity, especially gendered subjectivity, is lost, as is any unproblematized idea of representation. Cinema "after fascism," therefore, always underscores the instability of its own vision and narratives, of its constructions of temporality, causality and historiography, and desire. A highly unstable subject comes "after fascism:" the structures of desire that produce and are produced by this shaky subject inhabiting the ruins inevitably lead us back to a metadiscourse about film and representation.

The films discussed here come "after fascism" in their construction of desire as well as their chronology. Desire, configured as a vehicle for self-reflexive analysis, is consistently problematized: it emerges repeatedly as metaphor in examining the fraught relationship between fascism, historiography, and the cinematic medium. Scopophilia is a ruling principle; the desire for visual pleasure substitutes all others. Fascism is eternally fascinating as visual fixation, and fascists are fascinated spectators: we, as cinematic audience, enter into this system as we are repeatedly invited to see our own spectatorship enacted on screen. It is not, generally speaking, a pretty picture. We see the problematic masculinity of Rossellini's soldiers, both Axis and Allied, who are more viable as spectators than as warriors, and much more interested in satisfying their desire for visual pleasure than they are in fighting. Graham Greene and Carol Reed ask us to consider our investment in the dubiously beguiling pleasures of the "snake charmer," popular culture and cinema. The statement, "such a good cover, I always think," echoes through *The Third Man*: the masculine drag of the pulp-novel cowboy is emblematic of the failure to "cover" persistent fascist structures of desire and spectatorship. Billy Wilder places us in the enthralled audience as a seductive Rhine-maiden of the rubble sings into being a performative subjectivity, which is the only model that can survive in the shattered capital of Nazism. Helma Sander-Brahms, Alain Resnais, and Bernardo Bertolucci all place spectatorship and the scopophilic imperative at the center of their consideration of cinema, historiography, and fascism: they offer us fragmented subjects whose desire is to achieve some measure of wholeness, however illusory, in an exchange of glances with the past, glances of simultaneous longing and revulsion. The subject is split between past and present, with unity an illusion that is bound to fail. Spectatorship emblematizes the predicament of the postfascist subject, as vision is inescapably problematized, and any stable relationship between subject and object collapses. Spectatorship and scopophilia also offer consolation, and an illusory wholeness and epistemological stability that ultimately proves untenable. This paradox, the ensnaring web that structures all three films, is encapsulated in haunting dialogue that begins *Hiroshima mon amour*, delivered in an eroticized context as pillow talk between lovers: "You have seen nothing in Hiroshima," is answered by, "I have seen everything." Vision promises to offer the possibility of a repaired, stable subject/object relationship, and fails utterly to do so, leaving us, once more, with a split, multiplied, impossible subject inhabiting a shattered physical universe. Finally, Rainer Werner Fassbinder confronts us with the intensity of our desire for the analgesic drug of visual pleasure as we try to find a "fix," to repair the unhealed wounds at the heart of postfascist subjectivity. Questions of historiography also echo through this film, in a haunting phrase: Veronika's performance of "Memories are Made of This" is, literally and figuratively, a "cover." The song becomes an invitation to consider the way the medium of film has structured the relationship between fascist past and postwar present. Fassbinder wraps his exploration of historiographic discourse in a variety of "covers," the wild excess of allusion and echo that simultaneously conceal and expose the "ghosts" in postwar cinema. Cinema "after fascism" invites us into the dream factory of desire; as the insistent, inane country music soundtrack of the film tells us, we have long since "sold [our] soul to the company store," inhabiting the specular economy of film. *Die Sehnsucht der Veronika Voss* is indeed a passion play: the passion is also ours. Desire is a historiographic operation in all the films discussed in *Cinema After Fascism*, as we continue to seek out familiar structures of spectatorship. With palpable longing, we continue to go "after fascism" in both chronology and desire.

I turn now to a discussion, necessarily brief, of some trends in European filmmaking, especially in Italy, in which the erotic becomes a defining element in historiographic discourse, and we are invited to come "after fascism" in particularly transgressive or unsettling ways. In Italy, the cinematic treatment of fascism underwent a radical change after the late 1960s. In my chapter discussing *The Spider Stratagem*, I analyze in some detail Bertolucci's complex positioning of his own work within the prevailing discourse of a generational shift in attitudes to the fascist past and its representations. Bertolucci acknowledges, affectionately if perhaps impatiently, his debt to the immediate postwar generation of neorealist filmmakers who established a national cinema based on the rejection of fascist-era aesthetics and ethics, and that placed itself clearly in opposition to the cinema produced by Cinecittà and the film establishment during the Duce's *ventennio*. It is in the context of this acknowledgment that Bertolucci, in his 1970s films, *The Spider Stratagem*, *The Conformist*, and *1900*, insistently questions and destabilizes the moral truisms that had previously dominated the Italian national discussion about fascism. Bertolucci's challenge is overtly Oedipal: he uses his stories of fathers and sons to take to task the generation of his cinematic "fathers," the postwar directors who established this preexisting discourse. Bertolucci's 1970s films are irreverent and defiant, rejecting the moral clarity of earlier representations of fascism and insisting, in contrast, on moral ambiguity as foundational. In this rejection of the clear lines of power and victimization that was the prevailing interpretation of the neorealist work of the founders of Italian postwar cinema—including among others the towering figures of Roberto Rossellini, Vittorio De Sica, and Luchino Visconti—Bertolucci was part of a larger trend that emerged in Italian film during the late 1960s and the 1970s.

Irreverence and a strong tendency to attack the sacred tenets that defined the antifascism of the postwar generation are shared by several important Italian directors of this period. The social "revolution" of the late 1960s, and the collapse into violence of its widespread radical ideals produced, as has often been argued, a generation of skeptics. This skepticism suffuses film of the period. Fascism and the historiographic acts of its later representation become an inescapable national preoccupation. Moral lines between those with power and the powerless, between fascist perpetrator and the victims of fascist atrocities, are increasingly problematized. Sexuality and desire become important metaphors through which this blurring of preexisting moral and political boundaries is explored. In the mid- to late 1970s, several films were released in Italy that engaged with fascism in the context of sexuality and desire, often offering statements of transgression against established social and cinematic codes. The best known of these films, perhaps, is Liliana Cavani's *The Night Porter* (*Il portiere di notte*), released in 1974. If Bertolucci's films dealing with fascism are focused on the Oedipal, the battle between "fathers" and "sons" about historiography and desire "after fascism," Cavani along with Lina Wertmüller, another female director, moves in a different direction. Instead of positing a generational transaction between men, with desire following an Oedipal pattern, she considers fascism in connection to structures of desire as traumatic reenactment. Cavani's film, which focuses on the sadomasochistic relationship between a concentration camp survivor and her lover, a former officer at the camp, explores connections between historiography, trauma, and sexuality. Like Bertolucci's films about fascism, especially *The Conformist* and *The Spider Stratagem*, *The Night Porter* handles time in a disorienting fashion: past and present are not distinct, but merge into each other in complex ways. The past reemerges as traumatic repetition; the victimization of a Jewish survivor of the German camps is recreated through her continued and reciprocated desire for the Nazi officer. The Holocaust survivor visits Vienna as a wealthy woman and discovers her former lover and torturer employed as the night porter of her luxurious hotel: the axis of power between them appears to be reversed, but the power of the relationship is recaptured through sadomasochism. Cavani's exploration of trauma and psychological repression implies a challenge to prevailing historiography, to the ways in which fascism has been narrated and understood. The relationship between past and present is governed here by repression and traumatic repetition. Fascism, in the historiography of the film, has not been "defeated," but continues to persist in the most intimate structures of desire; "resistance" here is a term for sexual game playing, not heroic opposition to oppression. In *The Night Porter*, sexual trauma structures historiography: desire reanimates the past in all its repressed horror and fascination. Cavani's film has often been dismissed as exploitative "Nazi porn." Indeed, it was the forerunner of such inimitable highlights of Italian cinema as Cesare Canevari's *Last Orgy of the Third Reich* (*L'ultima orgia dell III Reich*) and Luigi Batzella's *SS Hell Camp/Beast in Heat* (*La bestia in calore*), both released in 1977. However, it was part of a series of important films of the 1970s that recast the national discussion of fascism in terms of sexuality and gender.

Lina Wertmüller's *Seven Beauties* (*Pasqualino Settebellezze*) and Pier Paulo Pasolini's *Salò: The 120 Days of Sodom* (*Salò: le 120 giornate di Sodoma*) both released in 1975, also explore fascism through the lens of sexuality. Wertmüller's comedic antihero, Pasqualino, is an opportunistic small-time criminal and sexual exploiter of women. In a reversal of the gender relationship depicted in *The Night Porter*, Pasqualino finds himself, after a series of comically horrifying adventures, forced to make love to a female concentration camp commandant in order to survive the Lager. *Seven Beauties* is strikingly different in tone from Cavani's film. Rather than being structured by traumatic repetition, it follows a series of carnivalesque reversals and inversions of familiar narratives and relationships. In its anarchic humor and comedic embrace of the grotesque, however, it too questions acts of historiography. Pasqualino, as an archetypal "survivor," is the link between the postwar present and the past of the fascism and the holocaust. In a series of flashbacks that take us further into the past, from the Lager to Paqualino's prewar life in Naples, we see the venality and puffed up preoccupation with masculine "honor" that characterized his previous existence. Rather than presenting us, as Cavani does, with an exploration of the return of fascism through the continued power of its erotic "fascination" and the appeal of hypermasculinity as sadomasochistic fantasy, Wertmüller uses grotesque sexual comedy as her vehicle for an exploration of postwar historiography. *Seven Beauties* flashes back and forth in time between Pasqualino's life in fascist-era Naples and the Lager scenes, in which Pasqualino's masculinity, its stability previously upheld by his being both the subject and the object of reassuringly reliable heterosexual desire, collapses. The ridiculous hypermasculinity that served him well in Naples can't survive the version of heterosexual desire he encounters in the camp. In Wertmüller's version of the concentration camp, the sexually exploitative Nazi is not a chillingly elegant male SS officer, but a grotesquely voracious female commandant. Nazism, as personified in the commandant, is not an alluring sadomasochistic fantasy that can return in its gleaming elegance to structure our postwar desires: instead, it is a grotesque parody that produces the collapse of all gendered subjectivity based on desire.

Pasolini's *Salò*, like Fassbinder's *Die Sehnsucht der Veronika Voss* and Bertolucci's *La strategia del ragno*, offers us a cascade of allusion and referentiality, drawing on a wide variety of aesthetic, historiographic, and erotic discourses. Pasolini was always poised at the transgressive edges of political and social communities, an openly homosexual gadfly who was fully accepted by neither left-wing political groups nor Catholicism; he therefore occupies, like Cavani and Wertmüller, a position of outsider relative to the Oedipal transactions that were so compelling for Bertolucci during the same period. He places extremes of sexual exploitation, victimization, and transgressive desire in a highly aestheticized context, referring in very specific visual quotations to Italian artists ranging from Mantegna and Raphael to De Chirico and Balla. His use of eroticism is similar in flavor to Cavani's sadomasochistic craving originating in the German camps, though far more disturbing. We, the audience, as we come "after fascism," see transgressive desire brought home to the Italian shores of the Lago di Garda; Pasolini explores physical pain and psychological degradation not within a Nazi Lager, but in the precincts of a lakeside villa with beautiful neoclassical spaces and elegantly architectural sight lines. The body, especially the male body, is "excruciated" in a variety of ways that specifically refer to Christian iconography and religious art, turning the villa into a grotesque sacred space, framing a literal travesty of sacral rites and a dark parody of artistic and aesthetic traditions, at once both caricature and homage.[1] Pasolini's screenplay (written with Pupi Avati and Sergio Citti) is based on highly codified narrative structures drawn from sacred and profane textual archetypes of religion and eroticism: Dante and the Marquis de Sade. The language, therefore, echoes the cascade of referentiality, simultaneously scathing and affectionate, established by the visual mise-en-scène. The sacrificial, excruciated body—the body of pain, degradation, fear, and death—becomes the site at which our desire is denaturalized, both evoked and horrifyingly challenged as we identify both with powerless victims and sadistic perpetrators, who ultimately become indistinguishable.

In each of the films discussed in *Cinema After Fascism*, our own acts of spectatorship are represented to us, almost obsessively foregrounded through an emphasis on the act of looking and the creation of a series of spectator-surrogates, denaturalizing the process. The relationship between subject and object is problematized, each reciprocally constituting the other until the opposition can no longer be sustained—for the directors discussed here, a denaturalizing of epistemology is essential to cinema after the fall of fascism. There is no longer a separate object that can be "known;" the subject is considered as itself an epistemological construct, and knowledge and the nature of reality are deeply compromised concepts. The gaze of the spectator is also invariably politicized: a historically situated subject emerges in specific contexts in the decades after fascism. This spectatorial subject, then, comes into being as a creature of ideology as well as aesthetics: indeed, for all the directors considered in *Cinema After Fascism*, the two cannot be separated. They are almost obsessively aware of the ideological history that marks their medium in the aftermath of fascism, and rigorously cognizant of the embedded subtexts of their films. Ideology as well as desire—to the extent that the two are discrete at all—is repeatedly foregrounded and subjected to skeptical scrutiny. The weight of this baggage, the taint carried by the medium itself in the world left behind after the fall of Hitler and Mussolini, burdens these films; the ideological and aesthetic traces of fascism are searchingly explored. On the shattered screen of cinema after fascism, the failure of representation is the only remaining imperative.

Notes

Introduction

1. For a very illuminating discussion of Crocean thought in relation to fascism, see Dalle Vacche, *Body* 10–15.

1 In the Ruins of Fascism

1. Luchino Visconti's *Ossessione*, which came out in 1943, is the other contender for the label "first neorealist film." In fact, many other fascist-era films, including Rossellini's, incorporated elements that would later come to be identified with neorealism. Rossellini's early work, and neorealist films in general, were critically and financially much more successful outside Italy than within it; this may partially explain why foreign—and many Italian—scholars have tended not to discuss neorealism in terms of a prior national cinema or culture. André Bazin, especially, was important in constructing neorealism as a transnational phenomenon. See Bazin 93–100.
2. Rossellini's personal relation to fascism was complex. Biographers and critics, including Brunette, *RR* 16–18 and Gallagher 60–65 make clear that he was never a convinced fascist; he took whatever opportunities were offered to make films and developed within the constraints of the fascist system many elements of what would later emerge as a distinctive individual style. See Ben-Ghiat, in Forgacs, *RR* 20–35, points out that the fascist film studios of the 1940s were highly collaborative institutions. Therefore, the films in Rossellini's early trilogy, especially *La nave bianca*, also bear the mark of other filmmakers, most notably Francesco de Robertis. Ben-Ghiat also stresses the paucity of scholarly discussion of the fascist war trilogy.
3. For a rare discussion of the transition from fascist cinema to neorealism, see the historian Ennio Di Nolfo's illuminating "Intimations of Neorealism in the Fascist Ventennio," in Reich and Garofalo 83–104. Di Nolfo's opening sentence is an excellent summary of the prevailing scholarly view of the relationship between neorealism and fascist cinema: "Since its inception, many critics have regarded Italian cinematic neorealism as a splendid and sumptuous flower that bloomed miraculously, almost by chance, among the ruins of a country ravaged by war" (83).
4. For a discussion of the heterogeneity and commercial aspirations of fascist-era films, see Bondanella *RR* 5. He states: "the fascist regime took a genuine interest in the health of the film industry and wanted it to flourish, without,

however, insisting on ideological purity…the totalitarian regime's model was Hollywood, not the rigidly controlled popular culture of Soviet Russia or Nazi Germany."

5. By the late 1930s, attitudes toward popular culture had changed, becoming more restrictive. Ricci points out a number of measures taken by the state to control the influence of Hollywood film, including mandating dubbing (a skill for which Italian studios are still known) that amounted to censorship of content and, in 1938, the passage of laws limiting distribution of non-Italian films (157).

6. See Tag Gallagher's comments on Rossellini and De Robertis' enthusiasm for Eisenstein and the influence of Eisenstein on the *La nave bianca* 70–72. Gallagher also defends the film as being covertly antifascist.

7. See Rossellini's autobiography *My Method* 44.

8. Millicent Marcus, in her very illuminating analysis of *Paisà* in *After Fellini*, comments on the double, almost paradoxical quality of the film, arguing that it attempts to achieve two different and perhaps contradictory goals. She states that it "stands as a powerful example of filmmaking as a foundational act, as a building of national consciousness out of the ravages of Fascism and war. But Rossellini's insistence on historical representation is counterbalanced by an equally intense awareness that *Paisan* is a filmic artifact, a complex aesthetic construction that transcends its documentary or didactic scope" (10).

9. See Mirella Serri, *I Redenti: Gli Intelletuali che vissero due volte* 7–24. I am indebted to Frank Adler for drawing my attention to this very useful book.

10. See Gallagher 47–49.

11. See Gallagher 83. Gallagher also notes that the screenplay for the film was written by a well-known fascist journalist and editor, Asvero Gravelli.

12. The title is translated into English as *Paisan*—clearly not by a native speaker of Italian. The English title is misleading: in an Italian context, the word *paesano* (of which *paisà* is a dialect version, evidently in Romanaccio, the popular dialect of Rossellini's native city) usually refers to someone from your *paese*, your home village or small region, and therefore underlines the regional loyalties of Italians and works against a formulation of national unity that the film ostensibly espouses. Italian Americans tend to use the word much more broadly, referring to other Italian Americans: it is ironic that an Italian film title is translated into an idiom that is only comprehensible once the language has "emigrated." Marcus, in her very illuminating chapter on *Paisà*, also points out this contradiction relating the fragmentation it suggests to the episodic structure of the film and its effect of montage (*AF* 14–19).

13. See Bondanella *RR* 65–67. Bondanella points out that *Paisà* does, in some areas, come closer to fulfilling some of the conditions associated with neorealism than Rossellini's previous film, *Roma, città aperta*, especially in the use of nonprofessional actors in some key roles and shooting some of the exteriors in the "real" locations depicted. However, he also points out that Rossellini deliberately muddied this issue and in fact "fooled" critics by his flawless fakery.

14. The relationship between neorealism and "the real" has engaged many critics. Rossellini's contemporaries, most notably André Bazin, champion Rossellini's films for their attainment of a "higher" or "truer reality," a concept that is not

questioned as such. More recent critics, including Brunette and Bondanella, tend to see the question of "realism" in terms of Rossellini's relation to traditional Hollywood coding. What Bazin saw as a radical new way of approaching "truth," later writers see as the substitution of a new set of cinematic conventions—the hallmarks of neorealism that, to Bazin, Zavattini, and the like, indicated "truth"—for the familiar Hollywood techniques. See Brunette *RR* 105, which argues: "this film, like all films, cannot offer an unproblematic, transparent window onto a direct experience of reality, but remains forever a constructed, and thus 'unnatural' artifact."

15. The question of whether the episodic structure of *Paisà* is a failing or strength has been discussed at length by various critics. See Bazin 34. Bazin makes an interesting argument that the film resembles a collection of short stories—reminiscent, to him, of authors as diverse as Saroyan, Hemingway, and Faulkner. See Brunette *RR* 70 for an alternate view. He argues the unconventional narrative structure of the film, which insists on fragmentation, works against any attempt to show Italy as unified, and a positive connection between Italians and Americans.

16. The animated maps appeared only in versions of *Paisà* intended for English and American release—there were several different versions of the film. I am working here from the version that played in American theaters. On the differences between the Italian and foreign releases, see Wagstaff 191–192.

17. Tom Conley, in *Cartographic Cinema* 2, discusses this paradoxical quality of maps in the context of film: "a map in a film is an element at once foreign to the film but also, paradoxically, of the same essence as film. A map underlines what a film is and what it does, but it also opens a rift or brings into view a site where a critical and productively interpretive relation to the film can begin" (2). Also see Conley 65–82, an extensive and illuminating discussion of *Roma, città aperta*.

18. For a discussion of the use of documentary footage, see Brunette, *RR* 71. Brunette argues that, although it has frequently been read as making the film's "reality" more "believable," the documentary footage in fact undercuts that very claim. This, according to Brunette, is due to the fact that these sections present themselves as "past" rather than in "present, individually dramatic terms." This creates a tension that, ultimately, forces the viewer to confront the constructedness of the film. Brunette posits the maps as having a contradictory function—ostensibly they are not only a unifying device, but they also insist on the regionality and geographic separateness of the landscapes of the film, undercutting claims of unity, whether aesthetic or ideological. Also see Bondanella, *RR* 65. He accepts the documentary footage as creating "actuality" and "immediacy." In an interesting aside, Dalle Vacche points out that the moving arrows representing military maneuvers on the maps accompanying the voice-overs can be seen as violating the surface of Italy, represented as a passive surface. Dalle Vacche argues that the map of Italy serves the same function as the dead body of Carmela at the end of the first segment: they both represent Italy as battleground, passively acted on by outside forces (*Body* 199).

19. See Gallagher 180–182.

20. Again, many critics are in agreement about the importance of communication—failed or successful—as a theme throughout *Paisà*. See

Bondanella, *RR* 77, Brunette, *RR* 65, and Marcus, *AF* 19. The initial moments of dialogue in the film underline this. What we have at the beginning is a total failure of communication between the Italians and Americans.

21. See Wagstaff 202. He tells us that most of the segment was in fact shot near Vesuvius and in Amalfi, with the final shot of Carmella's body lying on the rocks filmed in Anzio, near Rome, not in Sicily.

22. Bondanella comments on this snippet of dialogue, seeing it not as a self-reflexive reference to Hollywood coding, but stating that it is ominous and shows that "danger is lurking everywhere" (*RR* 69). He sees it, along with what he refers to, interestingly, as "expressionist lighting," as a kind of foreshadowing, preparing the audience for "something horrible." Marcus also singles it out, explicating it as parodic of genre films (*AF* 22).

23. The popular fascist anthem, *Facetta Nera*—still widely recognized and immediately locatable on YouTube in a 1930s rendition—captures the flavor of Italian colonialist racism. The lyrics are spoken by an Italian "liberator" and Latin lover to the African woman to whom he has brought the gift of "civilization:" *Faccetta nera, bell'abissina/Aspetta e spera che già l'ora si avvicina!/ quando saremo insieme a te/noi ti daremo un'altra legge e un altro Re...Faccetta nera, piccola abissina,/ti porteremo a Roma, liberata.* ("Little black face [girl] beautiful Abyssinian/Wait and hope that the hour approaches/when we will be with you/we will give you another law and another king. ...little black face, little Abyssinian, we will bring you to Rome, liberated." My translation.) Not surprisingly, the rhetoric of "liberation" at the end of the Second World War crosses over with fascist and racist rhetoric: the scene in the puppet theater relies on the audience realizing this.

24. See Marcus, *AF* 24–25, for an illuminating discussion of the layering of symbolic meanings of black and white in this scene.

25. It is perhaps worth noting here that the preeminent film journal of the fascist period—and into the postwar period—was called *Bianco e nero*, or *Black and White*.

26. For a very interesting comment on "Joe's" gaze at this moment, see Steimatsky 43: "Rossellini's emissary observer is here, as so often in his films, an outsider under whose look material conditions and an altered consciousness coalesce in phenomenological realization. ...By the disclosure of his own deprived background, by his very silence and his turning away, the MP, and Rossellini's camera in turn...enact in the face of this ruinous space a mode of seeing that is itself haunted, fragmented, traumatic. ...The ruin is internalized, inscribed in the film's body that itself emerges as a ruinous edifice, redefining Rossellini's realism, and his modernity, in an exemplary intersection."

27. Bondanella, in a brief discussion, also posits the scene in the puppet theater as a "moment of cinematic self-reflexivity to remind us that the story he recounts is composed of equal elements of fact and fiction" (*RR* 73). Gallagher also points out that the thematization of American racism is quite daring on Rossellini's part; however, a segment that was originally scripted but never filmed was much more critical of American society, and does not end with the black GI realizing how much "better" his life is. See Gallagher 195.

28. For a very interesting analysis of the fascist reconfiguration of Rome, see Painter, *Mussolini's Rome.* A discussion of the Via dell' Impero can be found on pp. 22–25.

29. Some of these maps remain, a bit worse for wear; the Via dei Fori Imperiali is still the site of a huge annual military parade complete with artillery, running Bersaglieri troops in feathered hats, and tricolor jet trails overhead.

30. See Wagstaff 196 for an interesting point about the critical reaction to the Rome segment: critics who saw it as "Hollywood cinema" used the word as a broad epithet, dismissive in the way the appellation "fascist cinema" might be.

31. See Marcus, *AF* 29: "This highly mobilized camera, whose speed of movement is synchronized both to his protagonists' hurried flight and to the urgent rhythms of the musical score, turns Florence into a dynamic, unfamiliar and uncomfortable space. It would be no exaggeration to claim that Rossellini's visual strategy alone tells us all we need to know about the Florentine Liberation campaign: this city museum has become a battlefield."

32. For a different interpretation of the retired major, reading the character as a committed participant, see Marcus, *AF* 27.

33. See Marcus, *AF* 20–30, for a very interesting comment on the Uffizi passage and Harriet's "passage" to knowledge.

34. The Apennine segment was also, like the Roman one, controversial, but for very different reasons. See Wagstaff 216–219. In the emerging cold war political alignments of Italy, there was a mounting anticommunist hysteria, enthusiastically encouraged and manipulated by the Catholic church and the Western Allied powers, leading up to the elections of 1948 that placed the Christian Democratic Party in power, a situation that endured for decades and sidelined the communists for the purposes of national government. (They were much more politically successful in local government.) Clearly, a segment that can be read as extolling the virtues of the church would be seen as retrograde by left-wing critics. *Roma, città aperta* extolled the cooperation between representatives of the church and the communists in antifascist struggle—in the response to *Paisà*, there is more controversy about Rossellini's treatment of Catholicism.

35. The monastery section is another that, like the Rome segment, is sometimes perceived as not "fitting" the rest of the film. Gallagher points out that contemporary reviewers responded negatively to Rossellini's apparent refusal to condemn the intolerance of the monks (91). Brunette says that the "ragged, recalcitrant difference of [this segment's] theme has resisted critical attempts at closure" (*RR* 93). While Brunette tends to see the monastery segment as characterized by irony and paradox—the illusion of impermeability of the monastery walls, the intolerance of these "holy" monks—Bondanella argues that it reflects the Christian faith espoused at this time by Rossellini, and by Fellini, who had a considerable hand in this segment. See Bondanella, *RR* 80. Brunette makes an interesting point that one way to read this segment is to privilege an early, casually dropped comment questioning whether the isolated monks are capable of worldly judgment and perception: "the thematically privileged position we normally assign to the main character's speech at the end of a narrative sequence, when all attention is solemnly focused on him or her and the rhetoric of language, image and music continues to underline

the moment's importance, would have to be completely overturned. A casual remark…would have to be privileged over the highly foregrounded, final dramatic scene towards which everything has been moving…critics find the whole episode absurd or confused because…it is not unified. A better reading might be to admit that the irreconcilable interpretations cannot, in fact, be reconciled, despite the uncomfortable lack of closure that results" (Brunette, *RR* 74).

36. The convention of showing the handwritten page of a diary—which, in the English version of *Paisà*, changes from the Italian language to English before our eyes—seems like a very "Hollywood" way of giving information to the audience. This is the first time Rossellini has resorted to this sort of cliché. It is interesting to note it is here, in the middle of his anti-Hollywood idyll, that he chooses to use this hackneyed Hollywood trope. (It's almost as familiar as the pages of a calendar blowing away in the wind.) This is an abrupt break in the "realist" conventions that have been operating and, perhaps, yet another instance of distanciation at work.

37. The Po Valley segment of *Paisà* has been consistently praised. For example, see Gallagher 205; he calls it "the great Italian national-populist masterpiece." (Gallagher rather undermines his praise, however, by suggesting that the innovative lighting—or rather, lack of light—is due to the fact that Rossellini had a date with his mistress and did not want to stay until the next day to shoot in daylight.) Bazin praises the Po segment as "admirable" and refers to the "subtlety of expression" of the camera work (characters are shot from a low angle, against the marshes and sky). He makes an interesting point about indeterminacy and the ellipses built into the episode: "the technique of Rossellini undoubtedly maintains an intelligible succession of events, but these do not mesh like a chain with the sprockets of a wheel. The mind has to leap from one event to the other as one leaps from stone to stone in crossing a river" (35).

38. See Wagstaff 285 for an interesting observation about the increasing importance of landscape in Rossellini's career. He places Rossellini in the context of different genres: the documentary (i.e., Flaherty), the Western, and the road movie, all of which center around the tension of "man against nature."

39. Wagstaff also points out the structural continuity between these two episodes. See 266.

40. Fred, perhaps, is remaining true to his namesake, Fred Astaire; he "wants" to be in a light, sprightly, frothily romantic film, and turns sullen and becomes passive and impotent, when he is suddenly thrown into a totally different kind of movie. Francesca, however, is content to be true to her namesake and accepts the role of Dante's Francesca, buffeted eternally by the winds of passion and misfortune, hoping eternally for reunion with her Paulo. Our last sight of Francesca is waiting hopefully outside, exposed to the elements, for Fred, who will never come.

41. In the specificity and audacity of his almost shot-by-shot quotation of *Hitlerjunge Quex*, a taboo film after the fall of Nazism, Rossellini appears to be engaging in a meditation very similar to Wilder's in *A Foreign Affair*, in which Leni Riefenstahl's *Triumph of the Will* is repeatedly quoted, again almost shot by shot. There is a crucial difference, however: Wilder left

Germany for the United States and was never implicated in Nazi cinema. Wilder was strongly antifascist and, because he was Jewish, he could only have become a victim of Nazism's genocidal machinery if he had stayed, never a co-perpetrator. Rossellini, by contrast, occupied a position of privilege in fascist Italy, an intimate acquaintance of Mussolini's son and a successful director in Cinecittà.

42. Apparently, the actor, Edmund Meschke, did resemble Rossellini's dead son, Romano. Rossellini modeled some of the child's behavior in the film on memories of his son. See Gallagher 242.

43. Again, the aerial panoramas that open some versions of *Germania anno zero* are highly reminiscent of the opening of *A Foreign Affair*, in which Wilder places us at the window of an airplane flying low over the city, quoting Riefenstahl's depiction of Hitler's plane approaching Nuremberg, and occasionally reversing the axis of view so that we can watch ourselves watching.

44. See Steimatsky 53 for a perceptive discussion of *Germania anno zero*, in which she suggests that it is not clear in this scene whether the ruined building from which Edmund jumps is in the process of reconstruction—if it is, in fact, a construction site. She relates this ambiguity to Germans' (and, by extension, Italians') ambivalence about "processing" the fascist past: "the inextricability of material and moral fronts—the physical reconstruction of homes and cities on the one hand, and the restoration of identity and community through monumental projects on the other—posited the most challenging questions for post-Nazi Germany. There was obviously an identity, a past that many were in a hurry to forget or to dismiss as a temporary aberration that now, in the process of reconstruction, may be neatly plastered over, along with these walls."

45. See Schulte-Sasse 267 for a very interesting statement: that *Hitlerjunge Quex* "unabashedly confesses the secret of Nazism as theater."

46. See Brunette, *RR* 86, for a discussion of the pietà in this scene. Brunette points out that it is remarkable for the lack of physical contact between the figures—it shows exhausted proximity, rather than an actual embrace of the dead body. Brunette sees this as a "refusal to symbolize, the refusal to refer to an extratextual religious and artistic iconographic tradition that could signal some semblance of human love and possibility" (86).

47. Shandley points out that the fatal fall of Rossellini's Edmund is similar to the death of a child who falls into rubble in the German "rubble film," made in 1946, *Irgendwo in Berlin* (*Somewhere in Berlin*) directed by Gerhard Lamprecht (124).

2   The Ghost in the Rubble

1. Mary Ann Doane comments on the presence of fascism as a "haunting" element in film noir in her indispensable analysis of Gilda in *Femmes Fatales* (115).

2. For an interesting comment on this scene, see Schulte-Sasse 122. Schulte-Sasse contextualizes the aircraft's shadow passing over Nuremburg as a visual metaphor later linked to the "eagle's wing" and "eagle's gaze" of Frederick the Great in Veit Harlan's 1942 film, *Der große Koenig*.

3. Galt comments on the use of documentary elements in both *A Foreign Affair* and *Germania anno zero* as well as Tourneur's *Berlin Express*: "Here it is the documentary force of the ruin image—familiar to the contemporary audience from newsreels—that anchors the films' claim on the real. Although the films variously involve romantic, political, and mystery narratives, their power to represent the stakes of the postwar German problem comes as an effect of the evidentiary quality of their ruined mise-en-scènes." She goes on to say that "this concern for the indexical truth of the ruin image is part of the averred work of the films" (187).

4. An interesting discussion of Wilder's relations with the Allied occupation authorities in Berlin around the making of *A Foreign Affair* can be found in Willett 28–39.

5. See Bernard F. Dick, *Billy Wilder* 63, for an illuminating discussion of the comedic elements of *A Foreign Affair*. Dick sees the film as simultaneously a "romantic" and a "political" comedy and comments on the ambivalence that characterizes this unlikely "comedy" set in the post-Holocaust rubble-scape of Berlin.

6. For an excellent discussion of *A Foreign Affair* in the context of its genre elements, see Gemünden 67–70.

7. In a typically sly snippet of dialogue, Wilder uses this scene to further undermine the gender stability of Pringle's character. When asked by his metamorphosing companion, Miss Frost, how he knows so much about women's clothing, Pringle makes the nonsensical reply: "My mother wore women's clothes." It is an explanation that explains nothing and leaves the question dangling. Pringle, the soldier who talks about sending "shorts to the cleaners and getting back a girdle," never comes to rest in any stable gender identity. It is also worth noting that in this scene Pringle adopts an analogous role to Mammy who dresses Scarlett in *Gone with the Wind*; he thereby not only casts himself as ambiguously gendered, but appears to cross racial boundaries as well.

8. It is worth noting that Miss Frost describes her goal as eliminating a moral "malaria," casting immorality as a tropical disease that can't exist in cold climates. She also uses metaphors of infestation—promising to "fumigate" Berlin.

9. See Bernard Dick 64 for comments on the importance of her hair in defining Miss Frost as a character. He describes it as "a coronet that looks like a halo." Gemünden also notes that this style was a favorite of the "Bund Deutscher Mädel" (69).

10. For a fascinating discussion of Dietrich, framing, and the femme fatale in film noir, see Mary Ann Doane's analysis of Josef von Sternberg's veiling and revealing of the face of Deitrich in *The Devil Is a Woman* (1935) and *The Scarlet Empress* (1934) (*Femme Fatales* 72–75).

11. See Gemünden 71.

12. Billy Wilder initially returned to Berlin at U.S. taxpayer's expense. He traveled to his former home city under the auspices of the U.S. Army Signal Corps to work on *Death Mills* (1945), a documentary designed to confront the German civilian population with the realities of the Holocaust. It is worth noting that Wilder's mother and grandmother died in Auschwitz. This casts an interesting light on his refusal to moralize about Nazism in *A Foreign Affair*. Erika's Nazi

associations, and the question of her complicity, are presented in the film as bureaucratic problems rather than moral ones: if she can get the right documentation from the Allied authorities, she will no longer be impeded by past associations.

13. The title is widely considered to be an allusion to T. S. Eliot's "The Waste Land," invoking the unseen but always present companion, the "third" ("Who is the third who walks always beside you?") and places the setting of the film within Eliot's cascade of cities, the "Falling towers" of "Jerusalem Athens Alexandria/Vienna London." See, for example, Rob White 52–55. This evocation of "The Waste Land" sets the stage for the dislocation, linguistic disorientation, and cascade of referentiality that are so characteristic of the film.

14. For a brief discussion of *The Third Man* in the context of British film noir, see Tony Williams "British Film Noir" in *Film Noir Reader* 2 (251).

15. For an illuminating discussion of the initial voice-over, see Rob White 8.

16. See Van Wert 345–346 for a discussion of the untranslated German dialogue in *The Third Man*.

17. Interestingly, the German language sequences were shorter in the American version of the film than in the British one—see Rob White 9. Presumably, European audiences were considered more able to tolerate indeterminacy and the suspension of meaning.

18. See Mitscherlich, *The Inability to Mourn*, and Santner, *Stranded Objects* for extensive discussions.

19. For a fascinating discussion of parodic echoes of the Western in *The Third Man*, see Palmer and Riley 14–21.

20. The balloon seller in *The Third Man* is an obvious and explicit homage to Fritz Lang's *M*, in which a similar character plays a pivotal role. There are several visual references to *M*, and many more to German Expressionist film generally, throughout *The Third Man*. See Rob White 40. This emphasizes, again, the film's self-referentiality; Reed continuously foregrounds his film *as* film, to be read as part of a broad intertextual matrix of images.

21. See Rob White 18–19. The unstable masculinity and the homoerotic subtext were at least partially conscious in the making of the film. Graham Greene's original name for the protagonist was Rollo. Joseph Cotten refused to play the character so named because the name seemed homosexual to him. Greene accepted the compromise "Holly" because it retained the "ridiculousness" he desired. David O. Selznick was evidently highly suspicious of the relationship between the two characters, referring to "buggery."

22. For a discussion of the resurrected Harry Lime as a vampire figure, and *The Third Man's* references to Gothic fiction, see Dern 46.

3   The Web of Spectacle

1. See Wagstaff's discussion of Bertolucci's antifascist views as expressed in his films of the 1970s (Bartram 202–213).

2. See Dalle Vacche, *Body* 18–22, for an illuminating discussion of Croce and the Italian philosophical tradition with regard to fascism.

3. Many discussions of Bertolucci's films of the 1970s stress their overtly Oedipal content, the complex interactions in which sons repudiate and overthrow literal and symbolic fathers. See Bondanella, *IC* 303–307; Dalle Vacche, *Body* 59; Liehm 274–260; Landy, *IF* 339.

4. To reach Draifa's villa outside the town of Tara, Athos has to negotiate an underpass—sometimes flooded—passing underneath a divided highway. The history of the autostrada system may be relevant here: the network of high-speed national highways was begun by Mussolini in the 1920s and 1930s, but expanded greatly in the postwar years. Draifa's house, itself a historic villa with what appears to be older frescos (perhaps eighteenth century) on the walls, therefore lies beyond the boundaries of Renaissance Tara, but its flirtation with modernity (the autostrada) represents a connection to both fascist and postwar Italy.

5. This is a reference to an Italian folk song, which begins "quand'ero piccina, piccina mio padre mi dava di ballar, mi diceva Ninetta vien grande" "When I was very small, my father told me to dance, he said Ninetta you're growing up"

6. See Dalle Vacche's extensive discussion on stylizations of the body in fascist and postwar film. She describes Athos the elder as having been transformed into a statue (*Body* 233–237).

7. As I argue elsewhere, especially in the discussion of Rossellini above, seeing neorealism purely as the antispectacle is somewhat reductive; the relationship of neorealism to spectacle and spectatorship is complex and ambivalent.

8. In the 1960s and 1970s, an impassioned debate around fascism in Italy centered on the questions of consent and complicity. Historians such as Renzo de Felice argued for what was labeled a "revisionist" approach to the history of fascism, seen by many intellectuals on the left as an apologia for it. The fourth volume of de Felice's biography of Mussolini, entitled *Gli anni di consenso* was published in 1974 and generated a furious response due to its arguments that Mussolini was a genuine, if flawed, political visionary and that fascism, at least initially, enjoyed widespread popular support and therefore had to be accorded some legitimacy by historians. Bertolucci was strongly antifascist and firmly on the left; however, *La strategia del ragno*, *Il conformista*, and *Novecento* do seem to have something in common with de Felice's approach. The "revisionists" tended to demystify the antifascist resistance, and to stress continuities between the fascist period and the rest of Italian history. For a very cogent discussion of the polemics around writing the history of fascism in Italy in the 1960s and 1970s, see Painter "Renzo de Felice and the Historiography of Italian Fascism," 391–405.

9. See Dalle Vacche, *Body* 60–62 for an illuminating discussion of the stone-like rigidity of so many figures in *La strategia del ragno*.

10. Bolongario 76 also points out Bertolucci's reference to *Gone with the Wind*. Kline 64 also briefly mentions the reference and suggests another interesting element incorporated in the signifier "Tara:" it is the first two syllables of the name of what he calls "the most dreaded of spiders," the tarantula. This obviously brings to mind the tarantella, a dance that, according to popular myth, originates with the tarantula's bite and causes involuntary rhythmic dancing.

11. As the mythical home of the ancient kings of Ireland, the site became part of the iconography of modern Irish nationalism. In this, too, it seems especially apposite to Bertolucci's discussion of historiography and myth. Irish anticolonial narratives about nation are perhaps prototypical in the discourse about empire that was so important an element of fascism in Italy in the 1930s.

12. The anti-Semitic racial laws were enacted by the fascist state in 1938. In the early days of fascism, Jews were largely assimilated into the movement, as they were within Italian society at large.

13. The fascist regime directly linked cinema to nationalism and militarism, as evident in the slogan: "La cinema è l'arma più forte" ("Cinema is the strongest weapon.")

14. Changes in Italian law in the late 1930s discouraged imported film.

15. The most well-known example (one of many) is Via dell'Impero (now Via dei Fori Imperiali), linking the Colosseum and the Capitoline Hill, which was constructed in the early 1930s. The construction destroyed a unique and still partially unexcavated archeological site and made clear that the fascists preferred myth and choreographed spectacle to "real" historical "knowledge."

16. Sabbioneta's famous Renaissance theater, built in 1590 for the Gonzaga family, and in which Bertolucci sets the climactic scene of *La strategia del ragno*, has a Latin inscription on the front reading *Roma quanta fuit ipsa ruina docet* ("This ruin teaches us how great Rome was"). This is another layer of managed nostalgia and targeted historiography: a Renaissance ducal family wished to associate their own buildings with the glory of ancient Rome, much as the Duce did in the twentieth century; they also anticipate the preservation of their own history for some distant future time, with the conceit that their creations will one day be grand ruins, like those of ancient Rome. The Gonzaga designed Sabbioneta as an "ideal city" and built it entirely between 1560 and 1591. The great theater is the centerpiece of a whole town that was originally conceived in theatrical terms.

17. Interestingly, it is in this sequence that we catch one of few glimpses of women in Tara; a middle-aged housewife is sitting outside by the colonnaded walkway, and we hear female voices in the background. The only other women who appear within the limits of the town (Draifa's villa is outside the city, though she does enter Tara proper to go shopping) are a group standing on an ox cart outside the theater, who appear confined to the platform of the cart, and to have been brought in as the chorus that comments on Athos senior's operatic demise.

18. Kline 66–69 points out that the composition of this shot is reminiscent of a Magritte painting, *La Reproduction Interdite*, 1937. Kline's discussion of the importance of Magritte's painting to this film is very illuminating; he emphasizes the dreamlike quality of *La strategia del ragno*, and the Borges story from which it is loosely adapted, and analyzes both in terms of Freudian dream work, pointing to structures such as condensation and displacement.

19. See Dalle Vacche, *Body* 223, for a very illuminating discussion of this scene, pointing out that the old men who inhabit Tara speak the "wrong" regional dialect. By inserting, presumably deliberately, this "mistake" into his

invocation of neorealism, Bertolucci underlines his problematization of neo-realism's claims of "authenticity" as an essential aspiration of cinema.

20. The relationship of neorealism to fascism is much more ambivalent and complex than is generally assumed—see discussion of Rossellini, above. And, of course, it is a mistake to think of Italian fascist film itself as monolithic. It incorporated a variety of genres, and often competed directly with the product of Hollywood, at least until protectionist legislation was enacted late in the fascist *ventennio*. The Duce's regime was surprisingly tolerant of "foreign" political influences in the arts, considering them fairly harmless and naturally of interest only to a small elite.

21. Bertolucci was much more willing to engage in more familiar political rhetoric in other films about fascism, most notably *Novecento*.

22. Dalle Vacche makes the very interesting comment that "to Athos' betrayal of antifascism corresponds Bertolucci's betrayal of neorealism" (*Body* 231).

23. This description, interestingly, reappears almost 35 years after Magnani's death in 1973 in the Adriano Celentano song, "Anna Magnani," from the hit album *Dormi amore, la situazione non è buona*, released in 2007.

24. The most famous use of "real time" in neorealist film is the lengthy sequence in De Sica's film, *Umberto D*, in which a young working-class woman wakes up, dresses, and prepares for the day.

25. The use of the opera, *Rigoletto*, is a reference to the mythology of the Risorgimento, which has a similar symbolic function to the Resistance in Italian cultural iconography. This reference brings together history and spectacle on many levels, from the nineteenth-century audiences chanting "Verdi" (the letters of which stand for "Vittorio Emanuele, Re D'Italia") to express their coded support for the unification of Italy to the condemnation implied by the famous "Maledizione" aria that, as Peter Bondanella points out in *IC* 300, provides the aural backdrop for the murder of the first Athos Magnani. Intertextual references to this opera in the context of the antifascist struggle appear in many Italian films; for example, in Rossellini's *Roma, città aperta*, a heroic priest, representing the resistance, condemns a Gestapo colonel with the word "maledetto."

26. In the opera, Rigoletto hires Sparafucile, an assassin, to murder the Duke of Mantua; Sparafucile, after Verdi's characters go through a complicated series of disguises, deceptions, and substitutions, inadvertently kills Rigoletto's beloved daughter.

27. Obviously, "Duca" and "Duce" are closely related words, both deriving from the Latin words *ducere*, to lead, and *dux*, a military leader.

28. It is interesting that, during the flashback scenes to 1936, we never see the physical markers of fascism in Tara. The extended sequence in which Athos Sr. dances mockingly to "Giovinezza," the fascist anthem, in defiance of glowering officials and citizenry, takes place at a town festival in an open area just outside the walls of Tara. We see black shirts and uniforms, and hear fascist music, but don't see how fascism would have resignified the spaces of the city itself. We never see any statues of Mussolini, or streets or youth clubs named after him, which would have existed in virtually every Italian city in the 1930s and to which, in the postwar universe, the memorials to Athos correspond.

29. Kline quotes a statement by Bertolucci about *La strategia del ragno*, in which he calls it "a film on the ambiguity of history" (64).

4   The Atomized Subject

1. It is interesting that the child in this documentary sequence bears a striking resemblance to some of the other children whose images "haunt" the rubble of German cities. He looks like Rossellini's Edmund from *Germania anno zero*, who himself resembles Heini from *Hitlerjunge Quex*. They both strongly resemble Gustav, the child in *Irgendwo in Berlin* who, like Edmund, dies by falling in a bombed-out building.

2. See Mercken-Spaas 245; she points out that "Resnais breaks from linear structure and sequential development. The sequence is no longer the semantic substructure of the filmic narrative; Resnais interweaves film fragments which are not recognizable as present moments and flashbacks. Sound and image are not necessarily synchronized; narrative units are suspended abruptly and unexpected takes inserted."

3. See Ropars-Wuilleumier 19 for a very interesting discussion of the film in terms of "the operation of transference by which atomic violence changes into atomized writing."

4. See Moses 163 for a brief but very interesting discussion of the series of "non narrative links"—such as the cut between the woman's hand caressing the man's body and the shriveled hand of a bomb victim that thematically and visually connects the past and present.

5. See again Moses 163: "from the first, Resnais undermines the power of his images. The opening paradox initiates the subversion by introducing counterpoint between soundtrack and image track. Subsequent exchanges between the two voices continue this counterpoint."

6. The cross is, of course, suggestive of far more than modern medicine. The film is also a sustained critique of traditional Christian morality, which becomes absurd in the context of Hiroshima. Both protagonists, but especially the woman, live outside conventional morality; it is sexual moralism, combined with nationalism, that forces the Frenchwoman into the dissolution of self in the cellar at Nevers.

7. The parallels between the river scenes in *Hiroshima mon amour* and the final Po Delta segment of *Paisà* are striking. The river has a similar symbolic function in both films: both posit a landscape of flow, without boundaries, as an epistemological "wilderness," similar to the ruptured structures of urban rubble.

8. See Cardullo 39–41; he makes the point that this linguistic substitution of the Japanese man for the German soldier has a denaturalizing effect, encouraging us to see the film on a symbolic rather than a literal level. He also argues that the relationship between the Frenchwoman and the Japanese man represents the difficult rapprochement between former enemies after the war.

9. Riva is the name of the actress who plays the woman.

10. The "disorder" here also refers, on a more prosaic level, to the social conditions in Vichy France immediately after the Germans departed.

11. See Bammer 93 for a discussion of this shot: "As this opening shot suggests, our access to what we call 'history' can never be immediate; it is always mediated by the forms of its re-presentation."

12. Laura Mulvey's essay from 1975, "Visual Pleasure and Narrative Cinema" is probably the best-known and most influential articulation of what later became

a familiar feminist analysis of this structure of woman-as-image, denoting the concept of "something-to-be-looked-at," a function as spectacle.

13. See McCormick 196 for a very illuminating discussion of the voice-over narration in *Deutschland bleiche Mutter*. McCormick argues that it is one of many distanciation techniques that work toward breaking down naturalistic codes within the film: "An examination of the film's formal structure makes clear how close the film's project is to that of Fassbinder and Brecht, and indeed how often the discursive nature of its 'story' is foregrounded. The most obvious device for distanciation that Sanders-Brahms uses is voice-over narration, a technique reminiscent of Brecht's own use of an on-stage narrator."

14. See Bammer 94 for a discussion of contemporary responses to the film. She sums them up this way: "Either the emotional power of its depiction of the subjectivity of history was acknowledged and it was then criticized for not limiting itself to this 'purely personal' focus, or its 'subjectivism' was attacked as *too* limited."

15. See Kaplan 302 for an opposing view, positing the autobiographical element as implying an attempt at transparency: "the spectator is in the strange position of at once experiencing cinematic processes that break with classical codes, and sensing the attempt at transparency."

16. See Seiter 572–573 for a critique of Sanders-Brahms for an excess of "subjectivity" in her emphasis on the mother–daughter dyad: "[the film] illustrates the problem with all types of feminism which mythologize the mother. The emphasis on the psychological self-sufficiency of the mother and daughter relationship results in the detachment of women from social, economic and political relationships." Seiter also critiques Sanders-Brahms for excessive use of melodramatic coding that "obscures the ability to read the family narrative in political terms, rather than pathetic ones." This reading of the film as "belonging unmistakably to the tradition of domestic or family melodrama" is very interesting—however, I do not agree that this makes it inherently politically regressive.

17. See Kaes 150 for the perceptive comment that "the spectator notices the manipulation of the documentary footage and feels uneasy about the unquestioned appropriation of historical material into the fictional world. Kaes, like other critics, argues that Sanders-Brahms is manipulating the documentary to give a "personal" view of "history" that has the effect, intended or not, of letting women in general off the hook, absolving them from responsibility for Nazism; this absolution is seen as politically suspect. See Brunette's interview with Helma Sanders-Brahms, *Conversation* 36–37, which allows Sanders-Brahms herself to respond to these charges, perhaps to her own detriment: "I have spent years and years and years just blaming my parents for what happened. . . . That doesn't help the horrible crimes the Germans have committed. Maybe there should be a film that is more accusing. . . . But when I see all these American films that have never really accused the Americans of all the crimes they did to the Indians, for example . . . I ask myself, how dare they accuse my parents."

18. See McCormick 198: "the documentary footage . . . breaks up the fiction at the same time as it contextualizes and is contextualized by it. The illusion of reality in the Hollywood film ('a beautifully closed object' as Metz writes) depends

in part on its apparent self-sufficiency; in Sanders-Brahms' film the fiction is called into question by the documentary footage that intrudes upon it."

19. See Hyams 47. Hyams states that, in the fairy-tale sequence, Sanders-Brahms introduces a "severely polarized" distinction between men and women in which women, representing life and nature, are once again exonerated to some degree from responsibility for Nazism. Women are, Hyams argues, viewed by Sanders-Brahms as passive victims rather than participants. Hyams also says that the film's treatment of Lene's rape by American soldiers continues this model of passive victimization into the postwar period, rendering the Allied powers equivalent to the Nazis in brutality: "The Germans in this film are implicitly as brutalized by American imposed de-Nazification as they were by Nazi totalitarianism."

20. Kaplan 302 takes her to task for this; in addition, Kaplan argues that Sanders-Brahms is not sufficiently critical of the use of the allegorical figure of Woman by Nazism.

21. See McCormick 190–198 for an extremely interesting discussion of allegory and essentialism. McCormick also argues that the poem is used in an antiessentialist way. His argument is that Sanders-Brahms portrays the mother—Lene—in such a morally ambiguous light that the allegorical figure is deconstructed. The allegorical Woman is eternally nurturer and blameless victim; by contrast, Lene, though definitely a victim, is clearly implicated in at least two incidents as an active—if thoughtless—participant in anti-Semitic persecution, and in the last section of the film is also a persecutor of her child.

5 The Passion of Veronika Voss

1. See Watson 221 for a comment on Veronika's drug addiction as metaphor for the pleasures of cinema viewing.

2. See Elsaesser, *FG* 112: his highly illuminating discussion of *Die Sehnsucht der Veronika Voss* defines the focus on spectatorship as a "mise-en-abîme of German history into private history."

3. See Elsaesser, *FG* 114, and Watson 222–223 for an analysis of the citation of film noir in *Die Sehnsucht der Veronika Voss*. The most obvious film noir influence is Billy Wilder's *Sunset Boulevard*, which also deals with the love of a younger man for a faded movie star, and is a murder mystery.

4. See McCormick 177–185 for an illuminating discussion of the cinematic discourses of the 1970s around historiography and aesthetics in relation to Germany's Nazi past.

5. See Elsaesser, *FG* 113, for a comment on the spectral qualities of many of the women in Fassbinder's BRD trilogy. He says of Veronika: "A figure with a past, a figure from the past, she steps on the tram in the Englische Garten like a ghost, which of course is partly what she is." He goes on to say this about her relationship with Robert: "Veronika is for Krohn a figure from an overdetermined history—the diabolical past of Nazi cinema—spreading a very cold but intense light."

6. See Kuzniar 70 for a very interesting discussion of the similarities between Veronika and Zara Leander, the major Nazi film star, commenting

on Fassbinder's use of citation to emphasize his construction of femininity through specularity and as masquerade. The plot of the film is loosely based on the life of Sybille Schmitz, a film star during the Third Reich, who struggled to survive after the war, becoming a drug addict and ultimately committing suicide.

7. I am indebted to Don Eric Levine for pointing out this connection to me.

8. See Sheehan 287.

9. See Kuzniar 73 for an illuminating comment on this scene, underlining the primacy of the image in the reproduction of the Nazi past: "Those that appreciatively recognize [Veronika] like the proprietor of the jewelry shop, are also nostalgic for the Nazi regime, signaling that the draw of this recent past occurs via its image repertoire."

10. See Silverman, *Male Subjectivity* 133 for a discussion of the "desperate attempts" by Veronika "to orchestrate lighting and music in such a way as to create the impression that she 'really' is the star which her publicity stills declare her to be."

11. I refer here again to the extensive scholarship regarding the psychoanalytic concepts of mourning and melancholy as structures governing Germany's confrontation with its Nazi past. See Mitscherlich and, for more recent discussions, Santner 1–56, Homans 1–42, and Flinn 29–69 among others.

12. See Elsaesser, *FG* 113, for a discussion in which he refers to *Die Sehnsucht der Veronika Voss* as "the drama of a woman who cannot hold on to her image, yet is a prisoner of that image."

13. It is notable that the victims of Nazism are also present as revenants in this film. An important role is played by an older couple who are concentration camp survivors, and Dr. Katz's name suggests that she is Jewish.

14. Minnespiel, Op. 101, No. 6: Lied—"O Freund, mein Schirm, mein Schutz." This is also an ancient Marian prayer, seeking the intercession of the Madonna.

15. Fassbinder is well known to have been a soccer fan; see *The Anarchy of the Imagination* 108 for, among the more important interviews and discussions with Fassbinder, a list of his favorite players (108).

16. Elsaesser, *FG* 116, also points out the connections between the uses of soccer in both films. He offers a broader and very illuminating discussion about the complex function of Fassbinder's soundtracks.

17. For an interesting discussion of the Brechtian function of soccer on the soundtrack of *Die Ehe der Maria Braun*, see Moeller 102–107. Moeller also reminds us of the importance of Germany's victory in the 1954 World Cup as a source of resurgent nationalism, complete with the singing of the "Deutschlandlied"—the anthem closely associated with Nazism—by thousands of fans in the stadium, including the verse, "Deutschland, Deutschland über alles," which had been banned by the Allied occupying powers after the war.

18. I refer again here to Mussolini's famous dictum, "il cinema è l'arma più forte:" "cinema is the strongest weapon."

19. The poem, in Fassbinder's version of Eich, is entitled "Fortschritt," and reads: "Entlaert von Gedächtnis/Ich war fünf Glaskugeln/ohne Laub, ohne Ausblicke/Gestern ware ein guter Tag zum Sterben gewesen/Heute beissen/den letzten die Hunde." ("Drained of memory/I was five glass spheres/without

leaves or prospects/yesterday would have been a good day to die/today the dogs are biting the hindmost." Translation from film subtitles.)

20. This dictum tended to produce writing bound to everyday objects, of noticeable flatness and concreteness—this rejection of the "literary" did engender many poems of great power. Perhaps the preeminent example is Eich's most famous poem, "Inventur," first published in 1945.

Afterword

1. See Marcus, *Auschwitz* 155, for the quotation of a very pertinent phrase from Pasolini's critical essays: "delirious with aestheticism."

FILMOGRAPHY

U.S. release title and/or original language title, director, country or countries of production, production company or companies, year of first release.

1860, dir. Alessandro Blasetti. Italy, Societa Anonima Stefano Pittaluga, 1934.

1900/Novecento, dir. Bernardo Bertolucci. Italy, PEA/Artistes Associès/Artemis Films, 1976 (in two parts).

Amarcord, dir. Federico Fellini. Italy, FC Produzione/PECF, 1973.

The Ballad of Berlin/Berliner Ballade, dir. Robert Adolf Stemmle. West Germany, Comedia, 1948.

Berlin Express, dir. Jacques Tourneur. United States, RKO, 1948.

Berlin Alexanderplatz, dir. Rainer Werner Fassbinder. West Germany, Bavaria Film, 1980.

The Bicycle Thief/Ladri di biciclette, dir. Vittorio de Sica. Italy, PDS-ENIC, 1948.

Bitter Rice/Riso amaro, dir. Giuseppe de Santis. Italy, Lux Film, 1949.

The Blue Light/Das blaue Licht, dir. Leni Riefenstahl. Germany, Leni Riefenstahl-Produktion, 1932.

The Cabinet of Dr Caligari/Das Kabinett des Doktor Caligari, dir. Robert Wiene. Germany, Decla-Bioscop AG, 1920.

Casablanca, dir. Michael Curtiz. United States, Warner Bros, 1942.

Christ Stopped at Eboli/ Cristo si é fermato a Eboli, dir. Francesco Rosi. Italy, RAI, 1979.

The Conformist/Il conformista, dir. Bernardo Bertolucci. Italy, Mars Film, 1970.

The Damned/La caduta degli dei/Götterdämmerung, dir. Luchino Visconti. Italy, Pegaso, 1969.

Day of Freedom/Tag der Freiheit—Unsere Wehrmacht, dir. Leni Riefenstahl. Germany, Reichsparteifilm, 1935.

Death in Venice/Morte a Venezia, dir. Luchino Visconti. Italy, Alfa Cinematografica, 1971.

Death Mills/Die Todesmühlen, dir. Hanus Burger. United States, US Army Signal Corps, 1945.

The Earth Trembles/La terra trema, dir. Luchino Visconti. Italy, Universalia, 1948.

Fist in His Pocket/I pugni in tasca, dir. Marco Bellocchio. Italy, Doria, 1968.

A Foreign Affair, dir. Billy Wilder. United States, Paramount, 1948.

The Garden of the Finzi-Continis/Il giardino dei Finzi Contini, dir. Vittorio de Sica. Italy, Documento Film, 1970.

Germany, Pale Mother/Deutschland bleiche Mutter, dir. Helma Sanders-Brahms. West Germany, Helma Sanders-Brahms Filmproduktion, 1980.

Germany Year Zero/Germania anno zero, dir. Roberto Rossellini, Italy/Germany, Produzione Salvo D'Angelo, Tevere Film, 1948.

Gone with the Wind, dir. Victor Fleming. United States, MGM, 1939.

Goodbye Children/Au revoir les enfants, dir. Louis Malle. France, NEF, 1987.

The Gospel According to Saint Matthew/Il Vangelo secondo Matteo, dir. Pier Paolo Pasolini. Italy, Arco Film/Lux CC, 1964.

The Great Dictator, dir. Charles Chaplin. United States, Charles Chaplin Film Corporation, 1940.

Hiroshima mon amour, dir. Alain Resnais. France, Argos Films, 1959.

Hitler: A Film from Germany/ Hitler—ein Film aus Deutschlan, dir. Hans-Jürgen Syberberg. West Germany, TMS Film GmbH, 1977.

Hitlerjunge Quex/Hitler Youth Quex, dir. Hans Steinhoff. Germany, UFA, 1933.

Icicle Thief/Ladri di saponette, dir.Maurizio Nichetti. Italy, Bambù/Reteitalia, 1989.

Ilsa, She Wolf of the SS, dir. Don Edmonds. United States, Aeteas Filmproduktions, 1975.

The Iron Crown/La corona di ferro, dir. Alessandro Blasetti. Italy, ENIC-Lux, 1941.

Lacombe Lucien, dir. Louis Malle. France, NEF, 1974.

The Last Metro/Le Dernier Métro, dir. François Truffaut. France, Les Films du Carrosse, 1980.

Last Orgy of the Third Reich/L'ultima orgia dell III Reich, dir. Cesare Canevari. Italy, Cine Lu Ce, 1977.

The Leopard/Il gattopardo, dir. Luchino Visconti. Italy, Titanus, 1963.

Life is Beautiful/La vita è bella, dir. Roberto Benigni. Italy, Melampo Cinematografica, 1997.

Lion of the Desert/Omar Mukhtar, dir. Moustapha Akkad. United States/Libya, Falcon International Productions, 1981.

Lili Marlene, dir. Rainer Werner Fassbinder. West Germany, Bayerischer Rundfunk, 1981.

Lola, dir. Rainer Werner Fassbinder. West Germany, Rialto Film, 1981.

M/M Eine Stadt sucht einen Mörder, dir. Fritz Lang. Germany, Nero-Film AG, 1931.

Man With a Cross/L'uomo della croce, dir. Roberto Rossellini. Italy, Continentalcine, 1943.

The Marriage of Maria Braun/Die Ehe der Maria Braun, dir. Rainer Werner Fassbinder. West Germany, Albatros Filmproduktion, 1979.

Marriage in the Shadows/Ehe im Schatten, dir. Kurt Maetzig. Germany, DEFA, 1947.

Metropolis, dir. Fritz Lang. Germany, UFA, 1927.

Miracle in Milan/Miracolo a Milano, dir. Vittorio de Sica. Italy, ENIC, 1951.

Murderers Among Us/Die Mörder sind unter uns, dir. Wolfgang Staudte. Germany, DEFA, 1946.

The Night of the Shooting Stars/La notte di San Lorenzo, dir. Paolo and Vittorio Taviani. Italy, RAI, 1982.

The Night Porter/Il portiere di notte, dir. Liliana Cavani. Italy, Ital-Noleggio Cinematografico, 1974.

The Old Guard/La vecchia guardia, dir. Alessandro Blasetti. Italy, Fauno, 1934.

Olympia Part One: Festival of Nations/Olympia 1. Teil: Fest der Völker, dir. Leni Riefenstahl. Germany, Olympia Film, 1938.

Olympia Part Two: Festival of Beauty/Olympia 2. Teil: Fest der Schönheit, dir. Leni Riefenstahl. Germany, Olympia Film, 1938.

One, Two, Three, dir. Billy Wilder. United States, Mirisch Corporation, 1961.

Ossessione, dir. Luchino Visconti. Italy, Industria Cinematografica Italiana, 1942.

Paisan/Paisà, dir. Roberto Rossellini. Italy, Organizzazione Film Internazionali (OFI), 1946.

A Pilot Returns/Un pilota ritorna, dir. Roberto Rossellini. Italy, Centro Cinematografico del Ministero della Marina, 1942.

Rocco and His Brothers/Rocco e I suoi fratelli, dir. Luchino Visconti. Italy, Titanus, 1960.

Rome, Open City/Roma, città aperta, dir. Roberto Rossellini. Italy, Excelsa Film, 1945.

Salò, or the 120 Days of Sodom/Salò, o le 120 giornate di Sodoma, dir. Pier Paolo Pasolini. Italy, PEA, 1975.

Salon Kitty, dir. Tinto Brass. Italy, Coralta Cinematografica, 1976.

Seven Beauties/Pasqualino Settebellezze, dir. Lina Wertmüller. Italy, Medusa, 1975.

Somewhere in Berlin/Irgendwo in Berlin, dir. Gerhard Lamprecht. West Germany, DEFA, 1946.

The Spider Stratagem/La strategia del ragno, dir. Bernardo Bertolucci. Italy, Radiotelevisione Italiana, 1970.

SS Hell Camp:Beast in Heat/La bestia in calore, dir. Luigi Batzella. Italy, Eterna Film, 1977.

Sunset Boulevard, dir. Billy Wilder. United States, Paramount, 1950.

Scipio Africanus/Scipione L'Africano, dir. Carmine Gallone. Italy, ENIC, 1937.

Shoeshine/Sciuscià, dir. Vittorio de Sica. Italy, Societa Cooperativa Alfa Cinematografica, 1946.

A Special Day/Una giornata particolare, dir. Ettore Scola. Italy, Champion, 1974.

Sun/Sole, dir. Alessandro Blasetti. Italy, Augustus, 1929.

Terra Madre, dir. Alessandro Blasetti. Italy, Cines, 1931.

The Testament of Dr. Mabuse/Das Testament der Dr. Mabuse, dir. Fritz Lang. Germany, Nero-Film AG, 1933.

The Third Man, dir. Carol Reed. United Kingdom, London Film Productions, 1949.

Triumph of the Will/Triumph des Willens, dir. Leni Riefenstahl. Germany, Leni Riefenstahl-Produktion, 1935.

Umberto D, dir. Vittorio de Sica. Italy, Amato Film, 1952.

Under the Southern Cross/Sotto la croce del sud, dir. Guido Brignone. Italy, Mediterannea Film, 1938.

Veronika Voss/Die Sehnsucht der Veronika Voss, dir. Rainer Werner Fassbinder. West Germany, Laura Film, 1982.

Victory of Belief/Der Sieg des Glaubens, dir. Leni Riefenstahl. Germany, Reichspropagandaleitung der NSDAP, 1933.

A Walk in the Clouds/Quattro passi fra le nuvole, dir. Alessandro Blasetti. Italy, Cines, 1942.

We All Loved Each Other So Much/C'eravamo tanto amati, dir. Ettore Scola. Italy, Dean Cinematografica/Delta, 1974.

The White Ship/La nave bianca, dir. Roberto Rossellini. Italy, Centro Cinematografico del Ministero della Marina, 1941.

The White Squadron/Lo squadrone bianco, dir. Augusto Genina. Italy, Roma Film, 1936.

BIBLIOGRAPHY

Allan, William Sheridan. *The Nazi Seizure of Power: The Experience of a Single German Town, 1922–1945*. New York: Franklin Watts, 1984.

Armstrong, Richard. *Billy Wilder: American Film Realist*. Jefferson, NC: McFarland, 2000.

———. *Understanding Realism*. London: British Film Institute, 2005.

Baker, Brian. *Masculinity in Fiction and Film: Representing Men in Popular Genres, 1945–2000*. New York: Continuum, 2006.

Bammer, Angelika. "Through a Daughter's Eyes: Helma Sanders-Brahms' *Germany, Pale Mother*." *New German Critique* 36 (1985): 101.

Bartram, Graham, Maurice Slawinski, and David Steel, eds. *Reconstructing the Past: Representations of the Fascist Era Past in Post-War European Culture*. Keele, Eng.: Keele UP, 1996.

Bazin, Andrè. *What Is Cinema?* Trans. Hugh Gray. 2 vols. Berkeley: U of California P, 1971.

Ben-Ghiat, Ruth, and Mia Fuller, eds. *Italian Colonialism*. New York: Palgrave Macmillan, 2005.

Benshoff, Harry, and Sean Griffin, eds. *Queer Cinema: The Film Reader*. New York: Routledge, 2004.

Berezin, Mabel. *Making the Fascist Self: The Political Culture of Interwar Italy*. Ithaca, NY: Cornell UP, 1997.

Bergala, Alain. "*Lettre a Helma Sanders-Brahms sur un Cinéma sans Consolation*" ("Letter to Helma Sanders-Brahms on a Cinema without Consolation"). *Cahiers du Cinéma* 329 (1981): 19.

Berger, Maurice, Brian Wallis, and Simon Watson, eds. *Constructing Masculinity*. New York: Routledge, 1995.

Bergstrom, Janet. *Endless Night: Cinema and Psychoanalysis, Parallel Histories*. Berkeley: U of California P, 1999.

Bertellini, Giorgio. *The Cinema of Italy*. London: Wallflower, 2004.

Bertolucci, Bernardo, Franco Arcalli, and Giuseppe Bertolucci. *Novecento: atto secondo (Nineteen Hundred: Second Act)*. Turin: Einaudi, 1976.

Bolongario, Eugenio. "Why Truth Matters: Ideology and Ethics in Bertolucci's *The Spider Stratagem*." *Italian Culture* 23 (2005): 71–96.

Bondanella, Peter. *The Films of Frederico Fellini*. Cambridge, Eng.: Cambridge UP, 2002.

———. *The Films of Roberto Rossellini*. Cambridge, Eng.: Cambridge UP, 1993.

———. *Italian Cinema from Neorealism to the Present*. New York: Continuum, 1991.

Bono, Paola, and Sandra Kemp, eds. *Italian Feminist Thought: A Reader.* Oxford: Basil Blackwell, 1991.

Bonsaver, Guido. *Censorship and Literature in Fascist Italy.* Toronto: U of Toronto P, 2007.

Bridenthal, Renate, Atina Grossmann, and Marion Kaplan, eds. *When Biology Became Destiny: Women in Weimar and Nazi Germany.* New York: Monthly Review P, 1984.

Brunetta, Gian Piero. *Intellettuali, cinema e propaganda tra le due guerre (Intellectuals, Cinema and Propaganda Between the Wars).* Bologna: Pàtron, 1972.

Brunette, Peter. "Helma Sanders-Brahms: A Conversation." *Film Quarterly* 44.2 (1990): 34–42.

———. *Roberto Rossellini.* Oxford: Oxford UP, 1996.

———. "Rossellini and Cinematic Realism." *Cinema Journal* 25.1 (1985): 34.

———. "Unity and Difference in Paisan." *Studies in the Literary Imagination* 16.1 (1983): 91–111.

Brunette, Peter, and David Wills. *Screen/Play: Derrida and Film Theory.* Princeton, NJ: Princeton UP, 1989.

Bruno, Giuliana. *Streetwalking on a Ruined Map: Cultural Theory and the City Films of Elvira Notari.* Princeton, NJ: Princeton UP, 1993.

———. *Atlas of Emotion: Journeys in Art, Architecture, and Film.* London: Verso, 2002.

Bruno, Giuliana, and Maria Nadotti, eds. *Offscreen: Women and Film in Italy.* New York: Routledge, 1988.

Burnett, Ron, ed. *Explorations in Film Theory: Selected Essays from Ciné-Tracts.* Bloomington: Indiana UP, 1991.

Butler, Judith. *Bodies That Matter: On the Discursive Limits of "Sex."* New York: Routledge, 1993.

———. *Gender Trouble: Feminism and the Subversion of Identity.* New York: Routledge, 1990.

———. *The Psychic Life of Power: Theories in Subjection.* Stanford, CA: Stanford UP, 1997.

Cardullo, Bert. "The Symbolism of *Hiroshima, Mon Amour.*" *Film Criticism* 8.2 (1984): 39–44.

Cassels, Alan. *Fascist Italy.* Arlington Heights, IL: Harlan Davidson, 1968.

Cestaro, Gary P., ed. *Queer Italia: Same-Sex Desire in Italian Literature and Film.* New York: Palgrave Macmillan, 2004.

Clark, Martin. *Modern Italy, 1871–1982.* London: Longman, 1984.

Conley, Tom. *Cartographic Cinema.* Minneapolis: U of Minnesota P, 2007.

Corrigan, Timothy. *New German Film: The Displaced Image.* Bloomington: Indiana UP, 1994.

Dalle Vacche, Angela. *The Body in the Mirror: Shapes of History in Italian Cinema.* Princeton, NJ: Princeton UP, 1992.

———. *Cinema and Painting: How Art Is Used in Film.* Austin: U of Texas P, 1996.

———. *Diva: Defiance and Passion in Early Italian Cinema.* Austin: U of Texas P, 2008.

———. *The Visual Turn: Classical Film History and Art History.* New Brunswick, NJ: Rutgers UP, 2003.

Davidson, John E. *Deterritorializing the New German Cinema*. Minneapolis: U of Minnesota P, 1999.

De Felice, Renzo. *Autobiografia del fascismo: antologia di testi fascisti, 1919–1945 (Autobiography of Fascism: Anthology of Fascist Writing, 1919–1945)*. Bergamo: Minerva Italica, 1978.

———. *Intellettuali di fronte al fascismo: saggi e note documentarie (Intellectuals Confront Fascism: Essays and Documentary Notes)*. Rome: Bonacci, 1985.

———. *Le interpretazioni del fascismo (Interpretations of Fascism)*. Rome: Laterza, 1995.

———. *Mussolini*. Turin: Einaudi, 1965.

———. *Storia degli ebrei italiani sotto il fascismo (The Jews in Fascist Italy: A History)*. Turin: Einaudi, 1962.

DeGrand, Alexander. *Italian Fascism: Its Origins and Development*. Lincoln: U of Nebraska P, 1982.

Dern, John A. "The Revenant of Vienna: A Critical Comparison of Carol Reed's Film *The Third Man* and Bram Stoker's Novel *Dracula*." *Literature/Film Quarterly* 33 (2005): 4–11.

Derrida, Jacques. *Limited Inc*. Trans. Samuel Weber. Evanston, IL: Northwestern UP, 1988.

———. *Writing and Difference*. Trans. Alan Bass. Chicago: Chicago UP, 1978.

Dick, Bernard F. *Billy Wilder*. New York: Da Capo, 1996.

Dixon, Wheeler, W. *It Looks at You: The Returned Gaze of Cinema*. Albany: State U of New York P, 1995.

———. *The Second Century of Cinema: The Past and Future of the Moving Image*. Albany: State U of New York P, 2000.

———. *Straight: Constructions of Heterosexuality in the Cinema*. Albany: State U of New York P, 2003.

———. *The Transparency of Spectacle: Meditations on the Moving Image*. Albany: State U of New York P, 1998.

Doane, Mary Ann. *The Desire to Desire: The Woman's Film of the 1940s*. Bloomington: Indiana UP, 1987.

———. *The Emergence of Cinematic Time: Modernity, Contingency, the Archive*. Cambridge, MA: Harvard UP, 2002.

———. *Femmes Fatales: Feminism, Film Theory, Psychoanalysis*. New York: Routledge, 1991.

Duras, Marguerite. *Hiroshima mon amour*. Paris: Gallimard, 1960.

———. *Hiroshima mon amour*. Trans. Richard Sever. New York: Grove, 1961.

Dyer, Richard. "Resistance through Charisma: Rita Hayworth and *Gilda*." *Women in Film Noir*. Ed. E. Ann Kaplan. London: British Film Institute, 1980: 91–100.

Eich, Günther. "Inventur." *German Twentieth Century Poetry*. Ed. Reinhold Grimm and Irmgard Hunt. London: Continuum, 2001: 108.

Elkins, Richard, and Dave King. *Blending Genders: Social Aspects of Cross-Dressing and Sex-Changing*. New York: Routledge, 1996.

Elsaesser, Thomas. *European Cinema: Face to Face with Hollywood*. Amsterdam: Amsterdam UP, 2005.

———. *Fassbinder's Germany: History Identity Subject*. Amsterdam: Amsterdam UP, 1995.

Elsaesser, Thomas. *New German Cinema: A History.* New Brunswick, NJ: Rutgers UP, 1989.

Engelmann, Bernt. *In Hitler's Germany: Everyday Life in the Third Reich.* Trans. Krishna Winston. New York: Shocken, 1986.

Fassbinder, Rainer Werner. *The Anarchy of the Imagination: Interviews, Essays, Notes.* Michael Töteberg and Leo A. Lensing, eds. Trans. Krishna Winston. Baltimore: The Johns Hopkins UP, 1992,

Fehrenbach, Heide. *Cinema in Democratizing Germany: Reconstructing National Identity After Hitler.* Chapel Hill: U of North Carolina P, 1995.

Flinn, Caryl. *The New German Cinema: Music, History, and the Matter of Style.* Berkeley: U of California P, 2004.

Forgacs, David, and Robert Lumley, eds. *Italian Cultural Studies: An Introduction.* Oxford: Oxford UP, 1996.

Forgacs, David, Sarah Lutton, and Geoffrey Nowell-Smith, eds. *Roberto Rossellini: Magician of the Real.* London: British Film Institute, 2000.

Frieden, Sandra, Richard McCormick, Vibeke R. Petersen, and Laurie Melissa Vogelsang, eds. *Gender and German Cinema, Feminist Interventions.* 2 vols. Oxford: Berg, 1993.

Friedlander, Saul. *Reflections of Nazism: An Essay on Kitsch and Death.* Bloomington: Indiana UP, 1993.

Gallagher, Tag. *The Adventures of Roberto Rossellini: His Life and Films.* New York: Da Capo, 1998.

Galt, Rosalind. *The New European Cinema: Redrawing the Map.* New York: Columbia UP, 2006.

Gemunden, Gerd. *A Foreign Affair: Billy Wilder's American Films.* New York: Berghahn, 2008.

Gledhill, Christine, ed. *Home Is Where the Heart Is: Studies in Melodrama and the Woman's Film.* London: British Film Institute, 1987.

Greene, Nathanael, ed. *Fascism: An Anthology.* New York: Crowell, 1968.

Hake, Sabine. *German National Cinema.* New York: Routledge, 2002.

———. *Popular Cinema of the Third Reich.* Austin: U of Texas P, 2001.

Hay, James. *Popular Film Culture in Fascist Italy: The Passing of the Rex.* Bloomington: Indiana UP, 1987.

Hewitt, Andrew. *Political Inversions: Homosexuality, Fascism, and the Modernist Imaginary.* Stanford, CA: Stanford UP, 1996.

Hewitt, Leah D. *Remembering the Occupation in French Film.* New York: Palgrave Macmillan, 2008.

Hillman, Roger. *Unsettling Scores: German Film, Music, and Ideology.* Bloomington: Indiana UP, 2005.

Homans, Peter, ed. *Symbolic Loss,* Charlottesville: U of Virginia P, 2000.

Hyams, Barbara. "Is the Apolitical Woman at Peace? A Reading of the Fairy Tale in *Germany, Pale Mother.*" *Wide Angle* 10.4 (1988): 46.

Jarausch, Konrad H., and Michael Geyer, eds. *Shattered Past: Reconstructing German Identities.* Princeton, NJ: Princeton UP, 2003.

Kaes, Anton. *From Hitler to Heimat: The Return of History as Film.* Cambridge, MA: Harvard UP, 1989.

Kaplan, E. Ann. "The Search for the Mother/Land in Sanders-Brahms's *Germany, Pale Mother.*" *German Film and Literature: Adaptations and Transformations.* Ed. Eric Rentschler. New York: Methuen, 1986. 289–304.

Klessman, Christoph. *The Divided Past: Rewriting Post-War German History.* New York: Berg, 2001.

Kline, T. Jefferson. *Bertolucci's Dream Loom: A Psychoanalytic Study of Cinema.* Amherst: U of Massachusetts P, 1987.

Knight, Julia. *Women and the New German Cinema.* London: Verso, 1992.

Koon, Tracy H. *Believe, Obey, Fight: Political Socialization of Youth in Fascist Italy, 1922–1943.* Chapel Hill: U of North Carolina P, 1985.

Koonz, Claudia. *Mothers in the Fatherland: Women, the Family and Nazi Politics.* New York: St. Martin's, 1987.

Krauss, Rosalind E. *The Optical Unconscious.* Cambridge, MA: MIT P, 1993.

Kuzniar, Alice A. *The Queer German Cinema.* Stanford, CA: Stanford UP, 2000.

Landy, Marcia. *Fascism in Film: The Italian Commercial Cinema, 1931–1943.* Princeton, NJ: Princeton UP, 1986.

———. *The Folklore of Consensus: Theatricality in the Italian Cinema, 1930–1943.* Albany: State U of New York P, 1998.

———. *Italian Film.* Cambridge: Cambridge UP, 2000.

———. *The Historical Film: History and Memory in Media.* New Brunswick, NJ: Rutgers UP, 2001.

———. *Stardom, Italian Style: Screen Performance and Personality in Italian Cinema.* Bloomington: Indiana UP, 2008.

Lang, Robert. *Masculine Interests: Homoerotics in Hollywood Films.* New York: Columbia UP, 2002.

Lasansky, D. Medina. *The Renaissance Perfected: Architecture, Spectacle, and Tourism in Fascist Italy.* University Park: Pennsylvania State UP, 2004.

Lehmann, Peter. *Masculinity: Bodies, Movies, Culture.* New York: Routledge, 2001.

Levi, Primo. *I Somersi e i salvati (The Drowned and the Saved).* Turin: Einadi, 1986.

Liehm, Mira. *Passion and Defiance: Film in Italy from 1942 to the Present.* Berkeley: U of California P, 1984.

Linville, Susan E. "The Mother–Daughter Plot in History: Helma Sanders-Brahms's *Germany, Pale Mother.*" *New German Critique* 55 (1992): 51–70.

Lizzani, Carlo. *Attraverso il novecento (Through the Twentieth Century).* Turin: Scuola Nazionale di Cinema, 1998.

Loy, Rosetta. *First Words: A Childhood in Fascist Italy.* New York: Metropolitan Books/Henry Holt, 2000.

Lyotard, Jean-François. *Heidigger and "The Jews."* Minneapolis: University of Minnesota Press, 1990

Marcus, Millicent. *After Fellini: National Cinema in the Postmodern Age.* Baltimore: Johns Hopkins UP, 2002.

———. *Italian Film in the Light of Neorealism.* Princeton, NJ: Princeton UP, 1986.

———. *Italian Film in the Shadow of Auschwitz.* Toronto: U of Toronto P, 2007.

McCormick, Richard W. *Politics of the Self: Feminism and the Postmodern in West German Literature and Film.* Princeton, NJ: Princeton UP, 1991.

Mercken-Spaas, Godelieve. "Destruction and Reconstruction in *Hiroshima, Mon Amour.*" *Literature/Film Quarterly* 8 (1980): 244–250.

Mitscherlich, Alexander and Margarete. *The Inability to Mourn: Principles of Collective Behavior.* Trans. Beverley R. Placzek. New York: Grove, 1975.

Moeller, H.-B. "Fassbinder's Use of Brechtian Aesthetics: The Marriage of Maria Braun, Veronika Voss, Lola." *Jump Cut* 35 (1990): 102–107.

Moses, John W. "Vision Denied in *Night and Fog* and *Hiroshima Mon Amour*." *Literature/Film Quarterly* 15 (1987): 159–163.

Moss, M. E. *Benedetto Croce Reconsidered: Truth and Error in Theories of Art, Literature, and History*. Hanover: UP of New England, 1987.

Mulvey, Laura. "Visual Pleasure and Narrative Cinema." *Visual and Other Pleasures*. Ed. Laura Mulvey. Bloomington: Indiana UP, 1989. 14–26.

Nowell-Smith, Geoffrey. *Luchino Visconti*. New York: Viking, 1973.

———. *Making Waves: New Cinemas of the 1960s*. New York: Continuum, 2008.

Nowell-Smith, Geoffrey, James Hay, and Gianni Volpi, eds. *The Companion to Italian Cinema*. London: British Film Institute, 1996.

Painter, Borden. *Mussolini's Rome: Rebuilding the Eternal City*. New York: Palgrave Macmillan, 2005.

———. "Renzo De Felice and the Historiography of Italian Fascism." *The American Historical Review* 95 (1990): 391–405.

Palmer, James, and Michael Riley. "The Lone Rider in Vienna: Myth and Meaning in *The Third Man*." *Literature/Film Quarterly* 8 (1980): 14–21.

Parker, Andrew, and Eve Kosofsky Sedgwick, eds. *Performativity and Performance*. New York: Routledge, 1995.

Parker, Andrew, Mary Russo, Doris Sommer, and Patricia Yaeger, eds. *Nationalisms and Sexualities*. New York: Routledge, 1992.

Penley, Constance, ed. *Feminism and Film Theory*. New York: Routledge, 1988.

Petro, Patrice. *Aftershocks of the New: Feminism and Film History*. New Brunswick, NJ: Rutgers UP, 2002.

Peucker, Brigitte. *The Material Image: Art and the Real in Film*. Stanford, CA: Stanford UP, 2007.

Pickering-Iazzi, Robin, ed. *Mothers of Invention: Women, Italian Fascism, and Culture*. Minneapolis: U of Minnesota P, 1995.

———. *Politics of the Visible: Writing Women, Culture and Fascism*. Minneapolis: U of Minnesota P, 1997.

Pomerance, Murray. *Ladies and Gentlemen, Boys and Girls: Gender in Film at the End of the Twentieth Century*. Albany: State U of New York P, 2001.

———. *Where the Boys Are: Cinemas of Proximity and Youth*. Detroit, MI: Wayne State UP, 2005.

Pribram, Deidre, ed. *Female Spectators: Looking at Film and Television*. London: Verso, 1988.

Ravetto, Kriss. *The Unmaking of Fascist Aesthetics*. Minneapolis: U of Minnesota P, 2001.

Reich, Jacqueline. *Beyond the Latin Lover: Marcello Mastroianni, Masculinity, and Italian Cinema*. Bloomington: Indiana UP, 2004.

Reich, Jacqueline, and Piero Garofalo. *Re-Viewing Fascism: Italian Cinema, 1922–1943*. Bloomington: U of Indiana P, 2002.

Reimer, Robert C. *Cultural History Through a National Socialist Lens: Essays on the Cinema of the Third Reich*. Rochester, NY: Camden House, 2000.

———. *Nazi-Retro Film: How German Narrative Cinema Remembers the Past*. Toronto: Maxwell Macmillan Canada, 1992.

Rentschler, Eric. *German Film and Literature: Adaptations and Transformations.* New York: Methuen, 1986.

———. *The Ministry of Illusion: Nazi Cinema and Its Afterlife.* Cambridge, MA: Harvard UP, 1996.

Rentschler, Eric, ed. *West German Filmmakers on Film: Visions and Voices.* New York: Holmes and Meier, 1988.

Rheuban, Joyce, ed. *The Marriage of Maria Braun.* Dir. Rainer Werner Fassbinder, Rutgers Films in Print Ser. 4. New Brunswick, NJ: Rutgers UP, 1986.

Rhodes, John David. *Stupendous, Miserable City: Pasolini's Rome.* Minneapolis: U of Minnesota P, 2007.

Ricci, Steven. *Cinema and Fascism: Italian Film and Society, 1922–1943.* Berkeley: U of California P, 2008.

Richter, Gerhard. *Gerhard Richter, 18. Oktober 1977.* London: Institute of Contemporary Arts in association with Anthony d'Offay Gallery, 1989.

Roberts, David D. *Historicism and Fascism in Modern Italy.* Toronto: U of Toronto P, 2007.

Rodowick, D. N. *The Difficulty of Difference: Psychoanalysis, Sexual Difference and Film Theory.* New York: Routledge, 1991.

Ropars-Wuilleumier, Marie-Claire. "Film Reader of the Text." *Diacritics* 15.1 (1985): 18–30.

Rosenstone, Robert A. *Visions of the Past: The Challenge of Film to Our Idea of History.* Cambridge, MA: Harvard UP, 1995.

Rossellini, Roberto. *My Method: Writings and Interviews.* Ed. Adriano Aprà. Trans. Annapaola Cancogni. New York: Marsilio, 1992.

Santner, Eric. *My Own Private Germany: Daniel Paul Schreber's Secret History of Modernity.* Princeton, NJ: Princeton UP, 1996.

———. *Stranded Objects: Mourning, Memory, and Film in Postwar Cinema.* Ithaca, NY: Cornell UP, 1990.

Schulte-Sasse, Linda. *Entertaining the Third Reich: Illusions of Wholeness in Nazi Cinema.* Durham, NC: Duke UP, 1996.

Sedgwick, Eve Kosofsky. *Epistemology of the Closet.* Berkeley: U of California P, 1990.

Seiter, Ellen. "Women's History, Women's Melodrama: *Deutschland, bleiche Mutter.*" *German Quarterly* 59 (1986): 569–581.

Serri, Mirella. *I Redenti: gli intellettuali che vissero due volte, 1938–1948 (The Redeemed: The Intellectuals Who Lived Twice, 1938–1948).* Milan: Corbaccio, 2005.

Shandley, Robert R. *Rubble Films: German Cinema in the Shadow of the Third Reich.* Philadelphia, PA: Temple UP, 2001.

Shattuck, Jane. *Television, Tabloids, and Tears: Fassbinder and Popular Culture.* Minneapolis: U of Minnesota P, 1995.

Sheehan, Thomas W. *Dictionary of Patron Saints' Names.* Huntington IN: Our Sunday Visitor, 2001.

Sheil, Mark. *Italian Neorealism: Rebuilding the Cinematic City.* London: Wallflower, 2006.

Silver, Alain, and James Ursini, eds. *Film Noir Reader 2.* New York: Limelight, 1999.

Silverman, Kaja. *The Acoustic Mirror: The Female Voice in Psychoanalysis and Cinema.* Bloomington: Indiana UP, 1988.

Silverman, Kaja. *Male Subjectivity at the Margins.* New York: Routledge, 1992.

Sontag, Susan. *Under the Sign of Saturn.* New York: Vintage, 1972.

Spaich, Herbert. *Rainer Werner Fassbinder: Leben und Werk.* Weinheim: Beltz, 1992.

Steimatsky, Noa. *Italian Locations: Reinhabiting the Past in Postwar Cinema.* Minneapolis: U of Minnesota P, 2008.

Theweleit, Klaus. *Male Fantasies.* 2 vols. Minneapolis: U of Minnesota P, 1989.

Toplin, Robert Brent. *History by Hollywood: The Use and Abuse of the American Past.* Urbana: U of Illinois P, 1996.

Van Wert, William. "Narrative Structure in *The Third Man.*" *Literature/Film Quarterly* 2 (1974): 341–346.

Wagstaff, Christopher. *Italian Neorealist Cinema: An Aesthetic Approach.* Toronto: U of Toronto P, 2007.

Ward, David. *Antifascisms: Cultural Politics in Italy, 1943–46. Benedetto Croce and the Liberals, Carlo Levi and the "Actionists."* Madison, NJ: Fairleigh Dickinson UP, 1996.

Watson, Wallace Steadman. *Understanding Rainer Werner Fassbinder: Film as Private and Public Art.* Columbia: U of South Carolina P, 1996.

White, Rob. *The Third Man.* London: British Film Institute, 2003.

Willett, Ralph. *The Americanization of Germany, 1945–1949.* New York: Routledge, 1989.

Wilms, Wilfried, and William Rasch, eds. *German Postwar Films: Life and Love in the Ruins.* New York: Palgrave Macmillan, 2008.

INDEX